FORT WORTH

Fort Worth

Outpost, Cowtown, Boomtown

HAROLD RICH

University of Oklahoma Press : Norman

An earlier version of chapter 2 was published as "Strange Bedfellows: 'Longhair Jim' Courtright and Political Infl uence in Fort Worth," *East Texas Historical Journal* 46, no. 1 (2008): 27–32.

An earlier version of chapter 7 was published as "A Distinctive Legacy: Settlement Patterns of Fort Worth's Hispanic Community," *West Texas Historical Journal* 82 (2006): 35–51.

Library of Congress Cataloging-in-Publication Data
Rich, Harold, 1948–
Fort Worth : outpost, cowtown, boomtown / Harold Rich.
     pages cm
Includes bibliographical references and index.
ISBN 978-0-8061-4492-4 (hardcover : alk. paper) ISBN 978-0-8061-6911-8 (paper)
1. Fort Worth (Tex.)—History.   2. Fort Worth (Tex.)—Economic conditions.
3. Fort Worth (Tex.)—Social conditions.   I. Title.
F394.F7R53 2014
976.4'5315—dc23   2014004513

*"I suppose history never lies, does it?" said
Mr. Dick, with a gleam of hope.
"Oh dear, no, sir!" I replied, most decisively. I was
ingenuous and young, and I thought so.*

—*David Copperfield speaking in* David
Copperfield, *by Charles Dickens*

CONTENTS

Illustrations

TABLES

PREFACE

This book began as a doctoral dissertation at Texas Christian University and differs from that version largely by the addition of material with more emphasis on human history and the removal of some economic data, especially statistics that can be daunting for a wider audience than a dissertation committee. The story begins in 1880—rather than 1849, when an outpost was first established on the site, or 1873, when the city was incorporated—because it focuses not on Fort Worth's beginnings or its survival, which was assured with the arrival of a railroad in 1876, but on the successful struggle to grow into a city of substance. In addition, Fort Worth's early years have been well analyzed, leaving little to be gained from yet another retelling, but scant attention has been paid to the forty-year period that ended one century and began another. Much of the transformative process involved economic development, but this study provides a fuller, richer view for the reader in the hope that a wide range of topics will aid and stimulate future historians.

I owe thanks and more to those who helped both directly and indirectly. Most of all, warmest appreciation goes to my parents, Hugh and Edith Rich, two decent people who never saw the inside of a high school classroom but who sacrificed beyond any standard of expectation to provide me what they never had. They are my betters. This work would have been less than it is if not for Todd Kerstetter, who both guided and moderated, a difficult job done with tremendous grace. He and the rest of my dissertation committee, Clayton Brown, Steven Woodworth, and Mark Gilderhus, allowed me to realize a dream. Special recognition

goes to Ben Proctor, whose high standards forced me to a new understanding of English grammar and made it impossible to read a para-
graph without looking for the "Mother Hubbard." His students will
understand.

FORT WORTH

INTRODUCTION

In 1880, Fort Worth faced an uncertain future. What had begun as an army camp only thirty-one years earlier had grown to a town of 6,663 on the strength of post–Civil War cattle drives and railroads. The great herds began to fade at the end of the 1870s, leaving only a weak, poorly diversified economy hanging by thin rails; the Texas and Pacific Railway was the only significant commerce left, a condition shared by many frontier communities that eventually withered and stagnated. Fort Worth's outlook was made even more difficult by its location in a landlocked area of North-Central Texas, between the rich East Texas greenbelt and the arid, brown landscape of West Texas, where (before irrigation) agriculture was more subsistence than commercial and ranching required such vast acreage that only large operations proved cost-effective. Of course the Trinity River flowed, but it offered little, especially during the summer when the waters ran so shallow that they hardly deserved the term "river."[1] To the south and southwest, substantial cotton production represented true potential, but other towns that were neither smaller nor less naturally endowed than Fort Worth lay closer to the fields. In 1876, when its first railroad arrived, Fort Worth's population stood at 1,500; Waco, fewer than ninety miles south and with rail service since 1874, counted 6,000.[2] Neither enterprise nor natural advantages suggested that Fort Worth would become anything but another unremarkable burg of limited population and influence, similar to Jefferson and New Braunfels, Texas, both of which declined in the second half of the nineteenth century as Texas underwent economic transformations that shifted centers of commercial activity.[3]

Perhaps the biggest obstacle to a grand future lay not within the Fort Worth city limits or to the west or south but thirty miles to the east.

Dallas, an older, larger, and richer settlement, strategically located in the East Texas greenbelt, enjoyed overwhelming advantages that seemed certain to guarantee superior population and commerce. Development of two closely situated urban areas had proven successful in Minneapolis and St. Paul, Minnesota, and in Houston and Galveston, Texas. However, most observers assumed, with substantial justification, that proximity was not an advantage, that closeness tended to create zero-sum equations in which success for one city meant failure for the other. This dynamic quickly spurred strong competition between Dallas and Fort Worth for railroads, a critical first commercial step in an area without viable river or sea transport. Dallas acquired the Houston and Texas Central Railway in 1872, four years before the Texas and Pacific Railway arrived in Fort Worth, giving Dallas a head start. The two cities would remain competitive well into the twentieth century, and the desire to outdo Dallas became a major force inspiring Fort Worthians, suggesting the ironic possibility that Dallas's proximity aided Fort Worth's development.[4]

Competition may have driven the city and its citizens, but economic development represented the critical factor in Fort Worth's transition from a frontier outpost to a nationally-ranked metropolis. That would not have happened, or the outcome would have been remarkably different, without several key commercial events. Fort Worth's early survival and growth depended on timely commercial stimuli, a fact many historians, both professional and amateur, have recognized. Little doubt exists about the link between commerce and Fort Worth's rise.[5]

Commercial success did not come easily or without effort but was won in an uneven, hard-fought struggle with many stops, failures, missteps, and successes. Those who guided the process began with a single-minded commitment to railroads as the sufficient engine of prosperity, an idea that brought the great rail infrastructure that made Fort Worth the transportation hub of the Southwest and that, for a while and to a degree, seemed capable of fulfilling all the dreams. However, by 1890 many civic leaders realized that railroads, while impressive, were better at creating wealth for investors than jobs for multitudes. This epiphany began to shift their focus to industry at the same time that the Panic of 1893 struck, effectively killing any significant commercial advance for a decade. The arrival of Armour and Company and Swift and Company in 1903 ended that period of relative dormancy. As Fort Worth's first large factories, the packinghouses had great impacts and were primarily responsible for a rate of population growth between 1900 and 1910 that was the highest of all American cities. For a decade after 1903, the city's economy continued to grow steadily, despite persistent problems in supply and commodity prices. The continuation and seriousness of these issues were early signs that Fort Worth's economy suffered from a lack of diversity. As important as they were, Swift and Armour represented not a bold transformation into a new, multifaceted economy but an extension and expansion of the agriculturally-based cattle market that had existed since the 1860s. True transformation would not come until World War I. Then, the combination of government spending and the oil boom joined the packinghouse effect to create such radical economic expansion and diversification that Fort Worth seriously challenged Dallas's supremacy, a goal dreamed of by so many, for so long.

No facet of life exists in vacuum, and economic development is not just about dollars and cents but about people. Fort Worth would not have amounted to much without the efforts of some very determined and dedicated citizens who worked hard and risked much. Most major enterprises, including railroads, the packinghouses, and Camp Bowie, an Army training facility, would have been unrealized dreams if not for these people's efforts. Boardman Buckley Paddock and John Peter Smith are especially notable, but others also contributed. Among these largely unsung or forgotten figures were businessmen, local politicians, and municipal employees, including police officers, fire fighters, and those who worked to provide adequate supplies of safe water. Where possible, their contributions and names have been noted.

There were also those whose contributions were neither clear nor intentional and whose motivations were less than exemplary. Timothy Courtright and Luke Short, two men whose legendary gunfight is reenacted regularly, are only the best-known of many who filled the numerous saloons, casinos, and brothels of Hell's Half Acre. They and their contemporaries became an important part of the romantic West portrayed in literature, film, and television, but they also played an important role in economic development. Fort Worth tolerated the Acre and all its sins—including those prohibited by law, like gambling and prostitution—not because of moral laxity but because of a mindset that linked vice to commercial success. During the Civil War, Fort Worth declined precipitously, but it revived thanks to the cattle herds traveling the Chisholm Trail. As the last true town before Indian Territory (now Oklahoma), Fort Worth profited from trail hands patronizing both sides of Ninth Street, the mercantile shops to the north and the Acre's saloons and associated establishments to the south. That experience ingrained a belief in the Acre's importance to business, an idea that became the underlying justification that ensured its survival. In the 1870s, when strict enforcement temporarily shut down the Acre and drove trade west to Fort Griffin, it was the business community that rose in protest to force an end to the campaign. Hell's Half Acre remained a factor and a presence because succeeding generations bought into the argument that a thriving red-light district supported general commerce. Occasionally, morality movements emerged, usually around election time, but those campaigns never lasted long or had a lasting effect; and once they passed, it was business as usual. That finally changed during World War I when patriotism and the military joined the moral crusade, creating a vibrant and sustainable force able to overcome the economic defense. One of the marks of the new economy was the change in attitudes concerning the Acre.[6]

There were many others whose names and contributions are lost, largely because history does a disservice to the majority by taking little note of nonwhites and women. What few references appear usually involve sensationalized events, crimes, or moral transgressions. The record is somewhat better for Mexican Americans, largely thanks to a few published works that relied heavily on oral histories, but women seem to have existed on record only as wives, mothers, or prostitutes, and African Americans only as criminals or victims of a harsh racial code. Nonwhites faced a racism that was neither subtle nor limited but unapologetically blatant and pervasive, a most unsavory part the period's culture.

What happened in Fort Worth is part of a larger history of urban economic development, a major force in forming and shaping the United States. Scholars like Lawrence Larsen highlighted the rise of the urban West in the late nineteenth century, noting that Fort Worth's rise made it a serious rival to Dallas.[7] Perhaps the best-known urban study covering the nineteenth century, William Cronon's *Nature's Metropolis: Chicago and the Great West*, touched on many issues important to Fort Worth. For example, Cronon argued that entrepreneurs molded trade in commodities in ways that reorganized commerce and forged the modern economy. One of the transformative commodities he emphasized, livestock, created the great packinghouses that shaped new centers of power and allowed Chicago to extend its reach far outside the city limits. The parallel is striking and obvious because Fort Worth, on a smaller scale, owes much to its stockyards.[8]

The scholarship on Fort Worth's development generally centers around two broad historical themes. First, researchers agree that a handful of individuals drove development. Local boosters sacrificed in many ways to transform Fort Worth, but nothing was as important as their financial contribution; the best estimates of citizen-funded support to railroads run as high as $3 million, half in cash and half in land. A disproportionate number of these transformative boosters, called "go-getters" by historian Daniel J. Boorstin, were lawyers, including Paddock, Smith, and James J. Jarvis.[9] Second, scholars acknowledge the importance of several critical events: the establishment of the military outpost in 1849, the influx of Confederate veterans after the end of the Civil War, the advent of trail drives in the late 1860s, the arrival of the railroad in 1876, the railroad boom of the 1880s, the Armour and Swift packinghouses in 1903, the Texas oil boom that began around 1917, and the construction of the massive Consolidated Vultee Aircraft plant in 1942.[10]

The critical-events analysis carries strong arguments and deserves recognition, but it suffers an important failing. It neglects the impact of World War I and suggests that the only significant economic events between 1890 and 1920 were the arrival of packinghouses in 1903 and the Ranger oil fields of 1917. This view cannot be sustained, not because the packing plants and oil were unimportant, but because the analysis omits much. Beginning in 1914, Fort Worth strengthened its existing railroad economy, added commercial and ethnic diversification (both Hispanic and European), achieved substantial population increases, built military bases, and ended the reign of open vice in Hell's Half Acre. To a large degree, these events owed a lot to federal involvement, including vast expenditures during World War I to build Camp Bowie and three airfields. Local historian Susie Pritchett, archivist for the Tarrant County Archives, concluded that the building of Camp Bowie and the airfields "pulled us into the 20th century like no other event and changed us from provincial to worldly in outlook."[11] The combined economic effect of army camps, the rise of a major oil industry, and the packinghouses pushed Fort Worth at the end of the second decade of the twentieth century to its greatest level of relative economic standing in Texas and the Southwest. There is some evidence that an equal or greater economic leap may follow shortly, perhaps in the second decade of the twenty-first century. The answer to that question waits for the passage of time and another historian.

1

THE RAILROAD AGE, 1880–1884

In the first five years of the 1880s, Fort Worth would begin its great journey on steel rails. At the decade's start the Texas and Pacific Railway's one daily arrival and departure constituted the sum of Fort Worth's railroad traffic, but by 1884 five trunk lines ran nine daily arrivals and departures, and others lay under construction or in advanced planning stages. Railroad development had a multiplier effect that drove construction and trade, expanding opportunities in other fields, especially the dressed beef industry, where a serious effort began to develop national and European markets. The rail surge also spurred the beginning of a modern municipal infrastructure in water and sewage systems as well as street and bridge improvements. Railroads would prove insufficient in and of themselves to make Fort Worth a great city, but they provided the economic critical mass upon which all other advances would rest.

The frontier had receded so little at the beginning of the 1880s that the distance between civilization and mayhem often measured only a few miles. In 1879, American Indians killed a man just four miles west of downtown, and in August 1880 four men traveling southwest died in another attack. Within the city limits, remnants of the frontier persisted, most visibly in high levels of violence aggravated by the pervasiveness of firearms (despite state laws), a fact that the *Fort Worth Democrat* lamented in 1881. Fort Worth's 31 saloons, roughly one for every 225 residents, contributed to lawlessness by offering not just alcohol but all forms of vice. Even drugs were present. Ho Lee was fined $25 for running an opium den on Houston Street, and the *Fort Worth Gazette* published complaints from physicians and druggists about rampant morphine use. Little gentility existed to hide the rough edges. In 1880, a recent arrival described wooden sidewalks lining a Main Street of dirt that was traversed by a donkey pulling a small streetcar past saloons on every block from the courthouse south to the depot. One block boasted three saloons operating night and day. In fact, most bars and casinos ran seven days a week despite the requirement that they close from midnight Saturday until midnight Sunday, thanks to an alliance between saloon owners and city administrators willing to turn a blind eye in exchange for regular fines. Such accommodations became the norm, developing a working mode bent not on banishing vice but on isolation and profit-making. The center of that accommodation was Hell's Half Acre, an area occupying the southeast quadrant of downtown between the business district on the north and the rail terminal on the south. In the Acre almost anything went, but at a price. Outside the Acre, the rules tended to be a bit stricter, at least in maintaining appearances. In 1880, a house of prostitution on Third Street, several blocks north of the Acre, was closed after the *Democrat* called it a "public disgrace," while many such houses only a few blocks south continued uninterrupted operations. Even gambling houses in the business district had to follow some degree of decorum. The *Gazette* asked that the police make casinos on Second Street lower their blinds to restrict the public's view.[1]

Occasionally, especially around elections, the police launched crackdowns with great fanfare but with little lasting impact. One such campaign in April 1881 became notable for two reasons. First, it led to the arrest of Fort Worth Alderman H. P. Shiel, who was also a saloon owner and sometime city police officer. As a councilman, Shiel was known for championing the semiofficial backdoor arrangements that kept saloon cash registers ringing seven days a week. He admitted serving beer on a Sunday but argued the legal technicality that he had not collected until Monday. The 1881 raids extended beyond saloons, taking in other Sunday workers, including several tradesmen and an employee of the *Fort Worth Democrat and Advance*, a local newspaper known for criticizing the lack of enforcement. Those arrested faced prosecution under "blue laws" that prohibited most commercial activities on Sundays. In all likelihood the raids on more legitimate businesses were meant to discredit the crackdown and stimulate complaints, which were not long in coming. A letter to the editor of the *Democrat* from "Six Teetotalers" described the aggressive enforcement as "obnoxious" and "ineffective at reducing drunkenness." In truth, neither the police nor city aldermen nor businessmen objected to the Acre or its Sunday operations; they just went through enforcement motions occasionally to maintain the pretense of office.[2] By July 1881 the appearance of yet another litany of complaints about the Acre's flagrant behavior signaled that the latest aberration had passed and once again it was business as usual.[3]

The Acre survived occasional crackdowns because many respectable citizens believed it contributed to a vibrant urban center. This generally held assumption overcame the outcries, including the July 1883 recommendation of Marshal William Rea that the Acre and its endemic violence be shut down. Rea's idea was not original; many had made similar pleas using different motivations, but the Acre persevered. In April 1879, a group of 300 citizens publicly sought more enlightened enforcement after a round of increased police activity proved so effective that ranchers and cowhands avoided Fort Worth in favor of Fort Griffin and Albany, Texas, costing local merchants trade. That appeal led the council to ease the restrictions so that saloons only had to close between 9:00 A.M. and 4:00 P.M. on Sundays. At the same time, the council increased the frequency of $25 fines from monthly to weekly. Some continued to complain that this was easing too far, including an irate citizen who charged that the mayor had ordered the police not to fine saloons more than once a month. There was no question that gambling and prostitution were early growth industries. When the local supply failed to meet demand the Paragon Saloon imported several prostitutes from St. Louis.[4]

The criminal justice system displayed a frontier mentality in its lack of concern for basic rights. In 1881 a local reporter, J. W. Putnam, accused several police officers of pistol whipping him after he criticized (in print) their handling of an arrest. Mayor John T. Brown responded that he was glad to have an officer who would club a reporter since "they all deserved to be beaten on general principles."[5] That lack of restraint was more pronounced when African Americans were involved. In 1880, a *Democrat* editorial called for leniency for several white men on trial for attempting to lynch an African American who was charged with assaulting a white woman. The newspaper argued that anyone would have done the same. It excused the attempted lynching as a consequence of a "black demon's hellish lust" and asked, "Could they do otherwise?" When evidence later cleared the African American man of any involvement, the paper dismissed the exoneration as a technicality, arguing that the would-be lynchers should not be faulted, because the exculpatory information was unknown at the time. Even when blacks made it to trial, they faced a system so bent on speedy convictions that fairness was usually impossible. On March 16, 1881, Frank Vaughn, an African American man, was arrested for raping Laura Edison, a white woman who lived at Fleming's Toll Bridge over the Trinity River. The Grand Cyclops of the local Klan, calling himself Fang Foo Flop, passed around a circular headlined "Negro Rapist Must Die," urging quick action. The next day, a Saturday, Vaughn was tried, convicted, and sentenced to hang in two days. On March 19, just two days after conviction, Vaughn was placed on a pine box with a noose around his neck (the rope was thrown over a bar fixed overhead) and asked to confess. When he refused the box was kicked away, leaving him dangling. In a true Hollywood ending, a messenger arrived just in time with a ten-day stay issued by the governor. The press was certain it would only be a temporary delay.[6]

For all its roughness, Fort Worth had achieved a level of development by the end of the 1870s. Tangible results were seen in the 1880 census, when Tarrant County recorded the largest population increase of all Texas counties. This growth provided a contrast with the recent past and with adjacent communities. One who witnessed that transition was Boardman Buckley Paddock. Paddock had arrived in 1873, coming from Mississippi where he studied law after serving in the Confederate Army. Once in Fort Worth, he adopted the city as his own and for the next five decades served as a civic champion, including at times editor of the *Democrat*, and mayor. In 1879, while traveling through Comanche, Texas, (120 miles to the southwest), Paddock remarked that Comanche reminded him of "primitive days" in Fort Worth, when he and other leaders used "adjurations" to overcome apathy and attract a railroad. That same year, the two local daily newspapers lamented the passing of the "old days" when cowboys raising general mischief provided no shortage of sensationalism to report. In 1880, longtime police officer W. B. Thomas seconded that sentiment while lauding Fort Worth's remarkable progress from the days when railroad gangs and cowboys came into town bent for trouble.[7]

In the first half of the 1880s, Fort Worth added to its entertainment environment, especially in the development of legitimate theater. In 1880, George Holland turned the Theatre Comique at Houston and Second streets (originally the Adelphie) into the My Holland, joining Evans Hall (an upstairs theater on the northwest corner of First and Houston streets), and Van Zandt Hall at Third and Houston streets in offering comedies

B. B. Paddock, circa 1890. Photo notation identifies
him as president of the Spring Palace. Courtesy of
University of Texas at Arlington Special Collections.

and melodramas; the local German community attended the Deutscher
Verein Hall at Fourteenth and Houston streets. The first vaudeville theater, The Standard, at Twelfth and Commerce streets, opened in 1893 just
as theaters began adding electric lights and running movie reels during
intermissions. In 1881, an opera house seating up to 1,800 and featuring a
grand staircase was proposed for Fifth Street between Main and Houston streets. When that plan proved too exorbitant, supporters opted for a
smaller venue seating 952 and costing just $16,000 (it would become the
Greenwall Opera House in 1890). The theater scene developed to the point
that in the 1894–1895 season (mid-September to May), Fort Worthians had
the opportunity to attend 142 shows.[8] In addition, a horse track opened on
September 27, 1883, with a four-race card. The track also hosted some of

the first local baseball games, pitting the Dallas Brown Stockings against the Fort Worth Nationals.[9]

In the 1880s, Fort Worth became home to two colleges. On September 7, 1881, Fort Worth University (FWU), chartered by the Methodist Church, opened for classes with 123 students in temporary facilities at Jennings and Thirteenth streets, pending completion of the permanent campus where Trimble Tech High School now stands (College Avenue was named for the school). FWU did well at first, adding a law school in 1893 and a medical school in 1894, but the school left Fort Worth after the spring of 1911, eventually becoming Oklahoma City University. On January 9, 1883, Texas Wesleyan College (now Texas Wesleyan University) opened temporary quarters at Throckmorton and Seventh streets while a $40,000 building went up in the College Hill area east of town. The school obtained the land from the Texas and Pacific Railway and offered to name the institution after anyone donating $50,000. When that offer lay unmet the school demanded $10,000, threatening to move to Gainesville, Texas, if the money did not come through. Several local individuals and businesses contributed to a successful drive to prevent the loss.[10]

By 1881, the accoutrements of an urban commercial city existed, if only in primitive forms. The city council contracted for a street railway service with Prairie City Company and Fort Worth City Company and continued the contract for phone service, which had arrived years earlier and now boasted sixty-nine subscribers. The post office handled an average of 2,000 pieces of daily mail, but water, supplied by seventy-five artesian wells, continued to be sold by the barrel from wagons. The commercial sector listed 358 professionals and businesses, including twenty-five lawyers, fifteen carpenters, eleven doctors, eight blacksmiths, seven butchers, three dentists, sixteen dry goods shops, fifteen saloons, eleven hotels and wagon yards, seven stables and restaurants, six liquor suppliers, three banks, two newspapers, a single variety theater and a street railway.[11] In the fiscal year that ended September 1881, some 160 businesses shipped $2.3 million in goods, the Tidball and Van Zandt Bank handled $20 million and the City National Bank $40 million, and the grocery wholesaler Joseph H. Brown bought and sold $1.5 million in goods. The future offered hope for continued growth. In January 1880, the nation's eighth largest compress began reducing cotton bales to seven inches (standard had been forty-two inches). The need for such a device was clear; some 6,428 large bales had been waiting for railcar space in December 1880. In addition, the Fort Worth Ice Company contracted for new equipment capable of producing twenty tons daily.[12]

For all the advances, Fort Worth's population and economic growth lagged the surrounding area. From 1870 to 1880 the population of Tarrant County grew 326 percent, from 5,788 to 24,678, the largest increase of all Texas counties, and Tarrant County's assessed valuations of taxable property rose from $1.08 million to $4.83 million, or more than 347 percent. Comparable figures do not exist for Fort Worth's share of the total economy, but census data show it accounted for only 27 percent of the county's total population, or some 6,663 people (526 foreign born, 5,606 "whites," 1,054 "colored," and 3 Chinese). The city of Dallas accounted for 31 percent of Dallas County's population. Fort Worth ranked seventh in total population behind Galveston, San Antonio, Houston, Austin, Dallas, and Waco.[13]

Fort Worth's small share of the total county population reflected its underdeveloped industrial and commercial base. The manufacturing section of the 1882 *City Directory* listed only the Fort Worth Packing Company and a large iron foundry under construction, admitting that "our manufacturing interests are just in their infancy." With little industrial production, Fort Worth relied heavily on trade in agricultural products. Of the $2.3 million worth of goods shipped in 1881, only $200,000, or 8.7 percent, involved manufactured goods, largely flour and ice. The other 91.3 percent included 43,460 bales of cotton, more than 26,000 cattle, 300,000 pounds of wood, 310,000 pounds of hides, 500,000 pounds of bone, and 21,000 bushels of grain.[14]

A comparison of industrial development reveals differences that were disproportionately larger than the population. Compared with Dallas County, Tarrant County in 1870 had 39 percent fewer manufacturers, 59 percent fewer manufacturing employees, paid 92 percent less in manufacturing wages, had 87 percent less capital invested, and produced 87 percent less (see Table 1.1).

Between 1870 and 1880, Fort Worth's position relative to Dallas declined to 54 percent fewer manufacturers and 71 percent fewer total employees, but improved in wages, capital invested, and value of products to 74, 66, and 67 percent fewer respectively. In addition, Dallas County had nearly twice the taxable valuation, $8.44 million to $4.83 million. Such a marked disparity must have been obvious even to casual observers and probably contributed to an awareness that Fort Worth must expand commercially. In 1882, the initial meeting of the Fort Worth Board of Trade, similar to a chamber of commerce, devoted its agenda to attracting new businesses.[15]

TABLE 1.1.   Tarrant County's lag behind Dallas County in
             manufacturing, 1870

	Tarrant County	Dallas County	Absolute difference	Percent difference
Manufacturers	27	44	17	−39
Employees	48	118	70	−59
Wages	$ 2,050	$ 25,715	$ 23,665	−92
Capital	$13,940	$106,332	$ 92,392	−87
Value of products	$37,625	$279,983	$242,358	−87

Source: *Ninth Census of the United States* (Washington, D.C.: Government Printing Office, 1872), pp. 342, 346, 841–42.

Fort Worth's growing focus on industrialization rested on a realistic evaluation of what was needed to become a major city. Scholars emphasize a strong positive correlation between urbanization and industrialization and specifically note that the industrialization of the late nineteenth and early twentieth centuries was primarily responsible for a corresponding rise in urbanization that swept the United States. During that first wave of industrialization, the U.S. urban population increased from 10.8 percent of the total population in 1840 to more than 51 percent in 1920, at the same time that the number of cities grew from 131 to 2,722.[16]

Railroads had been Fort Worth's salvation in 1876 and would be its first major industry.[17] Paddock and other leading lights of the immediate post-Civil War era saw economic success arriving on steel rails. Paddock in 1873 had published the "Tarantula Map," a pictorial prediction of Fort Worth's future as a major rail center with nine lines radiating outward like spider legs. Paddock claimed that the depiction was more projection than prediction, that representatives of the Texas and Pacific assured him much earlier that Fort Worth would be the railroad's convergence point.[18] The initial results certainly supported the economic promises. As North Texas's most westward rail terminus, Fort Worth became the supply center for a wholesale trade area that stretched into West Texas. Between 1876 and 1880, the number of businesses served by the Fort Worth wagon trade increased from 59 to 460, and the population of the extended trade area grew from 40,000 to more than 400,000.[19]

From 1876 to January 1880, Fort Worth's rail service provided only one arrival and departure daily, not counting limited local service to Wills Point. By July 1880 the schedule doubled, to two eastbound trains and two

Texas and Pacific Railway locomotive, 1876. Courtesy of University of Texas at Arlington Special Collections.

westbound, and September 1880 marked the beginning of a rapid expansion of rail service that would make Fort Worth the railroad center of Texas and the American Southwest. First, the Missouri Pacific Railroad line from Sherman, Texas, opened following a $10,000 subsidy and donations of rights-of-way. Then, John Peter Smith persuaded the Gulf, Colorado and Santa Fe Railway to make Fort Worth the junction point for a new line running to Galveston through Cleburne, Waco, and Austin. According to Walter Gresham of the Gulf, Colorado and Santa Fe, the original plan called for a junction near Buffalo Gap (near Abilene, Texas) but John Peter Smith's relentless entreaties drew the company to Fort Worth, contingent on a $75,000 subsidy and rights-of-way from the Johnson County line. To make a great month incredible, the Missouri, Kansas and Texas Railroad offered an extension of its Denison line contingent on a $10,000 subsidy, giving Fort Worth a major route running from the Texas Gulf to St. Louis. The success of that venture raised the total of new rail lines to three and boosted hopes for a successful economic future.[20]

John Peter Smith became one of two major personalities behind Fort Worth's economic rise (Paddock is the other). Smith arrived in Fort Worth in the 1850s and served as a teacher before becoming a lawyer and a banker. He made a fortune in real estate and became the city's richest man with a net worth of $700,000. His home on Fourth Street ranked as one of the most expensive in Texas. His dedication to local development was so consuming and involved that he frequently returned home in the evening without his coat; a servant would later be sent out to recover the missing garment. Smith played cards weekly at the home of C. J. Swasey, and Swasey recalled having as many as six of Smith's coats before someone from Smith's household would collect them. Smith became such a prominent figure that the *Gazette* wrote that one "could not mention Fort Worth without thinking of him" and that he "more largely made Fort Worth than any other man."[21]

Thanks to the work of city leaders, Fort Worth had little trouble raising the subsidies and land donations to complete railroad transactions. For example, the Gulf, Colorado and Santa Fe required that Cleburne and Fort Worth contribute $100,000 and land for depots. Cleburne quickly subscribed its share, $25,000, and Fort Worth took only three days to raise the remaining $75,000, largely thanks to Smith who donated $5,200 and signed bonds guaranteeing rights-of-way and depot grounds. That level of commitment and involvement served as a tremendous asset aiding Fort Worth's development. Supporters gloated that Fort Worthians subscribed $75,000 in three days while it took Waco weeks to raise only $30,000 and that Dallas, seeking eastern and northern rail routes in 1880, had only collected $9,000. The *Democrat* did not attempt to hide its glee concerning Dallas's poor showing.[22]

Altruism did not rule the day completely. In January 1881 officials of the Gulf, Colorado and Santa Fe and the Texas and Pacific threatened to move their junction east after property owners demanded $12,000 for rights-of-way. The railroads had thought the rights-of-way would be donated and in any case were worth only $4,000. A group of city leaders—which included M. B. Loyd, Dr. C. M. Peak, Sidney Martin, A. J. Chambers, and C. L. Holloway—expressed regret that a few "sordid" citizens had upset the efforts of so many but agreed to fund $10,000 of the added cost.[23] Opportunistic valuations by property owners represented just one variation of a system open to abuse. Citizens often made sacrifices in the name of civic welfare while a privileged few profited from unethical manipulation of information. All too often, Gilded Age politicians operated in league with railroads, and railroads widely used inducements such as free passes, advertising dollars, and even direct payments to win support for subsidized lines of questionable worth.[24]

Railroad growth continued through most of the 1880s, again with the encouragement of boosters such as A. M. Britton, Ephraim Daggett, W. A. Huffman, Joe Terrell, Dr. C. M. Peak, and A. J. Chambers. In April 1881 a solicitation drive sought a $25,000 subsidy and funding for rights-of-way for the Fort Worth and Denver Railway slated to run northwest through Wise County. Although the estimated cost for rights-of-way ran no higher than $7,500, the railroad asked for a bond of $12,500, payable in five monthly installments. Mayor John Brown argued for the economic sense of the proposal, noting that taxable property values had increased $500,000 in just one year thanks to railroad investments. Due to the number of subsidies that already had been granted, the collection proved difficult, requiring some serious cajoling to reach even $4,000, but work began quickly once the finances were finalized. Construction proceeded at a rapid pace; contract specifications mandated the laying of one and one-quarter miles of track daily.[25]

In the flush of the railroad boom a group of twenty-six local citizens, each pledging $10,000, formed the Fort Worth and Southwestern Railway Company with John Peter Smith as president and Paddock as secretary. The original plan envisioned a southwest line linking Granbury, Stephenville, Comanche, and Brownwood, Texas, but the line was soon extended to make Laredo the terminus, bringing a name change to the Fort Worth and Rio Grande. The line's backers believed that construction would be relatively cheap, with only light grading needed and one major bridge over the Brazos, but the enterprise stalled when the affected cities proved reluctant to subsidize a railway they believed would largely benefit Fort Worth. W. W. Lawrence, the company's field man, pointed out that Fort Worthians had already invested $250,000 in rail subsidies and had reaped great rewards. His message succeeded, at least in Stephenville, where a hundred-gun salute greeted the survey crew.[26]

By 1882, four rail lines radiated out of Fort Worth: the east-west Texas and Pacific, the north-south Missouri Pacific, the Fort Worth and Rio Grande to the Mexican border, and the Gulf, Colorado and Santa Fe to Galveston. In addition, construction had begun on the Fort Worth and Denver and the Missouri Pacific lines, providing a direct route to St. Louis. Even in their initial phase to Cleburne and Denison, the two railroads covered a five-county trade area and portions of thirty more counties, a region larger than Pennsylvania. Eventually, the road would reach southward to Galveston, providing a direct route to the Gulf of Mexico and reducing land transport costs to the coast that previously had exceeded the cost of the sea route from Galveston to New York.

Railroad expansion offered Fort Worth many benefits, including construction and maintenance facilities employing well-paid artisans who were part of an urban rail infrastructure unequaled in the state. This development also transformed Fort Worth's south side, with the construction of the Missouri Pacific freight depot, the Union Passenger Depot—an L-shaped building of two stories that also housed offices of the Missouri Pacific and the Texas and Pacific—and roundhouse facilities transferred in 1881 from Marshall, Texas.[27] The *Galveston News* editorialized that Fort Worth was on its way to becoming an important railroad town because Jay Gould had designated it a point of intersection for the Missouri Pacific and the Texas and Pacific. Gould actually visited in April 1882, staying just over an hour before moving on to Laredo.[28]

The effect was seen rather quickly in increased arrivals and departures. In May 1881 eight regular passenger trains, four with Pullman cars, came and went: two Texas and Pacific trains traveling both eastbound and westbound, and two Missouri Pacific trains running both northbound and southbound. In January 1882 service began on the Gulf, Colorado and Santa Fe, and by February the line offered both express and local service daily, giving Fort Worth nineteen daily arrivals and departures: nine via the Texas and Pacific, four by the Missouri Pacific, and two each on the Gulf, Colorado and Santa Fe, the Fort Worth and Denver, and the transcontinental route. The rapid growth overwhelmed the sidetracks, the largest in Texas, requiring the laying of a two-track line from the Union Depot to just south of the Vulcan Iron Works, a distance of three-fourths of a mile.[29] Railroads also contributed to a building boom that included 180 new homes, three elementary schools, a high school, and a new hall planned by the Knights of Pythias. Much of this growth involved grand homes south of the railroad reservation (currently the area south of Vickery and adjacent to Hemphill), a section so remote at the time that no streetcar service existed.[30]

At this early stage, many believed that railroads offered more than just great transport, that they created opportunities for manufacturers that the *Democrat* termed "beyond computation." Business promoters quickly pointed out Fort Worth's advantages: excellent rail service, access to fuel from the coal fields of northwest Texas, a plentiful supply of lumber, and a location beyond the reach of a yellow fever epidemic. The growth of rail service also brought some tangible ancillary developments. A $100,000 solicitation for a cotton factory quickly garnered $25,000, and the Vulcan Iron Foundry, with a capacity to employ 1,800 making Rigby railcar wheels, opened on November 21, 1881, on land donated by Ephraim Daggett. The foundry was kept busy; the railway boom required fifteen new locomotives and 220 cars each month. The rush of development led over-exuberant boosters to claim that Fort Worth would become "the Lowell of Texas."[31]

At the same time Fort Worth's cattle trade increased, reaching a level that justified expansion. Starting with cattle drives after the Civil War, Texas had become a significant beef supplier, and Fort Worth was an important stop on the Chisholm Trail leading to Kansas. By the end of the 1870s those drives had seriously waned, but their end did not mean the end of Texas cattle going north. In one particularly busy day fifty-one rail cattle cars bound for St. Louis and Chicago left Fort Worth's three-acre stockyards, located just south of Leuda Street and east of Main Street. In fact, most Texas cattle went out of state due to the lack of local facilities. In 1880 Texas had only three small slaughterhouses employing just 132 workers to produce just $213,000 worth of meat, minuscule in comparison with Illinois's 143 plants with 10,217 employees producing $18 million worth, much of it from Texas beef. In that sense, railroad development worked against local commercial development because railroads provided an affordable means of shipping Texas cattle to other markets, cattle that might otherwise have been processed locally by local workers. The first attempt to correct this situation came in 1881 when Paddock convinced W. E. Richardson, an East St. Louis businessman scouting Dallas for a pork packinghouse, to build on six acres donated by Smith. The plans specified a facility capable of employing 350 and processing 100,000 hogs annually. The Fort Worth Packing Company began operation in November but quickly faltered due to poor supply.[32]

In 1883, another, grander effort emerged. In that year the Texas Continental Beef Company in Victoria, Texas, announced plans for a North Texas slaughterhouse capable of handling 250 cattle daily with an estimated annual trade reaching $2 million. Representatives from several communities sought the plant, including a Fort Worth group led by H. C. Edrington, president of Traders National Bank. The acquisition of the facility would, according to Edrington, be the "longest stride" for growth and prosperity and would bring thousands of new residents, a large stockyard, fertilizer plants, an oleomargarine factory, and perhaps a tannery. Moreover, area farmers would benefit from increased demands for grain needed to fatten cattle, and ranchers would gain from the elimination of shipping costs. The potential seemed immense but untested because, with the exception of New Orleans, little effort had gone into interstate marketing of Texas processed beef. In fact, the whole South lay open, as well as Philadelphia and New York and the rest of country east of western cattle lands.[33]

Fort Worth won the competition but its victory did not last. In August 1883, Continental Beef and Fort Worth investors reached a deal that stipulated local funding of half the estimated $120,000 construction cost. After Fort Worth subscribed its share, $60,000, construction began on twenty-seven acres in the southeast quadrant, and operations started in February 1884. The plant lasted only a year before going bankrupt and being taken over by Isaac Dahlman, who also went broke despite a farsighted plan to ship beef to the east coast and England. Dahlman failed for many reasons, including a depression in the cattle market, but the most serious factors may have been opposition from New York butchers, who united to shut out western dressed beef as a threat to their livelihood, and from railroads that feared a loss in revenue because dressed beef weighed one-third less than live animals. The attempt to enter the European market soured when the initial shipment to Liverpool, England, arrived spoiled.[34]

The vulnerability of a one-dimensional railroad economy was displayed in January 1880 when the Texas and Pacific announced an extension to El Paso, a distance of 750 miles. Many greeted the news with apprehension, fearing that the end of Fort Worth's favored position as the line's terminus would seriously affect the healthy western wagon trade supporting local warehouses and wholesale shops. The Dallas press returned Fort Worth's earlier schadenfreude by suggesting that every spike in the new line constituted a nail in Fort Worth's coffin. Locals tried to put on a brave face, noting that the route would bring transcontinental access. The *Democrat*, in "Fort Worth: The Young Giant of the Southwest," argued that the change would offer advantages that Fort Worth was in the best position to exploit due to its lack of debt, its natural advantages, and its leading men. Others were not so sanguine. City Mills Company announced the purchase of new equipment capable of producing 200 barrels of flour daily, stating that it made the purchase despite "discouraging circumstances" regarding the westward rail extension.[35]

The loss of terminus status did result in a noticeable faltering. In 1881 Fort Worth's population declined by 2,500 to 3,000, a sizable chunk out of the 7,000 calling Fort Worth home. The economy so soured that the *Democrat* suspended publication in February 1880 and the city council delayed opening public schools until January 1, 1881, citing insufficient funding for more than three months. Fortunately, the effect was short-lived. The newspaper resumed publication on July 4, 1880, and in September the Missouri Pacific Railroad arrived, creating an upswing that quickly restored confidence so that the population soared to 10,000, according to a generous estimate by the *Democrat*.[36]

Around the same time, a new perspective developed based on the idea that Fort Worth had passed a threshold, that progress and growth had reached a level that would necessitate changes in attitudes and in the municipal infrastructure. As early as 1881, the press suggested that Fort Worth was a city, not a town, and that citizens should dress in modern fashions to present a proper image, that its streets should have sidewalks and be cleaned and lighted, and that a proper waterworks should be built to replace the wagon entrepreneurs measuring out a barrel of water for ten cents. The last item was particularly critical, so much so that Mayor John T. Brown and an alderman took a tour of several cities, including Hyde Park and Evanston in Illinois, Peoria, Ohio, and Sedalia, Missouri. On their return they recommended the standpipe system used in South Bend, Indiana, and Bloomington, Illinois, arguing that it provided smooth pressure without delays. The proposal called for a $60,000 system with a standpipe of 200 feet placed on a bluff or the high point south of city with water distributed via five miles of piping not less than six inches in diameter. The plan not only would provide safe drinking water and free water for city operations but also would advance fire safety by supplying sixty fireplugs with enough pressure to shoot a 125-foot stream from a one-and-one-half inch nozzle.[37]

The council appointed a committee to select well locations and authorized a bond issue that included an additional $10,000 for street and crossing improvement, but serious opposition developed on many fronts. Some feared that the proposed funding, a 1 percent sales tax, would prove problematic due to state regulations that restricted such taxes to

Robert Jackson delivering water to Irish Town, circa 1895. Outlying sections continued to rely on water wagons into the 1890s. Courtesy of University of Texas at Arlington Special Collections.

cities of 10,000 or more. (Even the mayor admitted that Fort Worth's population did not exceed 9,000.) Some questioned the need for a new water facility, arguing that the approximately fifty artesian wells already provided an unlimited supply; others took the opposite stance, arguing that the proposal was too limited and insufficient for demand. One complaint accused the city of sending "excursionists" to Illinois and Missouri at a cost of hundreds of dollars (total travel expenses: $235.10) only to have them recommend an impractical "toy" system that was too small. Others thought well of the proposal but recommended that private enterprise should fund it, thereby avoiding a $70,000 debt when city government's annual income averaged only $16,000. In the face of opposition from many sides the council reversed itself and tabled the bond package.[38]

The impetus returned following a large fire that destroyed several businesses on Houston Street. Firefighters blamed most of the $85,000 in damages on a lack of personnel and poor water pressure. The council responded by establishing a $2.50 payment per volunteer per fire and by reopening the waterworks debate. In December 1881 the council reviewed a privately funded, $54,000 Holley system that used four piston pumps capable of providing 1.5 million filtered gallons from the Trinity River with sufficient water pressure to simultaneously shoot six streams over the courthouse tower. Under the plan, investors would build the water-works but the city would operate the system and repay the cost, plus a profit, from water revenue. The councilmen also reconsidered a munici-pal system funded via the sales tax if a population of 10,000 could be verified or the law changed. In case neither proved successful, the coun-cil also prepared a bond issue totaling $150,000 to $200,000.[39]

Instead, in May 1882 the city granted a franchise to the Fort Worth Wa-ter Works Company, a private organization formed by Paddock that same month. The company promised to install a Holley system built by Drake and Orton that would make the Fort Worth waterworks one of only two first class systems in Texas (Austin had the other). The contract, which ran for twenty-five years, stipulated eight hydrants, no fewer than nine miles of pipes, and free water for city uses with set monthly user rates in which barber shops paid $8.50 for first chair and $3.50 for each additional chair, billiard halls $1.00 per table, hotels $1.50 per room, restaurants $10.00 plus $1.25 per room, livery stables $2.50 per stall, breweries $0.05 per keg of beer and family homes of up to four rooms, $6.00. Meters were also avail-able with a monthly base rate of $ 0.045 per 100 gallons for the first 5,000 gallons, and declining rates for larger quantities.[40]

The decision was far from the end of the matter, and water remained a major problem dogging the city for decades. In March 1883 the council granted a request for a sixty-day extension for completion, with the stip-ulation that the company would be fined if it failed to repair streets dam-aged in construction. The system became operational on April 24, 1883, with six miles of piping and a pump station at the juncture of the Clear and West Forks of the Trinity River capable of supplying six million gal-lons daily. Just a few months later, in September 1883, a major fire did $10,000 in damage after water pressure took fifteen minutes to build and then remained erratic to the extent that most of the spray fell short. Still, the council began buying the system in 1884, completely taking it over in 1885.[41]

Serious issues remained concerning streets, sidewalks, and sewers. Some younger and bolder residents blamed the slow pace of development on a group of "old fogeys" on the city council who, they claimed, stymied improvements because they feared increasing taxes. That parsimony may have been rather costly in that, according to many, Main and Houston streets would have been lined with tax-paying businesses if they had been graded and paved in 1879. Some suggested utilizing an unenforced state law requiring resident males between eighteen and forty-five years old to work one day per month on city projects or pay a $1 fine. Instead, the aldermen stipulated that affected residents fund two-thirds the cost of street grading or graveling and sewer line connections. In 1883 voter approval of a $190,000 street and sewer bond issue accelerated street paving and sewage service.[42]

Fort Worth would struggle with the basics of municipal services for many years, eventually achieving some limited success in developing water and sewer systems but accomplishing very little in garbage collection. In the late nineteenth and early twentieth centuries, many emerging cities faced challenging environmental crises that were byproducts of urbanization. The first level of technical expertise developed with the rise of municipal water systems in the mid- to late-nineteenth century, when the number of municipal systems increased from 136 in 1860 to 598 in 1880, and the miles of municipal sewers grew from 8,199 in 1890 to 24,972 in 1909. The technicians who developed these systems eventually gravitated into refuse collection and disposal, but it took several years for their contribution to have an effect. Problems lingered unaddressed because most cities avoided more complex solutions in favor of the quick and inexpensive alternative of dumping, using either waterways or any available plot of land. As much as any issue, municipal officers struggled with problems in waste collection and disposal without a real solution.[43]

The need for proper waste collection and sewers became especially evident during outbreaks of smallpox and other contagious diseases. In 1882, during a major smallpox epidemic, city health officials set up a treatment tent south of the city hospital and required the placement of yellow warning flags around quarantined homes. By May 1882 City Physician Ed Broiles reported eleven cases, all removed to a "pest house" outside of the city limits. The link between disease and poor sanitation seemed evident to many. "TP" wrote to a local paper in May 1882 complaining that heavy rains had swept waste into the muddy streets, making the stench almost unbearable, and C. C. Cummings, a candidate for city council, called for an end to stagnant pools around "crowded tenements," opining that a viable sewer system ranked second in importance only to education. To relieve the immediate problems the city council ordered stringent enforcement of sanitation ordinances, but a long-term solution awaited greater utilization of city sewers, which many residents avoided due to cost. On July 17, 1883, the council mandated connection to the city sewage system, straining the old, under-sized system that often left the streets flooded. After one such downpour in September 1883, someone placed a humorous sign next to standing water on Main Street lamenting a poor soul who had drowned.[44]

For all the problems, Fort Worth had made many notable public and private improvements. The list of accomplishments included: donations for the establishment of a public reading room, a precursor to a library; the completion of the first true waterworks system, with nine miles of mains; the addition of four miles of mains to the gas works and two miles to the streetcar lines; the laying of Telford-Macadam pavement on principal streets; a contract with Smith Bridge of Toledo, Ohio, for an iron bridge across the Clear Fork of the Trinity River that would be one hundred twenty feet long, eighteen feet wide and nineteen feet high, with a load capacity of 100 pounds per square inch; $104,916 spent on streets and sewers; $25,000 for new schools, and $12,000 on the fire department. Other metropolitan touches included a $45,000 Opera House, a $10,000 convent, four banks, two newspapers, and expanded telephone and telegraph service. Local progress was noted by others including the St. Louis Post-Dispatch, which described Fort Worth as a place of 12,000 residents with four important railroads, seventy-five artesian wells, a conspicuous courthouse, and streetcars connecting all to the Union Depot. Overall, the city's economy showed vibrancy, with an annual cotton trade amounting to 50,000 bales and smaller quantities of wool, gain, and hides, but its industrial sector remained unimpressive, adding only planing mills and a slash and blind factory. [45]

In 1883, Fort Worth also established a public school system serving 1,200 students. The school board, given power by the city council to run schools , was largely composed of aldermen, such as C. B. Daggett, M. C. Clarke, K. M. Van Zandt, Joseph L. Hatcher, John Nichols, and C. C. Cummings, as well as Mayor John Peter Smith. By 1886 the board oversaw 1,362 students and thirty-nine teachers in seven elementary schools and separate high schools for boys and girls. The overall pupil-teacher ratio stood at approximately thirty-five to one, but in the "colored school" (Number Six), with 294 students and six teachers, the ratio was forty-nine to one.[46]

Medical care also reached a higher level of service in 1883. In January, complaints appeared that many indigents from Dallas, Waco, and El

Paso—which, it was alleged, did not take care of their sick poor—cost Fort Worth residents $7,000 annually. The outlay prompted serious discussion of closing the city hospital, which would have been a serious burden due to the degree of need. Faced with unabated demand but a need to curtail charity care, the council appointed a committee to entice the Sisters of Charity to take over operations.[47]

Fort Worth's railroads built their own facility. In July 1883 the Missouri Pacific and the Texas and Pacific offered to build a hospital to care for their employees who paid thirty-five to fifty cents monthly for medical coverage. Railroading was dangerous work in the nineteenth century, with an average of ten workers killed each day nationally, and the average brakeman had a life expectancy of fourteen years of service; the odds were that a brakeman would be killed by an on-the-job injury before his fifteenth year of employment. The railroads' offer required the provision of land at no cost under the threat that failure would move the hospital to Dallas, Denison, or Marshall, all standing in line to donate the space. Work began on a site two miles south of the courthouse of Main Street adjacent to and just east of the city hospital, and care began in June with the first 500 to 600 patients treated in six tents. The building opened in November 1883 with fifty-five patients, twenty suffering from injury accidents. Later, the Sisters of Charity from San Antonio took over, buying the land and building a three-story building that became St. Joseph's Infirmary (later St. Joseph's Hospital) with sixty beds.[48]

Both the progress and problems of 1883 carried over into 1884. In January 1884 a committee of five, including Paddock and W. J. Boaz, initiated a $200,000 fund drive for a woolen mill, and contracts were signed for a cottonseed mill capable of producing forty tons daily. Later, the City National Bank presented a design by local architect M. R. Sanguinet for a four-story building, the city's tallest, to be built at Third and Houston streets with completion set for June 1, 1884. Unfortunately, old problems also resurfaced. In 1883 the *Gazette*, upset at the number of fights, called the Acre a disgrace and suggested it was time to demolish it. An editorial blamed prevailing odors and outbreaks of typhoid on poor sanitation enforcement, especially the failure of all but 200 to 300 of more than 3,000 buildings to comply with mandated sewer connections. Many ignored the order to connect to avoid paying required fees, a frugality that left much of the city exposed to foulness and disease. Streets seldom received adequate care and maintenance. A reporter complained about numerous potholes, especially on Houston Street, a main thoroughfare, and in the area south of the railroad tracks, the extreme southern edge of Fort Worth where already more than 100 homes and the Texas Continental Meat Company had sprung up. If Houston Street had potholes, secondary routes must have been in poor shape indeed.[49]

Historians who saw 1883 as a watershed for Fort Worth, as did Paddock and Oliver Knight, were not wrong. Remarkable progress occurred, thanks to the work of men like Smith and Paddock. Knight credited Smith for first putting city government on a sound footing through the implementation of four major improvements: a waterworks, an organized fire department, a street-paving program, and the first sanitary sewers. Of the four, the waterworks was by far the most important, supplying not only human needs but also those of the fire department and the sewer service. None of the initiatives arrived in finished form with the ability to function smoothly for extended periods, but they were at least a beginning. Yet nothing would have been possible, let alone imaginable, without the rapid and significant expansion of the commercial base through railroads that occurred in the first half of the 1880s. To a very large degree, the municipal infrastructure that took shape was only a manifestation of that economic advance.[50]

2

A Vision beyond Railroads, 1885–1889

S till barely out of its swaddling clothes, Fort Worth maintained an existence on the ragged edge of uncertainty throughout the 1880s. The question of whether it would remain an overgrown village or become a grand city involved nothing so pedestrian or easily determined as reaching a certain population. To begin with, official standards concerning population were neither static nor universal. The 1880 U.S. census distinguished urbanity by a population of 8,000, but in 1920 the threshold was lowered to a mere 2,500, a level Fort Worth had passed years before. The lack of a solid definition did not imply local intellectual anarchy. As U.S. Supreme Court Justice Potter Stewart said of pornography, Fort Worth's leaders knew the characteristics of greatness when they saw them, and their vision extended well beyond status as a county seat and regional railhead. The city they envisioned had state and even national standing, preferably attained while eclipsing Dallas.[1]

Some observers, including Boardman Buckley Paddock, thought that the beginnings of mature city services during the first half of the 1880s marked the critical transition period. They pointed to subtle touches, such as shrubbery and shade trees, as adornments of delicacies and comforts that heralded the passing of frontier roughness. The 1885–1886 *City Directory* proclaimed that "a frontier town had blossomed into a cosmopolitan city" and that "Fort Worth is no longer a *town*, a place of strained existence and uncertain future; it realizes the full significance of the title *city*." The *Fort Worth Daily Mail* went further, bragging that the Fort Worth of 1885 could snap her fingers at the "village" that had begun on the three forks of the Trinity.[2]

While significant progress had occurred, Fort Worth still lacked some important elements. Major city status would require advancement on many fronts including population and city services, both of which were dependent on economic development, the critical force propelling urbanization. Many boosters maintained faith that railroad expansion would provide sufficient stimulus for a vibrant economy. As the decade waned they continued to court rail service successfully, making Fort Worth the railroad center of Texas and the Southwest. At the same time, others began to recognize that a railroad economy carried certain limitations, most notably and importantly an inability to create large numbers of jobs or added value, the rise in worth that occurs when raw materials are turned into finished goods. In contrast, manufacturing served both ends well. That realization became a critical epiphany that would bring about the transformation from a one-dimensional railroad economy to industrialization, the critical step in Fort Worth's development.

Fort Worth also continued to struggle with other problems, including the Acre where little to nothing changed. A local minister blamed the prevalence of open vice on a lack of backbone, but the evidence suggested that preferences rather than character faults kept the Acre going and that, given the option, most Fort Worth residents would have rejected strict moral restraints. For example, a statewide prohibition referendum carried Tarrant County by 3,126 to 2,988 but lost within Fort Worth, although in a close vote, 1,242 to 1,274. (It failed badly in state returns, 128,273 for to 221,627 against.) Furthermore, the Acre experienced steady growth, spreading by 1886 to cover at least a dozen blocks clustered around Twelfth and Thirteenth streets between Main, Calhoun, and Rusk. That expansion hardly suggested that saloons, casinos, and prostitutes lacked trade. The Acre's influence extended well beyond its geographic boundaries. In 1886, Dallas filed 400 gambling cases against twenty-five Fort Worth gamblers who had ventured east for the state fair. Gamblers were part of a demimonde that included many prone to violence.

One of those charged in Dallas, Luke Short, achieved some infamy as a gunfighter and the slayer of "Longhair Jim" Courtright outside the White Elephant saloon on February 8, 1887, in North Texas's most famous gunfight. The day before, Short had transferred one-third interest in the White Elephant to Jake Johnson, a move that likely infuriated Courtright, who was heavily involved in local gambling. Courtright's death may even have been due to a mistake by his wife. Vic Josssenberger reported years later that he was with Courtright on the day of the gunfight. He maintained that Courtright was unarmed but had sent someone to collect his pistol when he realized trouble was imminent. Courtright's wife, either through ignorance or mistake, sent a single-action revolver instead of a double-action weapon. Single-action required the shooter to pull the hammer back before pulling the trigger, while double-action required only movement of the trigger to fire it. Jossenberger claimed that Courtright was "fanning" the hammer when he was struck by Luke's shots. In any case, Short's killing of Courtright made headlines because of the notoriety of the participants, not because of its uniqueness. Less than a month later, another dispute between two "sporting men" had the same fatal result, and in 1890 Short was wounded in a shootout with another rival gambler at the Bank saloon, 1608 Main Street.[3]

Short's second victim in 1887, Timothy Isaiah Courtright, was one of Fort Worth's most flamboyant figures. Born in the American Midwest in the mid-1840s, Courtright fought for the Union during the Civil War, seeing action at Fort Donelson and Vicksburg and suffering wounds at Belmont. Following Appomattox he went west as an Army scout, earning the nickname of "Longhair Jim" after foregoing haircuts, an act of bravado in defiance of the scalping threat. Courtright then drifted as a buffalo hunter, gambler, guard, and performer in a Wild West show. Married and seeking a more genteel life, in 1873 he arrived in Fort Worth, where he worked as a laborer, fireman, jailer, and deputy city marshal before being elected city marshal in 1876, a post he held until 1879. Afterwards he became a private detective but continued, unsuccessfully, to seek reappointment as a deputy marshal.[4] By most standards Courtright fit the popular image of a westerner, standing well over six feet tall, sporting a distinctive moustache, and wearing a two-gun holster with the pistol butts faced forward. Even his end sounded like a Hollywood script; his dying lament, to a buddy, was, "Ful, they've got me." One of the frontier's heroic figures and Fort Worth's best-known lawman, Longhair Jim personified the popular western ideal of a man of action who relied only on a rigid code of ethics and a ready six-shooter.[5]

In contrast, a recently recovered remembrance suggests that Courtright's rather rapid rise to city marshal had less to do with qualities associated with the popular image than with crass municipal politics, especially elite manipulation of elections. That does not, of and by itself, constitute a major criticism of Courtright, whose participation involved more opportunism than corruption, more happenstance than planning, and whose term in office actually imparted stability and respect to a police department with neither. It does do damage to his image, but images are often shallow things that are easily shattered. The salient issue was not what the apparent election manipulation said about Courtright but what it said about the pervasiveness and transferability of power politics in the American West, particularly the early existence of nondemocratic influences capable of corrupting the electoral process.[6]

Fort Worth, incorporated the year that Courtright arrived, was a raw frontier community struggling to support the structure of city government, especially a competent police force. In April 1873 Ed S. Terrell, a former trapper and reputedly the area's first settler and first saloonkeeper (the First and Last Chance), defeated five challengers to become chief of four officers who worked twelve-hour shifts seven days a week, two patrolling by day and two by night. Even that meager force fell victim to economics on May 10, 1873, when declining city revenues forced the discharge of all four deputies. Marshal Terrell continued in office until October 1873, when he resigned following bitter wage disputes. Shortly thereafter municipal policing ceased entirely.[7]

The marshal's office soon reopened, but it struggled in the face of chronic unprofessionalism and high turnover. Tom Ewing, elected as Fort Worth's second marshal in April 1874, was a local physician (some accounts identify him as a dentist) who continued his practice while serving. At times, Ewing incorporated the tricks of that trade into his new calling by drugging the drinks of aggressive drunks, a method that may have been inventive and effective but which suggested official ineptitude at controlling rowdies. Ewing resigned after only eight months, followed by H. P. Shiel (one of the first four appointed officers), who triumphed in a special election in December 1874 only to resign after only ten months complaining about wages.[8]

Yet another special election on October 25, 1875, made Tom P. Redding Fort Worth's fourth marshal in thirty months. Redding proved to be the worst of a remarkably poor group. He had some experience, having served as an unofficial marshal during the Civil War, but was best known as the town barber, a trade that he continued after assuming office. "Uncle Tom," as he was popularly known, represented such a low level of authority and public standing that toughs commonly chased him off the street with lariats or by shooting at his feet. On February 8, 1876, after just over three months, the city council suspended him pending a final hearing to determine the wisdom of filing formal charges. Redding resigned the next day amid reports that his conduct would lead to a permanent suspension. (Unfortunately, the resignation precluded a public report.)[9]

The resulting campaign and election appeared to be just another unremarkable exercise in a process made common by the revolving-door nature of the city marshal's office. Following Redding's resignation in February 1876, the council appointed Deputy John Stoker interim marshal until the regularly scheduled municipal election in April. The ensuing campaign hardly made a ripple in the local press; as late as two weeks prior to voting, only one candidate publicly declared (Stoker) and no reports appeared concerning Redding or the incident leading to his suspension. Yet Timothy Courtright came from seemingly nowhere to defeat Stoker and four others, outpolling his nearest competitor by only three votes, 106 to 103. By all accounts and appearances, the victory was an unremarkable expression of the democratic process and unrelated to Redding's departure. Almost exactly twenty years later, in 1907, those perceptions were challenged by allegations of collusion and political payoffs that fixed the election for Courtright. If true, these charges posited the existence and vitality of an early Fort Worth elite with sufficient political muscle to control the 1876 election.[10]

The crux of the allegations rested on an incident reported by the *Fort Worth Democrat* on December 18, 1875, and the *Fort Worth Standard* on December 23, 1875 (the *Standard* was a weekly, which accounted for the delayed reporting). On the afternoon of December 16, 1875, two young men, William Nance, described only as a teenager, and Bingham Feild, nineteen years old, entered the Club Room saloon at 22 Main Street. Due to their ages and advanced states of intoxication, the bartender, Lem Grisham, refused service even under threats of bodily injury. Enraged by the rejection and having their bluff called, Nance and Feild fired several random shots in the street, continuing the rampage as they entered an alley between the City Bakery at 23 Main Street and an adjacent bowling alley. Deputy Marshal Courtright, responding to the sound of gunfire, found the two in a four-foot wide alley enclosed on one end by fences. Courtright approached from the alley's open end, advancing despite warnings and threats to shoot. Nance relented, surrendering his weapon, but Feild refused, stating he would rather die. Courtright, perhaps motivated by Feild's youth, moved to disarm him rather than answer the challenge, a forbearance that almost proved fatal. During the struggle, Feild's pistol discharged, striking Courtright's abdomen and traveling upwards toward his right shoulder. Several onlookers, led by David Crawford, broke down the fence, subdued Feild, and marched both miscreants to jail.[11]

Contemporary newspapers agreed that Courtright sustained serious injuries. The *Democrat* claimed "little hope is entertained" of his recovery. The *Standard* expressed deep sympathy, describing the wound as dangerous, if not fatal, and offering faint hopes. Despite the similarities, a letter to the editor in the *Democrat* from "B" on December 25, 1875, accused the *Standard* and a third local newspaper, the *Mortar* (lost to researchers) of exaggerating Courtright's wounds. The polemic noted that Courtright never considered his injuries life-threatening and laughingly refused when asked to make a dying statement, insisting that Nance and Feild were friends and calling the shooting an accident occasioned by the struggle over Feild's pistol. The "letter" may have been a disguised editorial; newspapers often used the façade of letters to the editor to hide editorial opinions.[12]

The matter remained closed until 1907 when J. B. Roberts, a local reporter of thirty-five years' service, recounted the incident in a newspaper article commemorating the leveling of a city hall built in the 1870s. Roberts first noted that one of the two errant youths was then a practicing physician in Oklahoma Indian Territory and that the other had died. He verified the initial fatal prognosis for Courtright but recalled that the melee began on Main Street at Bohart's saloon when Marshal Redding, not Deputy Courtright, responded to the sounds of Nance and Feild shooting at flies on the ceiling, only to be chased out of the building by the two drunkards firing at his feet, causing the hapless marshal to jump "like a cat on a hot griddle." Redding then retreated to city hall where Mayor G. H. Day ordered him to return and arrest both men. Perhaps realizing the marshal's limitations, Mayor Day also suggested that he seek the assistance of Courtright, who the mayor knew to be "game." Roberts contended that Courtright was not then a deputy marshal and had not taken any part in municipal affairs but that he agreed to help after Redding found him chopping wood on the Trinity River bottom. Courtright, unarmed, approached from the rear of the alley between Bohart's saloon and the Club Room, calling for the two to surrender. According to Roberts, both Nance and Feild then fired, with one shot striking Courtright through the body. Courtright, although seriously wounded, subdued and disarmed both men before walking them to jail and collapsing.[13]

Although the later report differed slightly from the contemporary accounts, its major impact lay in revelations about the shooting's aftermath. Roberts claimed that the suspects were scions of two of Fort Worth's most prominent families and that their criminal culpability in such a serious offense presented quite a dilemma for their kin and the rest of local society. The two were clearly guilty of a felonious assault and if tried would surely have been convicted and sentenced to the state penitentiary, possibilities that Roberts termed out of the question due to their community standing. One of the two, already a doctor according to Roberts, proposed that if Courtright dropped the matter, both families would use their influence to make him city marshal. When Courtright agreed they forced Redding's resignation, opening the door for a new election in which Courtright became marshal.[14]

Many problems exist with Roberts's version of the events, most of which may be an example of time corrupting memory. Clear and irrefutable evidence exists that Courtright had served several functions in the city's employ, including firefighter and jailer, and that he was a deputy city marshal prior to and during the shooting. On November 18, 1875, less than a month earlier, the *Standard* reported that "Deputy Marshal Courtright" had broken his right forefinger shooting a man the previous Saturday. The historical record also argues against the idea that the incident was responsible for Redding's resignation. Although the particulars of the suspension remained hidden, the press did report that it stemmed from an incident occurring on February 7, 1876, several weeks after Courtright's injury on December 16, 1875. Of course, the undescribed incident could have been manipulated, but that seems unlikely because it was not necessary. At the time, all city positions carried one-year terms, and elections were only weeks away, in April. Replacing Redding in February with an interim marshal accomplished little to nothing. In addition, according to contemporary press reports, Courtright stated that he was wounded during a struggle, contradicting Roberts's claim that he was shot as he approached. Furthermore, it is unlikely that either Feild or Nance held a medical degree in their teen years.[15]

Hero worship also may have corrupted Roberts's memory. Courtright's bravery in the face of fire approaches legendary status, but it would have been foolhardy for an unarmed person to approach aggressively intoxicated men who had recently fired on the city marshal. Also, for all his attributes, Courtright remained mortal and it stretches credulity to believe that, while seriously wounded, he subdued two young men and then walked them several blocks to the city jail. Exaggerations often develop around persons of notoriety. Several apocryphal tales surround Courtright, including a claim that he twice knocked down heavyweight champion John L. Sullivan while the fighter was in his prime.[16]

These exceptions noted, considerable circumstantial evidence supports the critical part of Roberts's account, the assertion that the two families arranged Courtright's election to reward his cooperation. Courtright won the election despite facing a lengthy recovery and having entered the race rather late. In late January 1876, reports noted that he was only beginning to walk, and no public mention of his candidacy appeared prior to the election. Yet he triumphed over four other opponents including Stoker, the acting marshal. Of course, Courtright probably received significant popular support by virtue of his heroism and the resulting injury, but the neatness of the developments suggests machinations.[17]

In addition, all we know indicates that Courtright was not the sort to let even a minor slight pass without retribution, making it unlikely that he would laugh off a serious personal attack without some reason. However, he did so, calling the shooting an accident that owed more to drunkenness than intent and even stipulating that, in the event of his death, the two should not face prosecution. Courtright's atypical forbearance suggests that ulterior motives might have played a major role.[18]

A rather curious phenomenon following the shooting tends to support the notion that the suspects' families were prominent and powerful. From the very first, press accounts demonstrated an unusual level of support and forbearance for two men who had critically injured a local police officer. The *Democrat* immediately adopted a conciliatory tone, writing that the "boys" were friends of Courtright, that it was Feild's first "spree," and that the shooting would not have occurred if they had not been "crazed" by liquor. The paper spoke of "a feeling of deep sympathy that pervades the entire community for the unfortunate youths and their friends and relatives," expressing hope that mercy would be shown the "unfortunate boys." The *Standard* excused the matter as a youthful episode gone wrong, reporting that drunkenness would be the defense. Calls for leniency, published excuses and discussion of defenses probably were visible effects of the high status suggested by Roberts.[19]

Professional advertisements in the local papers and city directories also indicate the prominence of the families and their possible political connections, especially that of Bingham Feild. Dr. J. T. Feild shared an office with Dr. W. P. Burts, Fort Worth's first mayor, at 53 Main Street at Third Street, relatively close to the scene. (Ironically, Drs. Feild and Burts treated Courtright just after the shooting.) In addition, W. Henry Feild maintained a law office at Main and Second streets. Henry Feild was not just any lawyer; he was the Fort Worth city attorney. No evidence definitively ties the professional Feilds to Bingham, but the shared, uncommon surname and indications that he became a physician strongly hint at connections to a family with strong associational links to city hall.[20]

Violence also took place in staid settings involving less flamboyant characters. B. C. Evans, owner of B. C. Evans Company Dry Goods and worth over $250,000, died at the hands of a six-year employee of his clothing department. On July 10, 1889, J. W. Davis, incensed at being passed over for promotion, arrived at work clearly under the influence of alcohol. After an ultimatum that he either quit drinking or find another job, Davis stormed out. But he soon returned with a .41 caliber handgun and shot Evans five times as he sat reading at his desk. Davis received a death sentence with execution set for August 10, 1891, but died in his jail cell, allegedly from self-inflicted head injuries suffered during an epileptic seizure.[21]

Although violence tended to dominate local news, financial malfeasance carried more significant implications for Fort Worth's financial heart. One such incident unraveled after Fort Worth Treasurer John Nichols, who was vice president of City National Bank, committed suicide in his bank office using strychnine he purchased just thirty minutes earlier. Nichols died while an audit was under way that would disclose that he had made $80,000 in fraudulent withdrawals from both private and municipal accounts. Subsequent investigations found that he had large debts and had recently transferred real estate holdings to his wife. The incident cast a pall over the bank, precipitating a run on reserves despite assurances of solvency. Eventually the Nichols estate settled some $75,000 in debts at fifty cents on the dollar, including $41,950 due the bank and $9,000 of the $17,000 the city had on deposit.[22]

Nichols's fraud aggravated the city's already strained financial condition. In August 1886, estimated annual expenditures totaled $91,966, but the treasury held only $28,735 to fund operations for nineteen months. Cash flow problems stemmed from several causes but mostly from interest payments, including $14,000 due annually on $200,000 in waterworks

bonds and interest on $34,000 in floating debt and $320,000 in street improvements bonds. The debt load became so large that it exceeded the
city's annual income by sixteen to one at the same time that tax revenues
declined from $111,073 in 1886 to only $57,348 in 1887, before rebounding
to $106,559 in 1888. In addition, income from fines fell as a result of a cam-
paign to eliminate rampant vice, one of many such drives that waxed
and waned. Prior to 1885, revenue from the Recorder's Court (the city
court) overfunded police wages and prisoner costs to the degree that the
council was able to transfer $7,360 to other departments. After 1885, that
income declined 57 percent when strict enforcement measures effectively
(but temporarily) closed saloons on Sundays, thereby eliminating fines
that contributed $140 weekly to city coffers. In fact, fines paid by saloon-
keepers and other Acre business interests constituted the bulk of court
income and were an important part of city finances. In contrast, most
other arrests involved tramps and other indigents who sat out their sentences in jail, costing the city for their care and board. The combination
of reduced income and increased costs created a $7,500 shortage in the
police budget.[23]

In response, the council took several steps. It reduced the regular
police force from fourteen to eleven, eliminated the fire chief, although it
later reinstated the chief's position at a token $10 annual salary, and cut
two special policemen, an assistant engineer, and most street crews. The
council also increased the tax rate to $1.80 per $100 valuation and enacted
an occupation tax, an annual fee that varied from $2.50 to $50 according
to trade or profession. Still, the budget remained unbalanced, forcing the
council in January 1886 to borrow $935.40 from the street fund for police
salaries after officers had gone unpaid for two months. Eventually, the
aldermen resorted to paying wages in scrip, which merchants usually
discounted at least 15 percent.[24]

Scrip and indebtedness remained unresolved issues throughout the
1880s. Scrip added to the debt burden because the council raised the
standard daily wage from $1.50 to $1.75 to compensate for discounting.
Because the city remained obligated to redeem the scrip at full face value,
the council was, in effect, funding the discount to the benefit of merchants and workers, leaving taxpayers to foot the difference between the
value of scrip and actual money. Scrip, by increasing debts, reduced the
city's overall credit rating, which pushed interest on Fort Worth bonds
to as high as 10 percent. In addition, state laws limited municipalities to a

total debt of not more than 6 percent of assessed valuation, which set Fort Worth's 1888 credit maximum at $510,000 on tax assessments of $8.5 million. Unfortunately, the city's existing debt of $275,000 left only $235,000 in credit potential, insufficient to cover some $465,000 in needed improvements. To get around the limitation, the council raised tax valuations to their true market levels, $16.4 million, which increased the allowable debt ceiling to over $900,000. Property owners received some relief when the council lowered the tax rate from $1.85 to $1.00 per $100 valuation, but city tax revenue still increased from $157,000 in 1888 to $163,000 in 1889.[25]

The municipal treasury suffered, in part, because the waterworks hemorrhaged money, losing $11,000 since the 1885 takeover by the city and continuing to lose at the rate of $1,500 monthly, with no sign of relief. This was a major financial drain for a rather small system operating at the juncture of the Clear and West Forks of the Trinity River near the current Paddock Viaduct. A proposed solution involved expanding the customer base by adding more mains, which would require greater expenditures justified by expectations of increased returns later. Most agreed with the need to increase investment, including an 1886 mayoral candidate who excoriated the outgoing mayor John Peter Smith for buying the waterworks system. Smith agreed that the $56,000 outlay plus assumption of $200,000 in bonded debt had been substantial but claimed that the waterworks had increased in value to $300,000 with an annual income of $40,000 derived from 1,000 users. The man who would become mayor, Dr. H. S. Broiles, rose to Smith's defense, praising him for developing a package of improvements that was making Fort Worth the "Chicago of Texas." Broiles's remarks rested on potential more than reality; he hoped the water supply would attract a packinghouse supported by a significant livestock trade, an economic model drawn from Chicago's huge stockyards. Unfortunately, he was about seventeen years premature.[26]

A smallpox epidemic put more demand on resources while also exposing urban rivalries. In February 1886, Fort Worth health offices reported eight confirmed cases of smallpox, serious enough for the council to offer free vaccinations to indigents, a rare act of largesse when the budget strained to meet the mundane. Dallas's Mayor John Henry Brown cabled Mayor Smith for details and sent a health officer to investigate before issuing a quarantine denying entry to anyone coming from Fort Worth. Mayor Smith questioned the move, noting that smallpox had struck three times in four years without prompting a similar action, and the Texas

State Health Office agreed, ruling the quarantine unnecessary. Smith, along with many Fort Worthians, suspected economic motivations, suggesting that Dallas was making a covert attempt to discourage buyers from trading in Fort Worth. Their suspicion was bolstered when Dallas health officials boarded an eastbound train and put off Lee Herrod of Colorado City, Texas. The Dallas officials left the traveler stranded on foot in the middle of open fields, but they did not bother well-known Fort Worth residents who were also on the train. The Fort Worth papers fought back, running lists of out-of-town customers and asserting that the quarantine would not affect the underlying cause of Dallas's envy, Fort Worth's superior railroad facilities.[27]

Serious disease outbreaks also spurred an expansion of medical services. During the smallpox event of 1886, the lack of a dedicated care facility left most patients to suffer at home, many in high density population settings where they posed the greatest public risk. Alarm grew to the extent that officials feared a general panic, reaching a level that caused the county and city to set aside differences and share the $5,000 cost of a "pest house." In addition, in 1887 Drs. Beall, Adams, and Walker offered to build a hospital commensurate with Fort Worth's size if the city turned over the five acres where the inadequate city hospital then sat, an area off Main Street two miles south of the county courthouse. John Peter Smith led support for the transfer, arguing that the then current city hospital, a single-story frame building of six rooms holding 20 patients, was too small. Other supporters included railroads that were not served by St. Joseph's, which promised to send their injured workers to the new facility.[28]

The city fathers also wrestled with waste disposal problems, an important facet of city sanitation. In 1887 the owner of the existing dump site, the Chowning property, closed it for further use. The council tried leasing land across the Trinity River, but workers hauling city refuse were turned back by shotgun-armed neighbors opposed to a dump near their land. City council members then considered burning waste but rejected that option after learning that furnaces would cost $65,000. As filth and lawsuits piled up, the aldermen secured a temporary dump for sixty days and appointed a special committee to search for a permanent site, granting it the power to act without prior approval. For all its problems, Fort Worth remained parsimonious in sanitation, spending only $2,000 in 1890 compared with $24,000 spent by Dallas. Martin Melosi, among others, has documented the twin issues of urban waste collection and disposal during the late nineteenth and early twentieth centuries, finding that they constituted major problems that remained largely unresolved, which was certainly true for Fort Worth.[29]

Some infrastructure development continued, however. In October 1885, Fort Worth Light and Power Company contracted to provide electricity using an eighty-five horsepower engine. By December arc street lamps shone, at least until 10:00 P.M., but the demand quickly outgrew the limited capacity. In 1888 construction began on a $60,000 facility with a boiler producing 350 horsepower capable of illuminating 3,500 incandescent and 1,000 arc lights. Future plans were grander, envisioning a motor circuit capable of powering machinery.[30]

In 1885, the movement for economic development became formally organized. Twelve of the most active boosters, including Khleber M. Van Zandt (a founder of the Fort Worth National Bank), John Peter Smith, and Boardman Buckley Paddock, formed the Fort Worth Commercial Club, dedicated to advancing business. Membership soon reached 175, causing Paddock to urge construction of a permanent building in the business district. This initiative languished until 1888, when the board adopted plans for a six-story building at Houston and Seventh financed by borrowing $50,000 and raising another $50,000 through 500 shares offered at $100 each on generous terms requiring only $25 down and $10 a month. The contract that was let on June 5, 1888, totaled just $85,000; the reduction may have been due to defaulting investors, many of whom were sued by the board, including one set of partners who subscribed for twenty shares without making any payments.[31]

Railroads still dominated most commercial efforts. In October 1885, major infrastructure adjustments were needed around the Texas and Pacific reservation, an extensive railroad support network of machine shops and roundhouses south of Front Street (Lancaster Avenue). Paddock, Daggett, and John Peter Smith and colleagues traveled to the company's St. Louis headquarters to discuss bridges and street crossings as well as land condemnations needed to make the area passable. Meanwhile, expansion continued with work beginning on the Gulf, Colorado and Santa Fe line to Gainesville, Texas, with connections to Tulsa in the Indian Territory (now Oklahoma) and on to St. Louis. In addition, the Fort Worth and New Orleans Railway reached Mansfield, Texas, just eighteen miles southeast, a milestone celebrated by the arrival of the line's first locomotive into Fort

Major K. M. Van Zandt, president of Fort Worth
National Bank and Fort Worth booster. Courtesy of
University of Texas at Arlington Special Collections.

Worth on January 26, 1886. In the spring of 1886 the Texas and Pacific expanded its repair facilities, adding 200 skilled jobs paying high wages
($2.50 daily) that brought 500 to 1,000 new residents to Fort Worth.[32]

Paddock worked hard and traveled widely to promote the $40,000
bond issue funding construction of the Fort Worth and Rio Grande Railway. He also employed W. W. H. Lawrence, a principal in a New York firm
billed as "Promoters for New Railroads, Cattle Ranches, Texas Lands, Etc.,

Etc." In December 1885 Lawrence wrote that he would approach Cyrus Field about the matter with care; Field consulted often with Jay Gould. In March 1886 he met with financiers in New York City, and in August he took several prospective northern investors over part of the initial segment that stretched 140 miles southwest to Brownwood, Texas. Paddock sought funding for the excursion from the various cities on the route and received mixed responses. W. B. Cunningham, cashier of the Comanche (Texas) National Bank, replied that he would not ask his citizens to fund the expenses of millionaires who would do little more than glance out the train window as it rolled by. On May 1, 1887, the line's first passenger train was able to travel to a point some twenty-three miles southwest of the Tarrant County courthouse and sixteen miles northeast of the Hood County courthouse, celebrating the first leg's completion. The locomotive displayed an "On to Brownwood" sign and the famous Tarantula Map, a projection of future rail service first published on July 26, 1873. (The map received its name because the lines radiating from Fort Worth resembled a spider's legs.) Paddock, who rode with the first passengers, remarked that the projection that had seemed so ambitious at the time had been eclipsed. He credited much of the success to M. O. Hill, an engineer instrumental in laying out the route after others had failed. Paddock noted that Hill did so despite suffering from alcoholism. While off duty, Hill would drink until he ran out of money.[33]

Dallas entered head-to-head competition for several railroads. The two cities fought over a proposed extension of the Atchison, Topeka and Santa Fe to the northeast. The struggle added importance to the subscription drive, which some Fort Worth people described as the decade's most important for fear that a Dallas victory would embolden that city's future efforts. According to the railroad the decision favoring Fort Worth swung on a sense of permanence imparted by superior streets and sidewalks. Despite the loss Dallas did not surrender; it sent sixteen Dallas boosters to Texarkana in 1887 to woo the St. Louis, Arkansas and Texas Railroad with a $125,000 bonus. John Peter Smith intervened, convincing the company to bypass Dallas by offering $35,000 in cash plus rights-of-way and thirty acres for a depot.[34]

Possibly due to subscription fatigue, the pace of cash donations faltered, causing a large-scale campaign to hang in the balance for some time. In 1889, Fort Worth had difficulty raising $40,000 for the Fort Worth and Northwestern Railroad, a planned northwest route to coal fields that would supply cheap energy important for industrial expansion. Paddock pushed the proposal vigorously, suggesting that failure would open the way for a Dallas route around Fort Worth. The fear that Dallas lay in wait, eager to grab any spurned proposal, became a common rallying cry. On the other hand, a Dallas link would doom a proposal. The Fort Worth and Albuquerque Railroad received a poor response when word got out that the proposed route ran through Fort Worth to terminate in Dallas.[35]

Throughout the 1880s, Fort Worth added railroads at a rate that outdistanced every other Texas city. In 1886 its massive facilities served five trunk lines: the Missouri Pacific; Texas and Pacific; Atchison, Topeka and Santa Fe; Fort Worth and Denver; and the Houston and Texas Central. In addition, the northeast line of the Atchison, Topeka and Santa Fe and the Fort Worth and Rio Grande were works in progress, and the Gulf, Colorado and Santa Fe was well along in the planning stages. Fort Worth offered, or would soon offer, direct service from the Gulf to St. Louis via the Gulf, Colorado and Santa Fe; from Mexico to St. Louis on the Missouri Pacific line; and from the Atlantic to the Pacific on the Texas and Pacific. The proliferation of lines gave Fort Worth service monopolies to the Texas panhandle via the Fort Worth and Denver and to the southwest via the Fort Worth and Rio Grande, and ready access to most other regions. This meant that most travelers and goods coming into, leaving from, and/or transitioning across Texas passed through Fort Worth. In three months in 1886 (April, May, and June), Fort Worth received 14.9 million pounds via rail and shipped out nearly 11 million pounds. By 1888, when Dallas had just nine railroad outlets and Houston ten, Fort Worth counted eleven. Two other railroads, the St. Louis, Arkansas and Texas extension from Mount Pleasant, Texas, and the Fort Worth and Western, chartered to run to Albuquerque and Santa Fe, New Mexico, were scheduled for completion in 1889. Fort Worth's rise to railroad prominence was all the more remarkable considering that the first locomotive had arrived little more than a decade earlier, an anniversary saluted by a downtown parade and an eighteen-page special section in the *Democrat* on July 18, 1886.[36]

Railroads were a positive force but they also brought unintended consequences. In the second half of the nineteenth century, American labor challenged the great corporate empires created during the industrial revolution.[37] Many of these confrontations involved railroads, and Fort Worth's prominence as a rail center made it a major battleground in the

Great Southwestern Railroad Strike of 1886. The strike began in March after a union worker was terminated in Marshall, Texas, for attending a Knights of Labor meeting during work hours. (The worker claimed he had received management's permission.) On March 8, 1886, twelve Fort Worth area union locals met at the Knights of Labor Hall at Fifteen and Throckmorton, then marched 480 strong led by a brass band to the courthouse, where 3,000 listened to union speeches. The local effort focused on shutting down the Missouri Pacific, the city's second largest railroad presence, which would have crippled most rail operations including that of the largest, the Texas and Pacific. In the early stages, authorities took a watchful but subdued stance, including a Texas Ranger captain in town, he claimed, to visit friends and relatives. The strikers enjoyed considerable forbearance and a high degree of support in the city administration. In the council election that April, every successful candidate was a member of the Knights of Labor or open supporter, and Mayor Broiles publicly endorsed the stoppage. Others were not so supportive, and enough nonunion workers crossed picket lines to cripple labor's effectiveness.[38]

Frustrated by the failure of picket lines, union supporters resorted to more aggressive tactics to shut down rail service. On March 31, 1886, an estimated 500 protesters took over the Missouri Pacific yards and blocked a Missouri, Kansas and Texas train to Denison by uncoupling several cars and locking the brakes, making the cars impossible to move without first forcibly removing them from the train. A more serious incident was narrowly averted when calmer heads prevented an assault on a locomotive protected by armed company men threatening to shoot. The next day, unionists blocked an eastbound train and then shouted down the mayor's call for calm. On April 2, the company sought relief from the courts, securing and circulating 500 copies of a restraining order that forbade trespassing. At that point, the already volatile situation became a tense standoff between some 3,000 strikers and sympathizers, many armed or with firearms hidden nearby, and some fifty well-armed officers backed by a posse of armed citizens.[39]

Violence seemed assured when the railroads opted to move trains at any cost. On April 3, despite multiple threats, a Missouri Pacific train departed southward guarded by the entire Tarrant County Sheriff's Department and most of the city police. As it left, two women, one unidentified and the other named only as Mrs. Egan, the wife of a Knight, ran onto the tracks waving red flags. As the train approached one refused to move and was pulled away by her companion just as the locomotive passed. Mrs. Egan later said that she and her companion were trying to warn of some danger, perhaps referring to an ambush that waited two miles south. Near the junction of the Fort Worth and Denver and the Fort Worth New Orleans, called Tucker's Hill, a turned switch forced the train to stop. As the tracks were being reset, the guards spied four men nearby and another five armed with Winchesters in a gully 100 yards away. Officers Courtright, Fulford, Townsend, Thomason, and Charley Sneed arrested the first four without incident, but when they approached the armed group, a volley of gunfire killed Fort Worth Police Officer Townsend and wounded Sneed and Fulford. (Fulford would be the first officer to reach Courtright after his gunfight with Short.) During the battle, the four arrestees escaped. The next day the body of Frank Pierce, a known union man, was found near Sycamore Creek. H. Hemming was eventually convicted of killing Townsend and was sentenced to life imprisonment.[40]

After the shooting, Fort Worth took on the appearance of an armed camp; tensions escalated and more violence seemed certain. Seven to ten squads of militia arrived, including three from Dallas, two from Austin, and others from Sherman, Decatur, and Alvarado. The militias joined a contingent of ten Texas Rangers led by Captain McMurray (no longer just visiting, apparently) and up to 2,000 armed citizens deputized to ensure peace and operational rail service. Strike supporters seemed to be bracing for a fight. The following notice appeared around town: "To Trainmen of Freight Department: Please do not sacrifice your lives by being moved out on freights by government officers or Gould's petty officers. Last Call. Fair Warning. Determined."[41]

Fortunately, the Knights leadership intervened on the side of conciliation and nonviolence. With their cooperation, two trains left peacefully for Alvarado, one with a sheriff's posse of eighteen and sixteen members of the Grayson Rifles Militia commanded by Captain Lee Hall and the other guarded by ten militiamen. Both arrived without incident and were met by a Knights spokesman who publicly condemned violence. At a conciliation meeting with Fort Worth citizens, union representatives admitted that they had erred in allowing an out-of-stater to incite rancor and promised support for the prosecution of anyone committing violence. As calm returned the crowds and militias left, except for two companies of Rangers who vowed to remain until they were certain all was quiet. By mid-April conditions returned to normal, with railroads running without interference and merchants assuring customers that goods arrived daily. On May 1 the Knights national executive leadership officially ended the walkout, saying it did so to ease the suffering of workers and the nation. That same day, a general strike seeking an eight-hour work day began in Chicago. Three days later, on May 4, 1886, a bomb exploded at a labor rally in Chicago's Haymarket Square, killing seven policemen and dealing a crippling public relations blow to the labor movement. After Haymarket, Fort Worth unions tried to remain involved locally. A joint meeting of Farmers Alliance and Knights of Labor delegates on May 12, 1886, at Daggett's Hall resolved to create an Alliance cotton mill. Another meeting in June 1886, chaired by Mayor Broiles, planned a "people's ticket" for the next election. None of the initiatives was successful.[42]

The events of 1886 had major repercussions for the labor movement everywhere, including Fort Worth. The violence involving Officer Townsend's murder led to several indictments and a life sentence for H. Hemming, as well as the formation of Fort Worth's own militia, the Fencibles, commanded by Captain W. B. Ford and dressed in uniforms of dark green trimmed in blue and gold. The formation of a militia so soon after the 1886 strike was a clear expression of a growing distrust of labor. The adversity and hostility associated with the strike that led to the Fencibles also had a negative effect on what had been a rather vibrant local labor movement. Several local units of the Knights of Labor existed prior to 1886, including a "colored" lodge that hosted a Christmas day gathering at the Knights Hall, and unions were generally accepted and often successful. Before 1886, local carpenters had demanded an eight-hour day (with no reduction in pay) and city laborers had struck over scrip devalued as much as 30 percent. (They compromised on 15 percent devaluation.) After 1886, labor increasingly carried a negative stigma and its efforts met more resistance, both locally and nationally. Although the labor movement continued to deal with basic issues affecting workers, many on both sides lost sight of that aspect and only saw a broad movement dedicated to reordering society by redressing an imbalance of power favoring industries over workers. Walter Licht described the Great Railroad Strike of 1877 as a direct challenge to the growing political and economic power of concentrated capital, but his description applied equally well to 1886. Those on Fort Worth picket lines may not have formalized a connection with that larger perspective, but they would have understood that there were real issues involved and they were committed to the labor movement. After 1886, widespread support for unions diminished. In 1894, Fort Worth workers ignored the call of Eugene Debs, the president of the American Railway Union, to join Galveston and Dallas locals striking the Atchison, Topeka and Santa Fe, a refusal that the *New York Times* deemed "important, as nearly all roads center there [in Fort Worth]."[43]

Railroads remained the most important sector in Fort Worth's economy, but by the mid-1880s the city was developing a livestock trade that many ranked second in importance. Livestock became a viable local enterprise for many reasons—in particular, the city's well-developed rail service. Ranchers depended on railroads to provide feed and to ship livestock, both of which generated profits for the transport industry. In addition, the timing was fortuitous; the developing local market was concurrent with and benefited from a general livestock boom that lasted from the mid-1870s to the mid-1880s during which the price of steers increased 300 percent. This boom and the local industry drew strength from substantial British investment. In 1882, the Matador Land and Cattle Company, Limited, backed by three British investors, bought out the Matador Land and Cattle Company of Fort Worth, formed in 1879 by locals including Henry H. Campbell, Alfred Markham Britton, and L. W. Lomax. By the end of 1883, the company had grown to cover 374,717 acres and earn an annual profit of more than 15,000 British pounds, worth approximately $1.6 million in 2013. By 1890, it had expanded operations to 444,657 acres on which thousands of cattle pastured. The British contributed to one of Fort Worth's few non-rail enterprises by providing investment funds, by developing technologies in wire fencing, windmills and deep wells, and by crossbreeding shorthorns in conjunction with the Espuela Land and Cattle Company.[44]

The end of the livestock boom played havoc with the Fort Worth economy. Cattle ranching at the time faced many trials, such as the loss of grazing land to lumbering and other industries, but unusually harsh weather conditions proved disastrous. In the summer of 1885, a drought began that ran for two years at the same time that the nation experienced severe winters back-to-back, especially the winter of 1886–87, which became infamous for its harshness. The combined effects bankrupted many farmers and ranchers, leading to mass herd liquidations that drove cattle prices from $35 to under $5 a head. Even the Matador Company, which had been so successful, lost money in 1887 and eventually liquidated. The slump continued until the 1890s, when the livestock population reached such low levels that prices revived. In 1887, the *Gazette* blamed the cattle bust for stopping growth, suggesting that but for it Fort Worth would have been a city without equal.[45]

In addition to the weather, ranchers struggled in a market dominated by the great Chicago packers Armour and Swift. The two great butchers held such a complete stranglehold that they could dictate prices, a power that they exercised to the detriment of suppliers. The *New York Post* reported that cattlemen received only three of the twenty to twenty-eight cents per pound consumers paid for beef, with most of the rest going to the packinghouses. Such unfair financial distributions spurred development of regional slaughterhouses to challenge Chicago's monopoly. Regional packers had certain advantages, especially in eliminating the need or decreasing the distance to ship live animals via rails, which not only saved transport expense but also the travel stress that cost animals as much as 10 percent of their weight, a significant issue because cattle were often sold by the pound.[46]

Therefore, time and circumstances seemed to favor the establishment of a large packinghouse in Texas. Many cities, including Dallas, expressed interest in an industry with the potential to rocket its host to the level of cities like Chicago, Kansas City, or St. Louis, all of which benefited from sizable investments in meat processing. Fort Worth seemed a likely choice, thanks to its superior railroad facilities and the availability of a refrigeration plant—the closed plant that had been part of Isaac Dahlman's grand export plan—rivaled only by those found in Chicago and Kansas City. But Fort Worth suffered from the lack of a large stockyard. To correct this deficiency, a group of leading citizens organized, electing a board of directors heavily weighted with railroad men: John C. Brown of the Texas and Pacific; Morgan Jones of the Fort Worth and Denver; R. C. Kerens of the St. Louis, Arkansas and Texas; L. D. Voak of the Missouri Pacific; and J. J. Mulane of the Gulf, Colorado and Santa Fe. Financing came from 2,000 shares sold for $100 each, with only a $25 down payment. The Missouri Pacific, the Atchison, Topeka and Santa Fe, the Fort Worth and Denver, and the Texas and Pacific bought half of the $200,000 subscription, but the drive stalled $30,000 short. A grand public meeting successfully closed the deficit, largely thanks to Paddock, who bought the last $5,000. Construction began immediately on 258 acres located two miles north of the courthouse at the confluence of the Trinity River and Marine Creek.[47]

The enthusiasm that drove the project stimulated development on a much wider scale. The union stockyards, described as the finest south of Chicago, opened on January 2, 1890, with pens capable of holding 5,000 cattle, 10,000 hogs, and 1,500 horses and mules, as well as an exchange covering seventy-five acres. Several railroads, including the Atchison, Topeka and Santa Fe, the St. Louis, Arkansas and Texas, the Missouri Pacific, and the Fort Worth and Denver secured rights-of-way and began running tracks from Union Station. Support industries also appeared, such as the Fort Worth Tannery Company, the Dixie Wagon Company of Indiana, and the Texas Rolling Mill and Iron Works, employing seventy workers just south of the pens. The stockyards were a major step in the process that would make Fort Worth a beef processing center, but realization of that potential would take longer than most imagined.[48]

The stockyards also stirred development of streetcar service north of the Trinity River. This project required construction of an iron bridge because the existing wooden structures could only support pedestrians and light wagons. The city council, county, and stockyards agreed to share equally in paying the $24,500 bid submitted by Smith Bridge Company of Toledo, Ohio, for a crossing 34 feet wide and 930 feet long. The expenditure met considerable opposition, but proponents pointed out that the line would serve not only the livestock trade but also the St. Louis, Arkansas and Texas terminal and some 200 acres within the city that lay north of the river.[49]

The dispersion effect northward carried over into other suburban development. In 1887, H. B. Chamberlain began Arlington Heights on 2,000 acres west of the Trinity River, a location touted as healthier due to its elevation 150 feet above downtown. Chamberlain promised that the addition would become the city's most elegant, that it would have a grand boulevard and streetcar service, a resort with a hotel and a two-story pavilion with an amusement area at Lake Como. In the pre-automobile age, streetcar service made suburban development possible by providing quick access between residential and commercial zones. At the same time, the East Fort Worth Company, a group of investors that included several prominent railroad men, bought 414 acres north of East First Street, then a virgin forest, for the Sylvania Addition. The group dug its own well, set

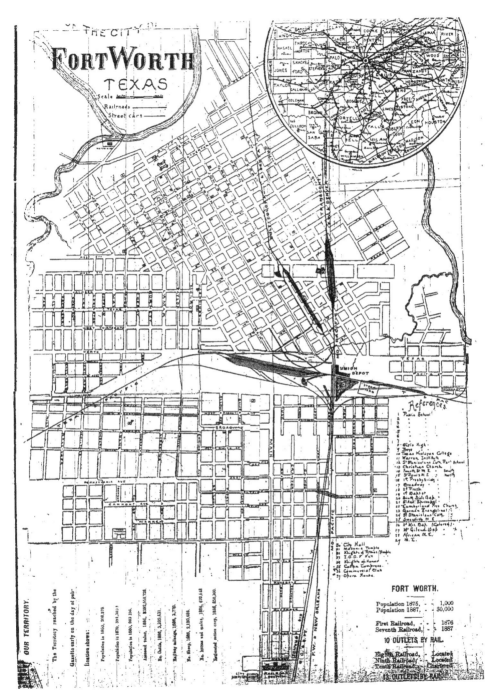

1887 map of Fort Worth. *Fort Worth Gazette,* May 25, 1887, p. 1.

The turn to industrialization was formalized in 1889. Paddock presided over a public meeting on July 22, 1889, that called on all supporting the "upbuilding of the city" to take the first steps in the new industrial era. Attendees listened to charges that Fort Worth had given railroads hundreds of thousands of dollars but that the more it gave the worse it had been treated. They agreed that the remedy to such ingratitude lay in switching focus to bricks and mortar, a process that would begin by funding subsidies of $100,000 for a woolen mill and $250,000 for a cotton mill. Paddock embraced the new cause as actively as he had wooed railroads. While in Boston seeking investors he complained of homesickness and of late hours promoting Fort Worth mills, but he maintained his resolve, writing "I *must* lay the foundation for doing some business this time, in a line that won't worry, harass and annoy the life (unreadable) me as that Railroad [sic] has."[61]

Railroads were not completely abandoned, either as an industry themselves or as tools promoting other industrial forms. Rail service had always complemented and promoted commerce, providing wide access to markets for livestock dealers and wholesale merchants and, beginning in the late 1880s, offering access to cheap coal. For years, Dallas had enjoyed the advantage of substantially lower energy costs due to its supply of coal at $3 to $4 a ton, arranged by its manufacturing association, giving it an edge that certainly contributed to attracting manufacturing investments. Little wonder that Fort Worth placed such importance on an 1887 proposal for a Fort Worth Western rail connection to the coal fields in Young and Jack counties, or that in 1889 the Fort Worth and Albuquerque line was deemed the city's most important agenda item because it included Thurber, Texas, where coal sold for only $2 to $3 a ton. With that link, coal would provide affordable energy to run water pumps and electric generators, but the salient force driving Fort Worth's interest lay in coal's contribution to industrialization. The matter was considered so vital that some suggested cheap coal would mean Fort Worth would not have to solicit factories, that it would not be able to keep them away, an assertion that represented little, if any, exaggeration. Walter Licht's remarkable study agreed, arguing that the importance of coal for nineteenth-century American industrialization could not be overstated, that a direct connection existed between the two.[62]

As their focus shifted from railroads to industries, boosters looked for ways to herald the change. A public meeting in January 1889 appointed a committee of fifty, including Smith, Van Zandt, and several railroad men, to consider a suitable promotional outlet. Their report recommended a grand exhibition of local products that became Fort Worth's Spring Palace of 1889 and 1890. The idea was not a committee original. R. A. Cameron of the Fort Worth and Denver Railroad, drawing inspiration from the Corn Palace of Sioux City, Iowa, and the Ice Palace of St. Paul, Minnesota, had pushed for such an exposition for months. Cameron, who became known as the father of the Spring Palace, had a profound understanding of the problems facing Fort Worth and the state. He described Texas as a large land mass with little urban development, no city of 50,000, no building of nine stories, and no factory worth $2 million. He might have added that no Texas city was listed among the nation's twenty-two largest, despite the state's overall ranking as sixth in population. This lack of urban development suggested that neither cotton, the South's premier agricultural product, nor railroads provided sufficient economic thrust for great progress and that real growth required factories. Cameron's proposal quickly gathered support, much of which was rather passionate, including claims that the exhibit would be more important for Texas than were the 1876 Centennial Exposition for the United States or the current Paris Exposition for France. The attendees wrote a charter that called for funding of $100,000 derived from selling shares but allowed for beginning implementation once $35,000 had been subscribed.[63]

The project seemed to take wings from the first. Planners scheduled the Texas Spring Palace for three weeks in June, Texas's best month, when grasses are green, flowers bloom, and fruits and vegetables ripen (some consideration went into calling it the Texas June Palace), leaving only a few weeks to build a suitable facility. Estimates for construction ranged from $26,000 to $35,000, reasonable considering that Sioux City's Corn Palace had run $30,000, with another $20,000 dedicated in contingency funds. Financing came from selling $10 shares with the full amount due at purchase. The organizing assembly named Paddock president, Smith vice president and Walter Huffman treasurer. Paddock and Smith started the campaign by each buying $300 worth of shares; Paddock then bought $500 more. Fundraisers were also held, including an Opera House event netting $6,160 that featured a "machine" projecting pictures of Great Britain and historical figures on a screen.[64]

The palace would be grand in dimensions and appearance. Various site proposals were considered, including locations in Sylvania and Northside,

General R. A. Cameron of the Fort Worth and Denver Railroad and father of the Spring Palace. Courtesy of University of Texas at Arlington Special Collections.

but the organization selected Lot 26 just north of the Texas and Pacific reservation (near the intersection of East Lancaster and Jennings avenues) that was available for $5,000 cash or $6,000 paid out over time. Following the design of Armstrong and Messer Architects, the Fort Worth Loan and Construction Company began work in March, allowing only forty days for completion. The project required 528,000 feet of lumber, 192 kegs of nails, and provided work for 106 laborers. The finished product, constructed of Texas products and modeled on Denver's Corn Palace, enclosed 60,000 square feet. The front and rear walls stretched 200 feet, with towers at the four corners and a sixty-foot center dome rising 125 feet high, surrounded by eight small towers. Agricultural products covered the interior and exterior surfaces, with wheat lining the dome, cotton and corn the sides, and wheat, sugar cane, beef horns, sheep pelts, or sea shells on

Interior exhibit area of the Texas Spring Palace, June 1889. Courtesy of University of Texas at Arlington Special Collections.

the towers and other walls. The first floor showcased mineralogy, stressing that Texas had more copper than Michigan, more lead than Missouri, and more iron than Wisconsin. The second floor displayed various fruits and vegetables, manufactured products, and agricultural goods. Other exhibits covered Texas's flora, fauna, and history.[65]

The Spring Palace opened on time and enjoyed a successful run. The inaugural procession on May 29, 1889, stretched two miles and featured the governors of Texas and Nebraska. Special attractions included a parody of *HMS Pinafore* and music provided by the local fire department band and the Elgin Watch Factory Band of Illinois that was paid $325 daily, including travel time, with $10 additional allowed the band leader for each solo. The exhibition averaged 3,000 patrons daily for a total attendance of 100,000, but reports that President Benjamin Harrison would attend proved false. At the closing on June 27, promoters expressed elation at an unqualified success.[66]

As the decade closed, Fort Worth saw some limited results of its turn to manufacturing. In November 1889 the foundation of the Dixie Wagon factory, a 15,224-square-foot building managed by H. L. Nichols of New Haven, Connecticut, lay almost complete, and its residential district had sold all but ten lots. In addition, a club house worth $50,000 and a St. Paul rolling mill employing seventy-five were planned for the Northside. For the week ending January 19, 1890, Fort Worth led the nation in percentage growth of clearing house receipts, with an increase of 110 percent over the same week in 1889 ($3.05 million, compared with $1.45 million in 1889) and even ranked above Dallas's total ($2.86 million), an impressive but isolated aberration. In 1890, Tarrant County's property tax assessments reached just $14 million, less than half of Dallas County's $29 million, which led the state.[67]

The 1880s represented a breakout period in which Fort Worth became more than just another county seat; it was a critical step on the road to greatness. This transition was largely due to the remarkable railroad development that made Fort Worth the transportation hub of the Southwest, with lesser but notable contributions from wholesale trade and livestock processing. Economic development made possible an incipient municipal infrastructure, including a waterworks system, however flawed it may have been. Two other events had less tangible contemporary effects but offered major implications for the future. The Northside stockyards disappointed investors by failing to attract a major packer in the 1880s or the 1890s, but they would be the catalyst bringing Fort Worth's first major factories in 1903. In addition, the years from 1885 to 1889 witnessed an emerging recognition that railroads were not sufficient for the level of urban development envisioned by Fort Worth boosters, an important step leading to a switch in Fort Worth's focus from transportation to manufacturing. In essence, the decade's second half brought the realization that the work of the first half was not adequate. This was, in its own way, just as important for Fort Worth as railroads or the stockyards. The new emphasis would face rough sledding in the 1890s, but in it lay Fort Worth's future.

3

THE STAGNANT NINETIES, 1890–1899

The 1890s were not kind to Fort Worth. The transition to an industrial focus that began in the late 1880s fell victim to the Panic of 1893, a national depression with aftereffects that plagued Fort Worth until the end of the nineteenth century. Boardman Buckley Paddock, always a keen observer, blamed the depth and length of the economic troubles on Fort Worth's dearth of industry, arguing that the lack of diversity left the local economy ill-prepared to weather declines in cattle and wholesale trades. Oliver Knight agrees that poor industrial development contributed to economic vulnerabilities, while J'Nell Pate sees the depression of the 1890s as a force destroying the hopes of many businessmen. Their perspectives share a common thread linking Fort Worth's poor economic vitality to its limited industrial base.

The confluence of negatives that prolonged and deepened Fort Worth's depression experience also aggravated other issues, often in dramatic fashion. Hard times contributed to the downfall of some highly respected residents and to the waning of organized boosterism, although a new, more limited form appeared as the decade ended. In addition, declining revenues and increasing debts drove Fort Worth's city government to the brink of bankruptcy, curtailing most initiatives, especially those having to do with recurring problems in the waterworks. Financial stress also affected, for a time, the official relationship with Hell's Half Acre. The historic justification for the Acre's longevity rested on its indirect commercial effects: the assumption that vice complemented and stimulated downtown trade. In the cash-starved 1890s, the argument turned more to direct revenue derived from fines.[1]

The 1890 U.S. census indicated that Fort Worth had grown significantly during the 1880s, although at a rate slower than Dallas. The population increased 246 percent, from 6,663 in 1880 to 23,076, an addition of
16,413. Fort Worth's population increase accounted for all but fifty-eight
of the county's total increase of 16,471 persons, a 66.8 percent upswing
from 24,671 in 1880 to 41,142 in 1890. The disparity in rates of growth between city and county meant that Fort Worthians now made up 56 percent of the county population, up from just 20 percent in 1880. As impressive as the statistics seemed, they failed to match projections. In 1880, local
wags had confidently predicted that the city's population would reach
40,000 by the end of the decade, and as late as 1890 the *New York Times*
postulated that significant growth trends in Southern urbanization would
push Fort Worth to 31,000 and Dallas to 39,000. Dallas came close to that
projection, achieving an 1890 population of 38,067, a 267 percent increase
that widened the gap between the two cities. Dallas was now 65 percent
larger than Fort Worth, up from 55 percent larger in 1880. A similar
growth pattern for Dallas County pushed it from 35 percent to 63 percent
larger than Tarrant County. The uniformity of statistics favoring Dallas
city and county suggested that Fort Worth's advance relative to Tarrant
County owed more to the county's poor growth rate than to a remarkable
performance by Fort Worth. In addition, the 1880s were a growth period
for all of Texas as it moved from the nation's eleventh to seventh most
populous state. Keen observers might have wondered how Fort Worth
could win the battle for railroad supremacy while losing ground relative
to Dallas in population growth.[2]

Still, many thought the present secure and the future bright. One analysis showed that Fort Worth enjoyed the state's highest wealth per capita,
$533, compared with $322 for Dallas and $388 for San Antonio. A later
report lowered the numbers and reduced the degree of separation but
still showed Fort Worth's per capita wealth at $466, ahead of Dallas's $342,
Austin's $323, Houston's $385, San Antonio's $400, and Galveston's $423.
However, these figures, derived by dividing tax assessments by population, were largely an effect of the 1888 increase in Fort Worth's property
assessments to true market value, while other Texas cities continued to
assess at a fraction of actual worth. In 1890, Fort Worth's assessed valuations totaled $22 million, equal to San Antonio's and larger than Dallas's
assessed valuation of $20 million. But both San Antonio and Dallas were
larger and richer than Fort Worth; they simply assessed property at lower

rates. When statistical analyses could not explain Fort Worth's smaller comparative population, boosters used history and geography. Fort Worth, they noted, was the "New Texas." It was the state's youngest major city, having incorporated just seventeen years earlier (1873), while Dallas had incorporated in 1856, Austin and Galveston in 1839, Houston in 1838, and San Antonio in 1837. In addition, Fort Worth's city limits covered only four square miles, compared with nineteen for Dallas and thirty-six for San Antonio. Supporters believed that these conditions would, over time, erode and that Fort Worth would reap the benefits of being the only large town in the Southwest established by army engineers. (Fort Worth began in 1849 as part of a westward line of army forts designed to control the American Indian threat.)[3]

Fort Worth's municipal infrastructure also had improved. In April 1890, outgoing mayor H. S. Broiles listed the accomplishments of his four years in office: increases in miles of paved streets from forty to fifty, of sewers from eleven to forty-six, and of water mains from eleven to more than twenty-six. In addition the city now owned and operated an electric plant that, along with two private generators, powered 200 arc and 1,000 incandescent lights. Broiles also bragged that the waterworks operated at a profit and that the gang-well system, complemented by 300 private artesian wells, yielded one million gallons daily, enough to supply all needs, including 175 fire hydrants and a public facility, the "Natorium," with a large indoor pool as well as Turkish and Russian baths. The positive cash flow generated by water service contributed to a municipal cash reserve of $222,824, with another $225,000 soon due from bond sales.[4]

Despite all the advances, and despite all its energy and boasting, Fort Worth remained little removed from its frontier beginnings. Boosters bragged of residences with fragrant gardens and of fifty-eight miles of sewerage piping, without mentioning that those sewers emptied untreated into the Trinity River or that downtown was a patchwork of contrasts where multistory granite structures housing retail giants stood next to dilapidated houses and tiny fruit stands. Gentility existed at such a low level that a proposal to end the use of women prisoners on rock piles met serious opposition. The criminal side of the frontier also remained on the municipal doorsteps. In December 1894, Sam Evans, the son of a prominent local family, and two other masked men made off with $140,000 after robbing an eastbound Texas and Pacific train near Mary's Creek, just six miles west of town.[5]

The undeveloped psyche of the period usually tied success to racial purity. In 1889, the *Gazette* opposed a plan to guarantee African Americans political representation at three-fifths their population, the same ratio by which the U.S. Constitution had counted slaves for congressional representation. The editorial argued that whites should retain absolute political control, that they "stood in a patriarchal relationship to the negroes [*sic*]," having done everything that could be done to give blacks an equal chance to succeed, including educating their children. The *Gazette* was a Democratic organ but whites on both sides of the political divide opposed black participation. In April 1892, Lily-Whites, a group of white Republicans, organized locally to shut blacks out of the Republican Party and politics in general. A link between assumed racial superiority and economic advancement was blatant in an 1890 advertisement bragging that Fort Worth was "distinctively American" with the smallest percentage "of negroes [*sic*], Mexicans or objectionable foreigners" of any Texas city. Also in 1890, John C. Ryan, a real estate developer, used horse-racing terms to tout the lack of racial diversity, arguing that the odds of winning the race for urban supremacy were "five to one on the thoroughbred Caucasian, Fort Worth." Fort Worth, Ryan claimed, was Texas's "whitest" city, with a population that was 90 percent white, 6 percent "colored," and only 4 percent "foreign," compared with Dallas with 25 percent "colored" and 15 percent "foreign." Opposition to the some of the more egregious manifestations of race prejudice surfaced occasionally but was muted. In 1894, Mayor Paddock promised to speak in opposition to lynching before a meeting of all "good citizens" at Mount Gilead Baptist Church, located at Jones and Thirteenth in the heart of an African American neighborhood. The local press probably considered itself quite gracious and liberal in describing the pastor, J. Francis Robinson, as possessed of as high a degree of mental development as could be "found in a man of his race."[6]

The press might have saved its patronizing tone for several miscreants holding responsible positions in politics, religion, and business. For example, Mayor W. S. Pendleton, married with five children, left all behind on July 5, 1890, to marry Addie Cullen, a "pretty telephone girl" described by the *Gazette* as "a second Venus." Pendleton had become involved with Ms. Cullen in August 1889 and obtained a sham *ex parte* divorce using a New York City law firm, a fact he concealed from his wife for six months. Mrs. Pendleton first learned of the divorce the day her husband left her, his office, and Fort Worth, taking $80,000 garnered from selling most of the family's property. Pendleton wed Ms. Cullen in New Orleans and sent his resignation as mayor after being charged with bigamy. The happy couple moved to New York City where Pendleton sued to recover the $267 that he had paid in legal fees for the invalid divorce, which he, a lawyer, should have known was fraudulently obtained. Both New York lawyers, W. Duryee Hughes and Patrick Campbell, eventually confessed to forgery involving the divorce, and the Pendletons left New York to settle in Amarillo. Another incident occurred in 1894 when the Third Ward alderman, Martin McGrath, shot and killed James Rushing inside Rushing's saloon. McGrath received a nine-year sentence but escaped from jail in March 1896, an act his attorney called foolhardy because he was sure to receive an executive pardon from the governor.[7] Other malfeasance by municipal officers concerned affairs of finance, including arrests of the city secretary and secretary of the waterworks for misappropriation of funds.[8]

In 1890 the religious community suffered from criminal fraud charges against a prominent Fort Worth pastor. Dr. W. Mitchell, pastor of Broadway Presbyterian Church, admitted forging the name of Martin Casey, a friend in the wholesale liquor trade, as a guarantor on loans totaling $2,500. Mitchell blamed the crime on a failure to live within his means but claimed emotional insanity, a plea supported by the superintendent of a New England "lunatic asylum" where Mitchell had previously been a patient. The court, obviously unimpressed, handed down a two-year sentence.[9]

The financial community had its share of misadventures. In 1891 L. B. Imboden, president of the local New England Loan and Savings Bank, received a four-year sentence for forging signatures on personal loans. Imboden came from a prominent Southern family whose ancestors included a general in the Confederate Army and an officer who had served in the Revolution under George Washington. In addition, his brother had served as both Tarrant County district attorney and judge. This family background probably contributed to the issuance of an executive pardon freeing him after only two years. Imboden left Texas but continued his life of crime, committing another forgery while president of Planters' Bank of Kansas City, Missouri, being implicated in 1903 in a scheme to obtain credit by fraud in New Jersey, and conspiring to wreck the Denver Savings Bank in 1905. A second incident involving Fort Worth bankers occurred in 1894, when R. W. Page shot and killed A. B. Smith in a private room of the Merchants' National Bank, the result of a long-simmering dispute involving bank affairs that dated to July 6, 1893. Unfortunately the details of their disagreement were not published.[10]

Public malfeasance did nothing to hamper the maturation of Fort Worth's railroad infrastructure. By 1890, Fort Worth not only had more rail lines than any other Texas city but was the clear rail center of the Southwest. Railroads were a great industry in and of themselves but they offered collateral advantages benefiting other industries. For example, the Fort Worth and Denver's access to Panhandle and West Texas grain fields fueled the growth of the local grain trade, leading to the construction of five elevators with a capacity of 500,000 bushels. Railroad development played a role in increasing tax evaluations from $16 million in 1889 to $22 million in 1890, thus boosting municipal revenue from a low of $57,348 in 1887 to $106,559 in 1889 and $231,514 in 1890—not all of which was attributable to Fort Worth's change in assessment procedures. The real estate market soared, so that city blocks that sold for $20,000 in 1887 commonly brought $200,000 in 1890. The rise in values encouraged speculation that replaced small buildings with grand edifices such as the new eight-story Hurley Building at Seventh and Main, described as the finest south of St. Louis. In 1890, the percentage increase in Fort Worth's bank clearings, the total of checks and monetary exchanges, often led the nation. The surge pushed the 1890 total to $98.4 million, more than three times the $31.7 million recorded in 1889.[11]

Despite all the positives, the Fort Worth economy remained agriculturally based with little manufacturing development. Wholesale trade continued to be profitable but stagnated. No major wholesale houses opened between 1882 and 1890, a reflection of uneven conditions in which a few large concerns controlled the most profitable trade while fifty jobbers jostled over smaller accounts. Industrial development occurred but at a rather anemic pace. In 1880, only 158 persons in all of Tarrant County worked in manufacturing, but by 1890, Fort Worth alone listed 2,368 industrial laborers earning $1.62 million in wages, mostly in agricultural-related enterprises. The 1890 *City Directory* list of significant businesses included five grain elevators, four flour mills, the stockyards, the iron foundry, and little else (but sixty-nine saloons). The directory, not known for admitting shortcomings, commented that only a beginning had been made in industrial development. The year 1890 saw the opening of a pork packer, a cotton mill, and Texas Brewing, located on Jones between Ninth and Eleventh, but 1891 added only twenty-one smaller businesses. The 1891 business list boasted of only four companies employing 100 or more: Fort Worth Packing (200), Fort Worth Rolling Mills (125), Fort Worth Iron Works (125) and Texas Brewing (120).[12]

Texas Brewing, fourth on the list of large employers, became a significant success. Construction began on the $100,000 facility in September 1890 after Fort Worth citizens subscribed a $20,000 subsidy. The brewery began distribution on May 20, 1891, selling 500 kegs by 4:00 P.M. that first day and 50,000 the first year, fueling a $200,000 expansion that increased output to become the largest in Texas. Texas Brewing so dominated the Fort Worth market that a "foreign" brewery (Anheuser-Busch) resorted to offering dealers free beer in an attempt to break the monopoly.[13]

In the early 1890s, Fort Worth tried once again to establish a packinghouse. Interest in beef processing traced back at least to an 1875 dressed meat plant built on six acres east of town (donated by John Peter Smith) that failed after a year and was converted into an ice house. In the mid-1880s, Isaac Dahlman began shipping beef to Europe via New Orleans, but the plan failed when poor refrigeration allowed the meat to spoil. In 1890, thirty investors revived the dream, forming the Fort Worth Packing and Refrigeration Company to build a $250,000 packinghouse just southeast of the stockyards. The business plan appeared well grounded; local processing eliminated the $12 per head cost of shipping to Chicago, giving the new industry a substantial cost advantage. Construction began in July but suffered from spiraling costs that reached $390,000, not including $181,000 for additions. The plant, which became known as Texas Dressed Beef and Packing Company, began slaughtering in November 1890 and was soon complemented by a refrigeration unit capable of holding 500 beeves and 600 sheep. After processing, the beef went on refrigerated railcars to New Orleans where it was shipped to the east coast and Liverpool, England, as part of another effort to open the European market.[14]

The packery did well initially but eventually crumbled under the weight of supply problems. The operation searched for new markets, even sending a test shipment of six carloads to New York City, spurring enough activity that in April 1890 Jay Gould arrived to assess the need for new rail lines. Gould found a busy market killing the 500 to 800 hogs arriving daily via rail and foot. In the first six months, the packinghouse returned a profit of $35,000, but problems developed when producers could not sustain the 1,500 head required daily for profitable economies of scale. In hindsight, critics suggested that the plan had been too ambitious, that the plant should have been one-fourth the size and cost no more than $50,000.[15]

After struggling to survive for several years, going through several owners in the process, the packinghouse merged with the stockyards on March 30, 1893, to become the Fort Worth Packing Company, with Greenleif Simpson of Boston as president and V. S. Wardlaw as manager. The two developed grand plans that envisioned a $5 million investment, but they were undone by tight credit during and following the Panic of 1893. Simpson, who did not admit defeat easily, remained confident of funding that would transform Fort Worth into the next Omaha, Nebraska (site of an important packinghouse operation). In November 1895, the Chicago Packing and Provision Company, described as one of the nation's top three packinghouses, bought the slaughterhouse but left the stockyards under Simpson. Simpson continued the faith, even seeking another packinghouse that he maintained would spur the type of urban growth seen in Omaha and Kansas City. The *Gazette* agreed, arguing that the stockyards and packinghouse had developed such a solid trade base that it was time for a second packery. Unfortunately, their optimism could not overcome lingering supply issues and other problems that reduced the enterprise to only a bare existence. Still, the dream did not die. At the 1899 opening of the new Union Depot, reputed to be the finest railroad terminal west of St. Louis, celebratory speeches predicted that Fort Worth would be the center of a great cattle market when Texas developed as a major consumer as well as supplier of beef. The prescience of these prognostications would finally be proven in 1903.[16]

Suburban residential development that had begun in the late 1880s continued. Arlington Heights, striving to become an aristocratic section, bragged of high-end homes and a $100,000 hotel in the works. Its developer, Chamberlain Investment Company, poured $500,000 into twelve miles of streets, including a boulevard 125 feet wide and three miles long graced by a triple row of trees, as well as the Lake Como amusement area, a forty-acre pond featuring rides and a lighted pavilion with music every evening. Fort Worth also pushed southward after 1890, when substantial residential growth began below the east-west railroad line on 320 acres that had lain undeveloped due to lawsuits contesting ownership. When the U.S. Supreme Court dismissed all the suits, developers moved quickly to establish the additions of Fairmont, Lexington Heights (by John C. Ryan),

Stanley Heights (bounded on the west by the new Cleburne Road), and Union Depot, advertised as within a "stone's throw of the Union Passenger Depot." Some suggested that the delay in settling such a large space adjacent to the center of railroad activity had severely stunted growth, that if development had occurred earlier Fort Worth would have grown much larger, much sooner.[17]

The growing importance of the city's new southern neighborhoods stimulated an initiative for a new city hall that the *Gazette* termed would be "in keeping with the city's grandeur." The existing dilapidated structure stood in an old section at Second and Rusk streets. The new plan, first proposed in 1887, called for building in the southwest quadrant as an accommodation to the southern growth trend. The council acted quickly that same year, adopting a site around Jennings Street over Mayor Broiles's veto, but construction stalled when the Texas comptroller refused to register the project's $84,000 in bonds. In 1890, John Peter Smith, who was elected mayor in August 1890 following Pendleton's resignation, revived the effort by proposing a $75,000 bond issue (payable on May 1, 1940) that would finance a three-story brick or stone building. Mayor Smith argued that rent savings alone would amount to $90 monthly, enough to cover one-third of the bond payments. Residents of wards one and two opposed removing the city hall from their section, and the city council's finance committee objected to increasing the debt load at a time when $844,000 in bonds lay outstanding and another $300,000 were scheduled for release. Despite these concerns, work began in January 1892 on a lot purchased from W. J. Bailey that occupied 125 feet on Jennings Street, 194 feet on Jackson Street, and 100 feet on Monroe Street. Construction by Smith and Barden was plagued by disputes over cost and defects that delayed completion until October 1893.[18]

In January 1890, discussions began on a second Spring Palace. The initial response was lukewarm, forcing supporters into aggressive solicitations based on the exhibition's commercial benefits, especially its focus on attracting factories rather than the cattle industry. Paddock worked hard to overcome apathy by reminding everyone that the first season had generated remarkable trade increases and had earned Fort Worth widespread publicity. He also noted that, during his recent New York trip, several northern investors had expressed interest in attending the next production. Encouraged, attendees at a subscription rally subscribed $19,000, then $26,000. R. A. Cameron of the Fort Worth and Denver Railway, a key

supporter of the original Spring Palace, also campaigned hard. He predicted that attendance would double in the second year, producing far
more gate receipts than the $60,000 registered in 1889, more than sufficient
to provide a profitable return on investments. The potential for profits
seemed high, with income derived both from ticket sales and from charging $3,000 for each of twenty-five exhibition spaces. Supporters, who
were not above strong-arm tactics if reason proved inadequate, urged a
boycott of non-contributing merchants. The combination of reason and
force pushed donations beyond the $50,000 level needed to begin reno-
vating and enlarging the existing facility.[19]

Fort Worth's Second Spring Palace Exhibition opened May 10, 1890, with
every expectation of another rousing success. Things got off to a good start
with a large opening-day crowd swelled by businesses that closed from
noon to 4:00 P.M. at the request of Mayor Broiles. Widespread notices in the
national press brought in significant numbers of out-of-staters, including
twenty-three New Englanders who arrived on one train while twenty Chi-
cagoans, including the mayor and the Cook County sheriff, arrived on another. The Board of Trade entertained and wooed visiting politicians and
industrialists with elaborate dinners, during which Paddock and others
lauded Fort Worth's commercial opportunities.[20]

Unfortunately, a great fire turned success into disaster. On May 31, 1890,
the final night, a crowd estimated at 4,000 including the elites of Texas attended a grand final dance. Around 10:25 P.M. a fire alarm sounded, just
as an exhibition vice president was reassuring a visitor who was worried
about the flammability of the structure and its exhibits. The fire signal
came from the "Gold Room," located in the northern section, where Mrs.
Harry Davis of Greenville discovered it. The fire reportedly began when
a boy stepped on a "parlor match" and spread rapidly, engulfing the structure in minutes. Most of the attendees escaped unharmed, thanks to ten
exits that made it possible to empty the building within thirty minutes.
The fire caused one fatality, Al Hayne, who collapsed while helping
others escape and had to be carried out by Jesse Williams, who was
described in press accounts as "A Brave Colored Man." Still, some thirty-
three people suffered injuries such as burns, broken bones, and sprained
limbs. The flames were so intense that they destroyed 700 feet of fire
hose, and the building, valued at $100,000 with only $15,000 in insurance,
was a complete loss. Private contributions funded a monument to Hayne,
commissioned to George Bowman, a local artist who planned to study

sculpturing in Paris, but the equally heroic efforts of Jesse Williams have lain unacknowledged for over a century. A bust of Hayne by Evaline Sellors was added in 1934 to replace a likeness worn by age.[21] Afterwards, discussions focused on ambitious rebuilding plans for a copper-covered stone structure featuring a center dome fifty feet wide and 200 feet high with five star points radiating out, each 180 feet long and 32 feet wide at their base. That idea died, as did Cameron's suggestion for an $82,000 Texas Spring Palace in Boston. Some two years later, Paddock denied rumors that he made unseemly profits from the exhibition, noting that he lost $1,700 in 1889 and that he was one of twenty-three in 1890 who signed a $23,000 funding loan that returned a small but undisclosed profit. No extravaganza of a scale commensurate with the Spring Palace would appear in Fort Worth until 1936, during the Centennial Celebration of Texas Independence.[22]

A few months after the Spring Palace disaster, Fort Worth hosted a smaller but still grand artistic production. In October 1890, fifteen citizens invested $1,000 each to bring to the city the "Last Days of Pompeii," a large theatrical production with a cast of 300 and lots of pyrotechnics that had only been produced in large eastern cities. It ran for two weeks, with general admission tickets selling for fifty cents and box seats for a dollar, but it was a financial failure, leaving each investor with a loss of $625. Such an elaborate production must have seemed strange in what was still a bucolic setting. A reporter walking down Main Street at the time counted seventy-two unhitched horses and saw children playing in the street while traffic rushed by. The sidewalks were no better, with much of their way blocked by shop wares or men congregating.[23]

Fort Worth had many other issues to deal with, including the continuing water crisis. In September 1891, firemen blamed insufficient water pressure for the destruction of the Ellis Hotel at Throckmorton and Third. Commercial engineering firms suggested upgrades, but the city council opted to forego private assistance in favor of researching facilities in Chicago and other cities. That assessment brought the hard but necessary realization that a system capable of supplying consistent water at steady pressure would cost at least $600,000, a huge sum for the day. The council accepted the challenge by authorizing a $650,000 bond issue that would provide twelve additional wells, some as deep as 900 feet, and equipment to pump emergency supplies directly from the Trinity River. At the end of 1892, after only eleven months, the improvements were operational

and by the second quarter of 1893, the waterworks reported a positive
cash flow with an income of $20,962 versus expenses of $17,222. This de-
lighted Paddock, who called the Fort Worth system the most complete in
the South. The financial report might have been even better if not for fraud.
City Secretary H. V. Burns was charged with misappropriation of funds,
and a water department official was prosecuted over a missing $531.[24]

The system may have been fine but the supply was not. By May 1894
Paddock, who had been so pleased, complained that daily output of wells,
the primary water source, had decreased to around one million gallons.
To make matters worse, the designated emergency source, the Trinity
River, tended to be at its lowest during high-demand summer months
when it was most needed. The city council tried to reduce demand by
fining residents for wastage and even considered installing meters, but it
soon realized that the only effective, long-term solution lay in increasing
supply, either through three small dams adjacent to the pumping station
or a large reservoir west of town.[25]

Water problems not only affected potability and public safety but also
aggravated health issues. The presence of contaminated water during a
cholera outbreak led local physicians to petition for rigid enforcement of
health ordinances and for establishment of a municipal health board.
The city council took its own actions, ordering the water committee to increase supplies of safer well water at any cost and beginning consideration
of filtering river water. The persistence and seriousness of water problems
should be viewed in the context of Fort Worth's geography in the American West. Norris Hundley described the West, except for the Pacific coast
and isolated mountain regions, as a region defined by its sparse rainfall
and few rivers. Hundley suggested that most Westerners understood the
implications of that aridity, that adequate water was crucial for a region's
(or a city's) industry, agriculture, and population distribution. Those in
the forefront of Fort Worth's industrial efforts recognized the negative
effect posed by undependable and questionable water supplies. The city
council called water a "matter of supreme importance" if the city were to
become "a commercial metropolis." This understanding led to a commitment to correct deficiencies even at the risk of increasing the already large
public debt.[26]

Dealing with expensive issues like water became more difficult when
the local economy began weakening. Wholesale houses were among the
first local concerns to feel the depression's hard edge. In 1890 Fort Worth's

Bateman Brothers, one of the largest wholesalers in Texas, filed for bankruptcy, listing liabilities estimated at $400,000, including $50,000 for coffee, against assets of $125,000; and in 1891 Randall Chambers Dry Goods Company went into receivership. By 1892 reports appeared regularly that falling cotton prices had depressed the Southwest and that Texas commerce suffered from reduced investment thanks to the Texas Alien Land Law, which imposed business investment limits on non-Texas residents. Hard times clearly affected the level of citizen support for potential development, especially proposals for a federal district court and an army post of fourteen companies promising an annual payroll of $578,000, both of which foundered when locals balked at granting inducements, particularly regarding construction sites. At the end of 1892 and into 1893 many felt, or hoped, that the worst was over. An 1892 visitor remarked on how well Fort Worth had weathered the economic difficulties, a sentiment repeated in the mayor's 1893 annual report.[27]

This optimism proved ill-founded. In 1892 Paddock was elected mayor, defeating Broiles despite losing the Third Ward (the Acre) and the support of African Americans who endorsed his opponent. As mayor he practiced extreme parsimony, vetoing $12,750 for a new Ninth Ward school building, and blamed deficits of $30,000 in the waterworks, $15,000 in the general improvement fund and $40,000 to $50,000 in the general fund. These shortfalls stemmed in part from falling property assessment values, including a decrease from $20.1 million in 1893 to only $16.7 million in 1894. Pressure from declining property values reduced the municipal budget from $567,263 in the fiscal year spanning 1891/1892 to $441,636 in 1892/1893 and to $333,543 in 1893/1894, a drop of 41 percent in just two years.[28]

The combination of reductions in tax revenue and a large debt load created budget gaps. In 1892 bonded and other debts totaled $1.34 million, a level, according to Paddock, that exceeded the city's ability to pay and which caused a local bank to refuse further loans. In the face of huge debts, declining revenues, and the inability to meet existing bills the finance committee urged the utmost economy. In response, the council cut salaries, reducing the mayor from $2,000 to $1,500 annually, but the city still failed to meet payrolls in December 1892. Problems continued as estimated expenditures for the last half of the fiscal year, running from April 1, 1892, to September 30, 1893, totaled $67,000 against income of only $60,300, based on an assumed but unlikely 100 percent collection rate.[29]

City finances struggled under many challenges. In 1894 the council reduced more salaries, which were already low compared with other major Texas cities, and ordered personnel reductions in many city departments, including streets, fire, police, and schools. Paddock traveled twice to New York City trying to save Fort Worth's credit, all the while remaining upbeat, even arguing in the mayor's annual state-of-the-city address that prosperity lay just around the corner. He was wrong. Economic deterioration worsened when the City National Bank failed, wiping out one-third of the city's annual cash. In January 1894 Max Elser, the city treasurer, refused to honor city-issued drafts or sell bonds, claiming they constituted too great a burden on the citizenry, which forced the council to seek court orders directing compliance.[30]

In July 1893 the Arlington Heights suburb also faltered. The Chamberlain Investment Company, with headquarters in Denver and offices in Fort Worth, San Antonio, and New York; closed, citing liabilities of $2.33 million and assets of $2.94 million. President Humphrey B. Chamberlain blamed heavy development costs in Arlington Heights and other areas, especially those associated with building and maintaining electric railways. Streetcars were so vital for suburbs that many developers assumed the construction costs, a decision that had little to do with altruism or fare revenue but a lot to do with spikes in property values generated by accessibility. Serious financial problems arose when the depression decreased or eliminated growth in real estate values, leaving the developers with large debts they could not pay.[31]

The Chamberlain Company's problems may have been aggravated by misconduct. In 1894 Humphrey Chamberlain was arrested in New York City on fraud charges filed by a wealthy shoe dealer who invested $5,175 in the Fort Worth project. The investor alleged that he had been assured that the company owned over 400 acres in Arlington Heights but found that Robert McCart and William Capps, both of Fort Worth, actually owned the land. The charges were eventually dropped after Chamberlain explained that he had formed a partnership with Capps, McCart, and Tallant to buy the land from K. M. Van Zandt for $188,240 ($429 an acre), paying $49,888 down with five years to pay the balance. Soon thereafter, in November 1894, a suspicious fire destroyed Arlington Height's Ye Arlington Inn, one of the state's largest and grandest hotels with luxurious furnishings in the Queen Anne style. The hotel, costing $300,000 with commensurate room rates but remotely situated, did well initially, but occupancy fell after its novelty wore off, creating annual losses that reached $10,000. The negative cash flow made the company's recent purchase of $36,000 in insurance rather timely, if not suspicious, especially since the owners had actually sought a higher value policy but were denied due to the hotel's suburban location and the company's receivership status.[32]

The drive for new factories had some notable successes, but grander schemes faced serious obstacles. On February 1, 1893, the *Gazette* wrote that "Fort Worth Marches on to the Head of the Commercial and Manufacturing Column in Texas" in announcing construction of a $100,000 distillery employing 100 on twenty-two acres between the Cotton Belt Railroad tracks and the Trinity River in North Fort Worth. The company chose a riverside site not to draw water for its liquor—for that the distillery would rely on wells—but for waste disposal. Also in February the McCord and Collins Wholesale Grocery Company opened, and work continued on a federal building and a new post office. In addition, J. M. Clark, the Chamber of Commerce secretary, lured several wholesalers from St. Joseph and Chicago to consider Fort Worth and wooed executives from the R. T. Davis Milling Company as part of Clark's grand scheme to make Fort Worth into the "Minneapolis of the South." The plan relied on Fort Worth's proximity and railroad access to the Texas Panhandle's wheat fields, but it would require a change in state laws limiting non-Texan stockholders in agricultural corporations to an investment of $500 without reducing their liability. Thus even small investments carried unlimited risks.[33]

In the meantime, Fort Worth returned to its commercial roots, railroads, which seemed to weather the panic better than most industries. Some lines actually improved their earnings in 1895 over 1894, and several continued to expand. In January 1893 the Chicago and Rock Island offered, contingent on a subsidy, an extension to Fort Worth connecting with the Missouri-Kansas-Texas, a railroad controlled by Standard Oil. In April the *Gazette* celebrated the successful subscription drive with a large edition listing all local railroad employees who, according to their estimates, put $100,000 in monthly wages into the local economy. The start of Rock Island operations on July 30, 1893, gave Fort Worth twelve lines of service, compared to ten each for Houston and Dallas.[34]

A drive also began to replace the old train depot that had become an eyesore. By 1893 Fort Worth was the nation's sixth most important railroad center, with service by all the trunk lines west of the Mississippi River and south of the Rocky Mountains, with twice as much rail traffic as New Orleans and more than Atlanta or any other city south of St. Louis, but the *Gazette* described its Union Passenger Depot as a "barn." Plans for a larger, nicer facility moved along quickly at first, using the Pueblo, Arizona, depot as a model, but the decision process became labored because of the need to coordinate each step among railroad executives in offices spread across several states. As the initiative struggled into 1895, four major lines finally agreed in principle to contribute up to $30,000 each, but even that basic understanding proved unwieldy and fell apart under constant squabbling. In 1897 the Bohemian Club, a local literary society with considerable civic presence, complained that Fort Worth still needed a first class rail facility. It took until 1899 for work to begin on a $125,000 Texas and Pacific Passenger Depot with 500 feet fronting on Front Street (now Lancaster Avenue) and 160 feet on Main Street.[35]

The few instances of commercial advancement did little to hide the economy's weakness. In 1893, real estate agent John F. Swayne conceded that business had not shown any great activity, and even the *Gazette*, noted for blatant civic cheerleading, admitted that advancement had slowed. The depression's dramatic effect can be seen in monthly clearinghouse receipts, which declined steadily from $6.15 million in January 1893 to $2.74 million in September 1893 before rebounding to more than $4 million in October, more than $5 million in November, and $5.75 million in December. Despite the year-end upsurge, the total for 1893 was just over $56 million, below the previous year's total by $2.67 million. The trend downward continued in 1894, when receipts fell 16 percent below 1893 and 26 percent under 1892, to the lowest total in nine years.[36]

The Dallas press exulted in Fort Worth's desperation. In 1896 the *Dallas Times Herald* argued that the "wind is out of Fort Worth," and that it was only a matter of time before businesses that had mistakenly built there would relocate east. The paper cited economic difficulties as clear evidence of the mistake made by cattle and sheep interests and land speculators in building a town without substantial manufacturing. "Of industries there is none," and Fort Worth's business lay "paralyzed," the *Dallas Times Herald* reported. The paper predicted that Fort Worth's underdeveloped economy was in for certain deterioration now that "boomers" had stopped dipping into their own pockets to fund promotions, a fact supported by the Fort Worth's daily newspaper going to its "long home," or out of business. The Dallas paper argued that North Texas had room for only one great city and that Dallas, due to its earlier start and superior industry, would be it. Dallas supporters moved to ensure that outcome by trying to entice Fort Worth railroads to relocate, which, they claimed, would make Dallas impervious to depressions. Dallas representatives approached the Fort Worth headquarters of the Rock Island, the Fort Worth and Denver, and the Fort Worth and Rio Grande, as well as the Ennis, Texas, headquarters of the Houston and Texas Central, the Marshall, Texas, shops of the Texas and Pacific, and the Missouri-Kansas-Texas facilities in Denison, Texas. Dallas was in a position to do so because its economy had recovered quickly from the Panic of 1893. In 1899, a letter to the *Fort Worth Register* from "JLC" complained that Dallas bank clearings rose $80,000 above the same week the previous year while Fort Worth's continued to decline. Further, Fort Worth's 1898 annual report lamented that a "tidal wave of prosperity" had stopped just east of the city limits, indicating that recovery had reached Dallas but no farther.[37]

Fort Worth's long road to full recovery was evident in fiscal and demographic statistics. Municipal tax revenues rose to $312,816 in 1894 but declined to only $183,481 in 1897 before beginning a slow rebound. Tarrant County property tax rolls also declined slightly from $20,949,500 in 1896 to $20,909,957 in 1897, while city tax rolls for the same period decreased from $16,236,764 to $15,508,088. Uncollected Fort Worth taxes amounted to $80,037 in 1897, almost half the total uncollected in the city's twenty-three year history. In 1897 seven national banks with assets of $2.23 million called Fort Worth home but by 1899 only six did so, with a combined capital of just $1.38 million. In 1898, suffering general economic hard times and a drought that depleted the hog supply, the Chicago and Fort Worth Packing Company closed. The plant reopened in 1899 as the Fort Worth Packing and Provision Company, but it struggled to stay afloat amid general instability in the meat-packing industry. Beset with so many economic problems, the population sank to the extent that even notoriously generous civic estimates showed a population decline from 39,141 in 1896 to 36,294 in 1897, a loss of 2,847, or more than 7 percent.[38]

The poor economy showed up in Paddock's household finances. In a September 19, 1895, letter he advised his wife to charge purchases at Turner and Dingee because it was a large concern better able to wait for payment. Paddock expressed shame over the state of his personal income but rationalized that many were in similar straits and that he, at least, still had the option of "sacrificing some property," if worse came to worst.[39] Other boosters admitted problems. In 1897 the Bohemian Club complained that Fort Worth lacked textile mills but that Waco, a smaller city just ninety miles south, boasted woolen mills worth $200,000, and the continuing slump forced more Fort Worth wholesalers out of business. The year of 1898 closed with some hope derived from slight trade increases, signaling that the economy, while struggling, might yet recover.[40]

Mayor Paddock's annual report for the fiscal year ending March 31, 1898, provided a candid and sweeping survey. Paddock saw many problems and was not shy about assigning blame, arguing that "it has seemed that every device which human ingenuity could suggest was being resorted to cripple and embarrass the administration of the business of the city."[41] Paddock was human and would, occasionally, display anger at individuals. He chastised unnamed litigants who dragged the city through "vexatious and harassing" lawsuits and marveled at the unreasonableness of citizens opposing taxation while clamoring for street improvements, more policemen, extending the electric light system, increasing the water supply, and using street sprinklers more freely. Improbably, he also boasted that the local financial condition was better than ever and that only seven of sixty-five cities between 25,000 and 40,000 had smaller debts and expenditures. Still, he called for strict economy, forecasting that resources would be thin due to reductions in the tax rate and assessed valuations.[42]

Paddock also analyzed sections of the municipal government. He boasted that the Public Health Department was so effective that only a mountain resort in North Carolina had a lower death rate, and he noted that Fort Worth was the only Texas city that did not quarantine travelers during a yellow fever epidemic in October 1897. He then returned to the attack on judicial interference, suggesting that court rulings had subverted municipal authority to enforce sanitary regulations and had encouraged "the improvident and careless in the violation of ordinances." Paddock praised the police for making up for their limited numbers with "activity and vigilance" and the fire department for having "no superior, if indeed it has an equal." But he stretched credulity by arguing that streets and alleys were superior to many large cities while admitting that they could be in better condition.[43]

The water department and schools received a mixed review but streetcar franchise operators earned unmitigated scorn. The mayor boasted of the water department's positive cash flow and described its machinery and pipelines as "ample and adequate" but regretted that pressure and supply had not reached a desired level. Paddock suggested that the answer to supply lay in a reservoir and basin, a solution he had advanced three years earlier. He found the school system hampered by "an unfortunate friction, to which your Mayor, the chairman *ex officio* of the Board of Trustees, was a party, that was not conducive to the welfare of the schools." Regrettably, he refused to spell out the matter on the ground that it would serve no purpose since everyone knew the facts, but he did mention that schools faced a facility crisis, lamenting, "Just what we are going to do about it, I am at a loss to conceive." In a particularly vitriolic review, Paddock accused street railway franchisees of criminal negligence and indifference for creating a defective and poorly maintained system that was a menace "to the lives, limbs and property of the people." He suggested selling future concessions, rather than giving them away, and using the proceeds for a victims compensation fund.[44]

Paddock took some pains to lambaste the city charter, laying much of the blame on his fellow citizens. He faulted citizens for restricting municipal power, especially in economic matters, charging that some well-meaning but misguided souls had amended the charter so restrictively that it was next to impossible to conduct regular business.[45] At one point he wrote to his wife that machinations by unnamed persons caused him to think about resigning as mayor so he could tell "them" his true opinion.[46] Paddock thought the charter outdated, that it had been framed for a city of 10,000, not 40,000, but he expressed more regret that its amendments reflected "personal views, whims, or caprices of individuals," creating such a mass of "contradiction, inconsistencies, and incongruities" that it was unsalvageable.[47]

Paddock's complaints concerning petty amendments to the city charter may have been a reaction to proposals affecting the powers and responsibilities of the council and mayor. In January 1897 the council proposed several amendments, including one to reduce representation from two to one alderman per ward, thus halving the seats from eighteen to nine, and another to limit the mayor to voting only in cases of ties. Both received popular support, but a third proposal proved controversial. That amendment would have authorized the mayor, with council confirmation, to appoint most department heads, including the city marshal and his chief deputy, the fire chief and his chief deputy, and the city secretary, judge, auditor, engineer, waterworks superintendent, and inspectors of plumbing and electricity.[48] Opponents submitted a counterproposal with more modest appointment privileges that included a reduction in the property tax rate and lowered salaries. On March 20, 1897, the Texas legislature adopted a mixed plan that reduced the number of aldermen and the property tax but retained the police chief and superintendents of waterworks and streets as elected offices.[49]

Paddock's concerns about poor water supplies reached a receptive audience, but one beset with financial problems. Many continued to favor wells because wells offered a cheaper alternative or because they believed well water was purer; others, including Water Superintendent A. W. Scoble and Paddock, realized that only a reservoir could provide adequate and clean water. Scoble stressed that poor water reserves and pressure had driven up fire insurance rates and that wells could never supply the quantities needed to operate the forty-three-mile sewer system and fifty-two miles of water mains. He warned that a repeat of an incident eight or nine years earlier, in which an obstructed pipe left the city without water for three days, would be disastrous in 1897. A council-appointed investigating committee concluded that the lack of natural water made a "storage basin" the best option and recommended a site west of town at the confluence of the Trinity River's Clear Fork and Mary's Creek, at an estimated cost of $100,000, including $16,000 to buy 300 acres.[50] The problem lay not in the proposal but in the treasury's red ink. The only available funding source, a bond issue, was problematic at a time when Fort Worth had difficulty meeting its existing obligations. For example, in September 1897 American Water Works Company sued in federal court to force payment of its $5,000 fee for plans and specifications of an improved water system. The council settled out of court with a $1,000 down payment and a promise to remit the remainder, plus interest, in eighteen months.[51]

After several more months of discussion and investigation, the reservoir succumbed under the weight of impecunity. In September 1899 Paddock proposed a $150,000 bond issue, but it drew little support because of finances and the intransigence of many who remained committed to artesian wells. W. F. Cummings, a former state geologist, argued that a well 300 feet deep costing between $25,000 and $75,000 would be a quicker and cheaper option, but reservoir supporters retorted that pumping costs would eliminate any construction savings. Another committee, made up of Hyde Jennings, W. W. Humphreys, and H. C. Edrington, considered three water plans. The committee eliminated a proposal for dams on the Trinity River adjacent to downtown due to the water's poor quality, but it reported favorably on both a giant well and a 400- to 500-acre reservoir on the Trinity's West Fork, where hills and terrain formed a half-moon basin. The council voted to take bids on both before making its final decision, but shallow pockets and deep debts forestalled more concrete action on either. It would be another fifteen years before a reservoir would become a reality.[52]

Economic liabilities became so pervasive that they consumed most of the leadership's energy. Paddock devoted considerable time and effort trying to borrow more money to meet existing bond payments. In 1895 he sought financing in Chicago, New York, and London to solve "these low questions on our bonds" while also trying to entice investors in his private enterprises involving coal fields and railroads. During one of his absences, in July 1897, the council ordered the city attorney to research statutes that might limit liability for water bond repayments, but acting Mayor J. P. Nicks argued that Fort Worth should pay its just debts and vetoed the resolution as unseemly. When Paddock returned he retightened purse strings, vetoing in November 1897 an appropriation of $175 for a typewriter as unjustifiable when the city could not meet bond obligations.[53]

Court decisions aggravated problems. In November 1897 a state district court prohibited cities from mandating that property taxes be paid in gold. That aggravated already difficult bond payments because Fort Worth, like many cities, had few other means to acquire specie required as the medium of exchange for most bond interest payments. In addition, an appeals court ruled that the local Board of Equalization assessed property at excessive values. The lawsuit had been filed soon after the council increased assessments to 100 percent valuation in 1888, but it took years to get through the court system. Despite all the problems, Paddock voiced optimism that the city would meet its interest payments. He was wrong again. In September and November 1899 the council repudiated payments, leading eastern investors to file federal court suits and to send James Baker, a Houston lawyer, to investigate Fort Worth's financial condition. Many investors, such as the Department of Finance of the City of New York and Blair Bankers of the same city, appealed directly to Paddock over missed interest payments on city bonds.[54]

The other perennial issue, vice in the Acre, received limited attention in the 1890s, with most efforts focused more on hiding than ending the problem. Concealment would have been no easy job given the size of the operation. The *Dallas News* reported that twenty-five gaming establishments operated in one two-block section of downtown Fort Worth.[55] Some called for strict controls, including the *Gazette*, which asked in 1892 how many victims had to be slaughtered and ruined before public sentiment demanded an end to the debauchery. However, most focused more on visibility, a persistent issue because the Acre lay between the train depot on the south and the respectable north end, forcing railway arrivals to take an unsavory tour. The city council decided against restricting the "disorderly houses" to secondary streets because this would move them closer to the suburbs and surely result in complaints from residents. In addition, decentralization of the Acre faced serious opposition from the police, who argued that concentration allowed easier and more effective control. As a result, the Acre enjoyed a largely unfettered existence in the 1890s. Sam Smith, a lifelong resident, reminisced that in 1897 saloons outnumbered all other businesses, and even the Board of Trade admitted to the existence of at least one hundred.[56] A minor flap occurred in 1893 when the council made a feeble attempt to close variety theaters, a class of saloons offering salacious performances, very loosely deemed entertainment, as a means of luring suckers who were then pressured into buying overpriced drinks for the women "entertainers." Warrants went out for George Holland for an operation at Main and Eleventh and Dan Andrews of the Honk-a-Tonk at Twelfth and Jones (Holland would take over that location in 1897), described by an alderman as a disgrace to civilization. The initiative waned after jurisdictional disputes caused significant delays which lapsed into amnesia.[57]

Violence survived in the Acre. In December 23, 1890, Luke Short suffered wounds to his hip and left hand and Charlie Wright's right wrist was shattered in an affray described as the most exciting since Short killed Courtright three years earlier. The shooting occurred at 1608 Main Street at the Bank saloon, where trouble had been brewing for some time between Short, who controlled gambling in the saloon, and Wright, who owned a gambling operation upstairs. Short entered Wright's place about 9:00 P.M. with his pistol drawn, seized a black porter as a human shield, and ordered everyone out. After the room cleared, Short ransacked the place, turning over tables and breaking lamps. Wright, armed with a shotgun, confronted Short and both fired. At the time Short, who was from Cooke County but had spent time in Arizona and Dodge City, was thirty-six and had been in Fort Worth since 1884.[58]

The de facto recognition and sanctioning of vice in the Acre via scheduled fines became an issue between city hall and the courthouse. Like
the city police, the Tarrant County sheriff's office, which had concurrent
authority, filed a set number of charges each month and feigned ignorance
of all the rest. Problems developed in March 1897 when incoming County
Attorney John Swayne refused to play along. Swayne stated the obvious,
that allowing saloon owners to remain open and gamblers to ply their
trade on Sundays in return for three fines a month was only the illusion
of enforcement, practiced to swell county revenues.[59] An 1899 grand jury
report agreed, stating that periodic prosecutions of habitual offenders
constituted "prostitution of the penal law for revenue, having no tendency to suppression, but rather the licensing of crime."[60]

Swayne's criticisms may have inspired Fort Worth Magistrate J. H.
Jackson to attack the city's similar arrangement. In July 1897 the *Fort Worth*

Tarrant County sheriff's office, circa 1899. Front row (*left to right*):
L. H. Dillard, Sheriff Sterling P. Clark, Tom Wren, Ralph Purvis.
Back row (*left to right*): Hardy Mayfield, Rufe Porter, James H. Wood,
Jim Fridge, John Smithey, Chief Deputy E. J. Brook. Courtesy of
University of Texas at Arlington Special Collections.

Register reported that "the best of feelings have not prevailed" between Judge Jackson and the police, that their war was "on good and strong" over the practice of allowing casinos to run openly while monthly fining three employees $6.00 each, netting the city treasury $18.00 per month, per operation. Jackson put his reservations into practice by refusing the city attorney's request to dismiss three gambling charges due to insufficient grounds. The real reason for dropping the charges was that the accused had already paid their quota for the month. When police officers tried to circumvent the process by having convenient memory failures, Jackson threatened them with fines. Jackson prevailed, leading to the conviction of two accused casino employees, who paid $10 fines, while the third won a dismissal.[61]

Jackson openly discussed his perspective, taking some pains to pose the matter in ethical terms rather than as a power struggle between him and the police. He stated that he entered office with no knowledge of the existing arrangement but with the conviction that gamblers should be prosecuted as vagrants and fined $5.00 plus $5.00 in court costs. His first knowledge of the sordid practice came when he fined five casino employees $10.00 and they complained that the fines were supposed to be only $6.00. Jackson said he had no idea where, when, or how the system originated but that he did not feel bound by it. He also expressed concern that police officers practiced selective enforcement, noting that twelve gamblers from four "white" operations had paid fines during the first two weeks of July 1897 while three houses run by "colored gamblers" had not been bothered.[62] Police officers certainly were familiar with what the Acre had to offer, perhaps too familiar. In August 1890, rules were adopted calling for the dismissal of any officer frequenting a saloon, place of prostitution, or variety theater.[63]

The major issue involving the Acre in the 1890s concerned neither control nor elimination but revenue. The economic side of the Acre had always existed, but before and after the 1890s its major economic justification was its ability to draw customers who also patronized downtown merchants. However, in the depression years of the 1890s tax revenue declined so markedly that city government became more concerned about its own ledgers than those of merchants. When the economy revived, the order of priorities quickly reversed to emphasize commercial benefits but, for most of the decade, income from fines was more important. An unseemly dispute between the city and county over a recent court decision provided evidence of the new level of importance that Fort Worth placed on revenue from fines. On July 2, 1897, Swayne, who had opposed fines for revenue generation, appeared before the city council to announce the appointment of an assistant district attorney to try state cases in municipal court. Swayne based his move on a new Texas Court of Appeals decision that made city courts part of the state judicial system. He argued that this ruling, in *Stewart vs. Harris County,* compelled the city judge to recognize the county attorney in all cases covering violations of the Texas Penal Code. Therefore, he said, the city court must collect the appropriate fines as demanded by the county, not the city attorney.[64] Instead of a legal argument, Fort Worth aldermen saw only a brazen attempt to seize the city's fines and fees. They retaliated by threatening to discharge all city police officers, except for the marshal, an assistant, and a clerk, and to require the county sheriff to police the city. This would be an impossible task because the state limited Tarrant County to six deputies, or three per precinct (Tarrant County had only two precincts at the time). Recognizing the impossibility of that option, Swayne backtracked, denying any financial interest and assuring that municipal court income would continue to go to the city treasurer. Swayne still sent an assistant, James S. Farmer, to municipal court to try cases, claiming only an interest in avoiding double jeopardy in charges likely to reach county court. Mayor Paddock remained skeptical, reiterating that the county sheriff would have to replace the city police if the county wanted all the fines and court costs.[65]

The issue resurfaced in 1899. On March 3, 1899, three aldermen again proposed discharging the police force, saying that the Court of Appeals decision had made municipal enforcement impossible. The council delayed a vote to allow the police committee to confer with county officials, then, on April 21, 1899, put the matter on hold pending an undescribed investigative report.[66] On May 5, 1899, Paddock's state of the city address lambasted the Court of Appeals, charging that it had divested the city of its crime fighting ability. Paddock complained that it was now impossible to punish offenders and effectively maintain law and order because the city police had become "little short of an adjunct to the state courts." Clearly, income from fines was the issue. Paddock noted that up to 90 percent of county and district court cases originated from Fort Worth arrests and that the loss of revenue arising from state law violations tried in municipal court would seriously reduce city services.[67]

In 1899 the state legislature resolved the matter by giving municipal courts concurrent jurisdiction in petty state offenses, a change Paddock

View of old jail, streetcar warehouse, and junkyard building, circa 1900.
Courtesy of University of Texas at Arlington Special Collections.

said would add $760 in monthly revenue from the estimated forty gam-
blers and sixty prostitutes who were fined regularly.[68] At the end of the
day, little changed, as evidenced in November 1899 when the majority of
the 165 indictments returned by the Tarrant County grand jury involved
gambling violations. Although Swayne demanded that casinos close or
face the consequences, most observers maintained a justifiable skepticism,
seeing Swayne's demand as more a reaction to a recent influx of gamblers
from Dallas fleeing a crackdown than a true resolve.[69]

The Acre existed largely through its exploitation of gambling and prostitution, neither of which left much in the way of a historical footprint.
Little is known about the hundreds of women who suffered deprivation
and abuse as prostitutes. A report of the Women's Industrial Home provides some insight into the plight of those trying to escape the lifestyle.
The home, existing through donations, provided housing at a cost of
$8.00 per month for women seeking a way out of the Acre. In 1892 twenty-
seven women entered along with their ten children, and another seven

babies were born at the residence (six surviving). These numbers suggest rather strongly that pregnancy played a major role in bringing women out of the Acre. Fifteen of the twenty-seven were single, ten of the remaining twelve were widows, and two had been deserted by their husbands. During the year, five women left after being taken in by individuals, seven found "situations," four left voluntarily, and two were dismissed, leaving nine still in residence. According to the report, two-thirds of the twenty-seven women took their first "misstep" after being abandoned by husbands or becoming pregnant while unwed and being turned out of their homes.[70]

One of the most famous and notorious local gamblers of the period was James M. Brown. Born in Kansas but reared in Texas, Brown had been sheriff of Lee County and, reportedly, had killed twelve men. After leaving law enforcement he focused on horse racing, both owning horses and betting on them, and made a fortune estimated at $1 million. He was wealthy enough so that he once turned down an offer of $30,000 from Montana copper millionaire Marcus Daly for a two-year-old colt named G. W. Johnson. In September 1892, Brown and two police officers were killed during a raid at Garfield Park in Chicago. The fray began as a rather minor matter, a raid because the park lacked an amusement license, but it turned deadly when Brown refused to submit to arrest and shots were exchanged. Following his death, his local stable was auctioned. G. W. Johnson brought $30,000, and other horses between $1,100 and $15,000.[71]

For all the bad economic news, Fort Worth was able to survive. Although affected, the city came out of 1893 with a few economic bright spots, especially when viewed against the backdrop of adverse national conditions. Area merchants and businessmen tried to stress the positive, claiming that things were on the upswing with a 25 percent population increase and a new trade territory recently opened to local wholesalers thanks to the Rock Island Railroad. The *City Directory* of 1894–95 boasted that Fort Worth had come out of the worst panic ever known less affected than most cities and with only a few business failures. Optimists saw hopeful signs in the packinghouse revival and in the state's largest brewery straining to serve ninety-eight full saloons and seven beer halls. The *City Directory* of 1896–97 kept faith, stating that, despite little speculation and declining real estate prices, Fort Worth had maintained steady growth for two years. There was enough activity to at least foul the air.

According to observers, the view of downtown from Arlington Heights, just to the west, lay obscured by a thick smoke layer.[72]

As the 1890s closed, Fort Worth experienced some effects from the Cuban revolution and the subsequent Spanish-American War. In December 1897 the U.S. Agriculture Department sent Simpson from the stockyards to report on the Cuban food situation. Shortly thereafter, a Spanish representative came to town seeking cattle to feed the Spanish army in Cuba. Sentiment in favor of American involvement, however, had already surfaced months before the USS *Maine* was sunk. As early as January 1897 a local man claimed he had thirty men willing to leave immediately to fight for Cuban independence. After the United States entered the war in April 1898, Fort Worth flourmills shipped one thousand barrels of flour to Cuba while locals mustered for battle. Captain George West organized a cavalry unit, the Fencibles became Company D of the Second Infantry under Captain Sam Rosenfield, and Lloyd's Rifles, organized in 1894, became Company H of the Second Texas Infantry commanded by Captain A. B. Kelly. All three were in Florida when the war ended, missing combat but suffering one fatality when Sergeant William Payne died from a heart attack during a wrestling match. (Payne was buried with full military honors in Oakwood Cemetery.) Fort Worth also played an economic role in the distant Boer War of 1899 to 1902 (a struggle between Britain and Dutch settlers for control of South Africa). The British made the Fort Worth stockyards their Southwestern center for acquisition of army mules.[73]

The state of the city reflected some progress. In 1897 Fort Worth claimed four electric streetcar routes, eighty miles of graded and graveled roads, thirty-five parks, and a school system with nine ward schools, including a high school at Jennings and Daggett and two "colored" schools, Number 10 at East Ninth and Pecan and Number 13 at 1217 Arizona Avenue. Tarrant County reveled in its new courthouse, a magnificent building costing $467,966, and work began on a new federal building costing $200,000. In 1897 the new Union Depot opened and telephone subscribers increased to 500, a rather limited addition of 173 since 1891, while telephone company income rose dramatically from $250 to $2,000 monthly, an 800 percent rise reflecting growth in commercial and governmental accounts. In addition, in 1899 the Fat Stock Show was made into an annual event with a permanent supporting organization. Although not especially ethnically diverse, Fort Worth did have seventeen Chinese laundries and a shop at 704 Houston Street dealing in Japanese and Chinese items.[74]

The transition from railroads to industrial development waned in the depressed 1890s, leaving railroads as the jewel in Fort Worth's economic crown. Each month, eight railroads ran on twelve trunk lines through Fort Worth terminals, producing a monthly payroll of $125,000.[75] Many still pushed for more, including Paddock who labored to build a route to Albuquerque, New Mexico, but the depression of the 1890s sapped the life out of the grand scheme. In November 1895 the Fort Worth Promotive Club organized with Paddock as chair. Paddock addressed the members, delivering a positive interpretation of the city's prospects and assuring attendees that discussions were under way with manufacturers of plaster, vinegar, and ropes. J. T. Powell, who would become mayor in 1900, was less sanguine. Powell argued that public lethargy had set in, that no major public activity had developed since the packinghouse deal in 1893. He suggested that Fort Worth needed an aggressive economic strategy more than ever because the depression had taught northern capitalists the value of their industries and they would fight dearly to prevent removal to the South.[76] Despite Powell's warning, Fort Worth's commercial efforts remained uncoordinated and divided. Some saw suburban expansion as the key because they believed that outlying communities would attract working masses who would, in turn, draw businesses. Others favored the opposite approach, focusing on new manufacturers that would draw workers. The city council opted to encourage "much-needed factories" by proposing a five-year tax moratorium for new manufacturers, but the plan died after City Attorney C. Templeton ruled it unconstitutional. Other initiatives appeared, including plans for cotton or woolen mills and a shoe factory employing 200, but little of substance developed.[77]

The proposals accomplished little, other than demonstrating the resurgence of positive attitudes. This revival contributed to the organization of the Men's Home Industry League, a group of leading citizens dedicated to building the industrial base. The group's leaders, including Judge J. E. Martin, J. W. McGraw, and Charlie W. Hoelzle, emphasized patronage of local businesses, the idea being to keep Fort Worth trade in Fort Worth. In the keynote address, Hoelzle claimed that the key reason so many Fort Worth residents remained poor was that seventy-five cents of every locally-earned dollar went outside the city limits. Paddock seconded the shop-at-home initiative and C. M. Brown read his own composition, a lengthy poem, "Forward, March," which included the lines:[78]

The factory's lazy hum will cure our ills,
And make us happy while we work and wait.
And while we wait, and watch, and work and pray,
To our dear city let us all be true.[79]

The effect of the buy-at-home movement was questionable. Hoelzle and the others worked diligently, often speaking at events such as the opening of the new City Market. The Bohemian Club backed the program, agreeing that hometown patronage would develop funding that would bring cotton and shoe factories. Yet the only tangible evidence of its efforts, other than public exhortations, involved charges leveled against Texas Brewing for failing to use local suppliers, which the company contested by providing receipts for local purchases. The buy-at-home effort was a well-intentioned but limited effort that accomplished very little.[80]

The answer to the city's poor commercial development lay not in an insular campaign but in the attraction of new industry. The lethargy that Powell identified in 1895 still retarded Fort Worth's development. In 1898 Alderman M. A. Spoonts traveled to Washington, D.C., seeking an army base. He reported that the War Department looked favorably on Fort Worth's health and transit advantages but that action would require strong citizen involvement. No sign of such activity or an army base appeared. Even amid the exaggerated boosterism of his annual message in 1899, Paddock admitted that securing new factories required immediate attention.[81] In 1899 an anonymous letter to the editor proved instrumental in resurrecting some of the lost zeal. The writer, later identified as Dr. J. L. Cooper, a local physician active in city affairs, summed up recent shortcomings, noting that Fort Worth had maintained steady growth in the past because of its railroads but had lost momentum because its citizens had done little or nothing for years. He proposed a new and dynamic organization. From this suggestion the city's top 100 property owners formed the Businessmen's League, which later became the Board of Trade. The members elected Paul Waples, a wholesaler, president and named thirteen directors. Mayor Paddock was nominated as a director but declined to serve, perhaps influenced by comments from T. J. Skaggs, secretary of the Texas Real Estate Association: that Fort Worth was a one-man town, and that everyone waited for Paddock to do everything. The Bohemian Club praised the new board but expressed regret that the absence of an organized effort had let many opportunities slip away over the course of the previous five years.[82]

Although the commitment and focus of local leaders remained decisively pro-business, a viable pro-labor sentiment survived, along with some examples of social activism. Strikes in 1899 closed five of the top six laundries, and Texas Brewing was idled when Local 109 of the Brewer's National Union struck for higher wages, shorter hours, and free beer every hour. The company yielded on the first two but retained consumption limits.[83] Mrs. B. M. Burchill operated the Benevolent Home for wayward children that was supported by donations, including $100 monthly from Tarrant County and meat from the Fort Worth Packinghouse; and in 1897 a kindergarten for high-risk children opened in the Acre on Fourteenth between Rusk and Calhoun. Chronic poverty cases still went to the county poor farm, while acute needs for food, heat, and clothing were directed to the Pauper's Fund administered by the Fort Worth police. In the twentieth century, the county would provide a home for the aged on Birdville Road and Cumberlands Rest Home for aged women, as well as an orphanage for children aged three to twelve on Stop Four of the Interurban streetcar line.[84]

At the end of the nineteenth century Fort Worth still remained more frontier than metropolis, suffering from economic stagnation brought on by the national depression and the failure of local leadership. Most city leaders realized the limits of the economy, although Paddock insisted as late as 1922 that Fort Worth in the 1890s had an array of commercial and industrial enterprises that qualified it as one the Southwest's great cities, an argument more a product of overwhelming civic boosterism than facts or logic. For example, Paddock also stated that not until the Armour and Swift packinghouses formed the cornerstones of greatness in 1903 did Fort Worth experience the conservative material growth and development necessary for a city of diversified resources, an admission that clearly indicated doubts about Fort Worth's commercial base prior to 1903. Those doubts were necessary precursors for bigger plans that came to fruition in the new century. For Fort Worth the end of the 1890s could not come soon enough.

Shortly before the curtain came down on the nineteenth century, however, a scene out of the romantic past played out in real life. On July 21, 1898, four masked men held up a Santa Fe train just north of the stockyards, shooting the engineer and foreman and using dynamite to blow the safe before shooting it out with police. A year later, on July 28, 1899, James C. Garlington was hanged for the crime.[85]

4

Taking a Giant Step,
1900–1903

In 1900 the failures of the 1890s became evident, suggesting that Fort Worth had become just another railroad crossroads, established well enough to survive but struggling under stagnant growth with few signs of prosperity. It remained a county seat, an important railroad center, and a regional trade center, but struggled with an underdeveloped industrial base that served a limited area and averaged only seven workers per shop. After a quarter century of incorporation, Fort Worth lacked an economy commensurate with its grand dreams. In the late 1880s Fort Worthians had begun to realize that the key to economic advancement lay in manufacturing, that factories would provide jobs, wealth, and population growth. Application of that idea was at its incipient stage when the Panic of 1893 struck disproportionately hard, effectively sapping energy from all initiatives. In the first years of the twentieth century, Fort Worth would face other trials: the death of one of its greatest supporters, yet another expensive but short-lived fix to the waterworks, and the continuing debate over the Acre. In 1903 all these issues were overshadowed by the arrival of two major packinghouses. Most observers thought Swift and Armour would propel Fort Worth into national significance, from a have-not to a city on the move. The packinghouses did change the scale dramatically, creating large increases in employment, wealth, and population that lasted years. Later, it would become clear that the effect, although significant, only expanded without diversifying, leaving the Fort Worth industrial economy larger but still limited.[1]

Fort Worth entered the twentieth century still recovering from the 1890s. The Panic of 1893 was a national depression, but statistics suggest that other Texas cities and the state as a whole experienced significant manufacturing growth during the 1890s, while Fort Worth suffered major declines. Between 1890 and 1900, the number of Fort Worth manufacturers fell 33.9 percent, the average number employed 38.8 percent, average wages 47.7 percent, and the total value of production 21.9 percent, while the state of Texas and all four of the other major cities—Dallas, Galveston, Houston, and San Antonio—increased significantly in every category, with the single exception that Galveston declined 12.4 percent in value of production (see table 4.1).[2]

Fort Worth's percentage decreases represented a drop in number of manufacturers from 316 to 290, in total capitalization from $3.19 million to $2.67 million and in value of production from $6.83 million to $5.33 million (see table 4.2).

TABLE 4.1.   Change in manufacturing measures for major Texas cities, 1890–1900 (in percentages)

	Number of businesses	Workers employed	Wages earned	Value of manufactured products
Fort Worth	−33.9	−38.8	−47.7	−21.9
Dallas	19.6	5.7	8.1	26.8
Galveston	55.3	27.6	2.1	−12.4
Houston	142.4	69.2	78.0	55.7
San Antonio	1.0	52.2	44.2	21.3
Texas (total)	133.3	38.4	35.7	69.5

Sources: *Twelfth Census of the United States,* vol. 8 (Washington, D.C.: Government Printing Office, 1901), p. 994; Robert Harris Talbert, *Cowtown Metropolis: Case Study of a City's Growth and Structure* (Fort Worth: Leo Potishman Foundation, Texas Christian University, 1956), p. 123.

TABLE 4.2.   Comparison of Fort Worth manufacturing, 1890 and 1900

	1890	1900
Number of manufacturers	316	290
Amount of capitalization	$3,194,032	$2,668,045
Value of products	$6,826,083	$5,332,804

Source: *Twelfth Census of the United States,* vol. 8 (Washington, D.C.: Government Printing Office, 1901), p. ccl.

Fort Worth's manufacturing decline was also incongruent when compared with Texas as a whole, the Southwest, the rest of the United States,
and even when compared with Dallas. While Fort Worth's value of manufactured goods fell almost 22 percent between 1890 and 1900, overall
the value of manufactured goods rose 39 percent nationally, 53 percent in
the Southwest and 70 percent in Texas. Fort Worth's declines came when
Texas's growth was the fourth largest among the states, trailing only Missouri, Louisiana, and Kansas. In addition, capital investment in manufacturing declined in Fort Worth while increasing 50 percent nationally and
75 percent statewide. The poor state of Fort Worth manufacturing can
also be seen in a direct comparison between Tarrant and Dallas counties.
According to the 1900 census, Dallas County was 67 percent larger than
Tarrant County in both population and number of manufacturers and
led by 146 percent in capital investments, 151 percent in factory workers,
116 percent in wages, and 108 percent in production.[3]

Fort Worth did outpace Dallas, however, in rate of population growth.
The 1900 census counted 26,688 Fort Worth residents, an increase of 3,612
since 1890, or 16 percent. This was considerably lower than the 246 percent
increase in 1890 over 1880 but was sufficient to make Fort Worth Texas's
fifth largest city, trailing San Antonio, Houston, Dallas, and Galveston in
descending order. Tarrant County grew slightly faster, adding 11,234 residents, or 27 percent, to reach 52,376. The disparity in growth reduced Fort
Worth's percentage of the county population from 56 to 51 percent. The
population of Dallas city reached 42,638, an increase of just 12 percent
that lowered Dallas from 65 percent larger than Fort Worth to only 60
percent larger. Dallas County also declined relative to Tarrant County,
dropping from 63 percent to 58 percent larger. Both Dallas's and Fort
Worth's growth rates appeared sluggish during a decade of significant
urban expansion that saw New York City grow almost 38 percent (to more
than 3 million) and Chicago add 54 percent (to 1.7 million).[4]

Fort Worth's results would have been even worse if not for wholesale
trade and railroads. The city's 60 wholesale houses and jobbers, with an
annual trade estimated at $6 million, employed 1,350 workers in town
plus 202 traveling sales agents. In 1900 Dallas had just 328 railroad laborers, but Fort Worth counted 755, the city's second most common occupation, trailing only general laborers with 936. Another 3,937 Fort Worth
workers were listed under the general category of Trade and Transportation. The total railroad workforce, estimated at 1,500, was 5 percent of Fort

Worth's population, most employed at general offices for the Fort Worth and Rio Grande, the Rock Island, or the Fort Worth and Denver as well as at the Texas and Pacific's machine shops and its large roundhouse with six stalls. In addition, the future looked bright as railroads in the late nineteenth and early twentieth centuries enjoyed vigorous growth. From 1890 to 1900 the nation's total track mileage increased 23 percent, from 29,162 to 35,813 miles, with much of the expansion located adjacent to Fort Worth. In 1902 the Southwest region added 1,245 miles of new track, more than half the national total of 2,314. The strength of these industries may have contributed to percentage population growth that exceeded Dallas's rate.[5]

The new century began rather poorly, with Fort Worth enduring a plague in 1901, the closure of a local institution, and the death of one of its most important boosters. In February a smallpox epidemic sent forty cases to the pest house with another six housed elsewhere. In the same month, the legendary White Elephant Saloon and Restaurant closed, citing debts in excess of $20,000. The Elephant had opened in 1883 on Main between Second and Third to acclaim as the finest saloon in Texas. In 1884 W. H. Ward, then a city councilman, bought the establishment and moved it to finer digs at 606 Main Street, where it remained popular for years. However, changes in times and tastes reduced patronage so that the once popular establishment became little more than a rendezvous for old-timers. On April 15, 1901, John Peter Smith, one of Fort Worth's earliest settlers and most active boosters, died in St. Louis, where he had stopped on his way to woo the Frisco Railroad in Chicago. On the evening of April 6, Smith left the Planter's House Hotel to see a friend off at the Union Depot, but he returned several hours later in a dazed state, claiming he had been drugged and robbed of $30. His condition deteriorated overnight into delirium before doctors at St. Mary's Infirmary diagnosed blood poisoning from infected lacerations of the tongue, probably caused by a broken tooth. Eventually swelling spread to the neck, making breathing impossible. The *Register* called Smith the "Father of Fort Worth," a title also given by some to Ephraim Daggett.[6]

Fort Worth mourned Smith as it struggled with deteriorating city finances. In 1900 municipal tax revenues reached $245,707 but expenditures totaled $317,072; in 1901 revenues dropped to $192,337 and expenditures to $283,758; in 1902 income rebounded to $223,317 but outgo hit a new high of $357,209. In these three years, the gap between tax revenue and expenditures increased from $71,365 to $133, 892. The actual budgetary shortfall was less due to the addition of other forms of revenue, such as water department fees and court fines. For example, in 1902, when tax revenue was $223,317, the city's total income reached $330,290, but even that figure left a deficit of $36,389. The city's financial difficulties, stemming largely from property tax shortfalls, provided a barometer of overall economic health. That Fort Worth's tax revenues dropped between 1900 and 1901 suggested a lack of commercial vitality, a condition also reflected in virtually stagnant property assessments that grew at a rate of less than 2 percent. The accompanying decline in tax revenue in 1901 may also have been an effect of tax defaults, another suggestion of economic weakness. The gap between income and revenue continued despite a rather high tax rate of $1.75 per $100 of assessed property.[7]

Many reasons were cited for the poor fiscal outcomes, including claims that other cities dumped their paupers, but the biggest factor remained an out-of-control debt load. The 1901 budget revealed the degree to which debt had become a significant factor: interest payments alone consumed 41 percent of tax revenue. In 1902, bond interest amounted to $58,113 while the sinking fund (funds dedicated to reducing indebtedness) required $30,066, creating a financial drain that exceeded the $65,000 spent on the waterworks and the $59,809 for schools. Faced with large and growing debts, Fort Worth began defaulting on interest payments. In 1900, H. W. Sage and Company of New York sued in federal court over nonpayment of bond interest. In 1901, the New York Security and Trust Company began organizing bondholders for legal action before agreeing to a relaxed bond redemption schedule, providing a brief respite.[8] Still, the problem was not solved. The fiscal year ending March 21, 1903, carried a projected income of $400,000 against expenses of $532,089; including $153,738 budgeted for interest payments. Mayor J. T. Powell, who candidly admitted that the city had been bankrupt and unable to meet its bond interest payments since 1895, remained opposed to a tax increase, favoring instead cutbacks and efforts to lower interest payments through debt refinancing. When this effort proved too slow for anxious bondholders, the State National Bank came to the rescue by granting the city a $170,000 overdraft that avoided defaults.[9]

In the face of municipal bankruptcy, the waterworks experienced yet another supply crisis. The situation became especially critical during summer months, when demand forced introduction of unfiltered river water, a move always obvious from the water's brown hue. In July 1900, the waterworks committee reported that wells had reached their limit and that further drilling within the "zone of interference" of existing wells would decrease rather than increase production. Questions about quality and quantity caused many residents to dig their own wells, aggravating supply problems and causing a drop in annual revenues from $60,000 to $56,000 against operating expenses of $30,000 and bond interest and other costs estimated at $62,500—a total of $92,500, or $36,500 more than income. The condition of the current system suggested that the existing underground aquifer had passed its peak production potential and had gone into an unalterable state of declining returns.[10]

The council hired Daniel W. Mead, a nationally known water supply expert from Chicago, to assess strategies for increased well supplies. Mead arrived on March 7, 1901, and stayed for weeks before filing a fifty-page assessment that estimated daily usage at 3.36 million gallons, with 960,000 gallons drawn from thirteen deep wells sunk in 1892 and 1893 and the remaining 2.4 million gallons coming from the Trinity River. The perennial problem was that both sources declined in summer, just when need stood at its greatest. Mead recommended several modifications, including connecting wells with a shaft 170 feet below the surface, steps that, he claimed, would permanently increase well flow to 5 million gallons daily. The waterworks committee recommended acceptance of the full plan costing $169,000, arguing that the city could not continue indefinitely losing money. The city council compromised, accepting a slightly reduced plan at $110,000 that promised 3 million gallons daily.[11]

Implementation began quickly and, once again, the waterworks seemed to work fine, at least at first. By September 1901, two new wells were producing 2 million gallons daily, giving residents immediate relief while work continued for months on a connecting tunnel and the installation of four pumps capable of moving 4 million gallons daily. In July 1903, the first test of the system, with only one pump operational, yielded water at a rate of 3.5 million gallons in twenty-four hours, but administrators remained cautious, stating that they would wait a year to verify a consistent supply before paying Mead. The system also offered cost savings to the consumer, billing at the rate of twenty-eight cents per 100 gallons for residential customers, compared with fifty cents in Dallas and Texarkana. The abundance of clean water at a fair price spurred connections, which increased income. In 1902, waterworks revenue totaled $64,627, or $16,157 a quarter, and in 1903 annual receipts reached $91,861, an average of

$22,962 per quarter, sufficient to cover both operating expenses of $40,851 and annual bond interest of $49,480 and still leave a surplus of $1,579. All seemed fine for the moment, but the moment would pass. In September 1903, the city physician urged everyone to drink only private well water, citing health threats from malaria and typhoid carried by river water in the municipal system.[12]

Despite its money woes, Fort Worth carried on a somewhat aggressive program of other civic improvements. By January 1901, Main Street, the city's principal commercial thoroughfare with solid store fronts stretching for twelve blocks, was paved with vitrified brick from the Texas and Pacific passenger depot to Seventeenth Street. Work was in progress to extend the vitrified brick paving to Fifteenth Street, and plans were in place for the remaining blocks to the courthouse. Other improvements included an agreement with the Texas and Pacific Railway to share the cost of a viaduct over the railroad reservation ($15,000 for wood or $30,000 for steel) to connect the Southside and downtown. The viaduct would begin on Jennings Street, at about the north end of the Texas and Pacific property, and would extend 600 feet south.[13]

Privately funded infrastructure development also contributed, especially in the Fort Worth's suburbs. J. B. Coffenberry of Cleveland bought the Fort Worth Street Railway Company and the Street Railway Company for approximately $400,000. Coffenberry, who already owned the Dallas and Fort Worth Electric Street Railway, spent $1 million to complete the Dallas and Fort Worth Interurban line. On June 18, 1902, officials from Dallas and Fort Worth celebrated the opening at Handley. The Interurban also provided instant streetcar access for the new suburb of Sycamore, which had started in 1901 on 450 acres east of downtown known as the Bob Maddox Tract. In 1900, Arlington Heights, which had been largely abandoned after the hotel fire and the crash in property values following the Panic of 1893, added twenty new homes and a country club. In 1903, the Southside experienced such dramatic growth that Police Chief William Rea asked the council for more officers to patrol south of the railroad tracks, an area that he described as constituting half the city. The *Register*, certainly given to exaggerated boosterism, called 1901 the best year in history, crediting sewer and street improvements, the Mead waterworks improvement system, issuance of 180 building permits, and commitments from the International and Great Northern Railroad and the Frisco Railroad. Revealingly, this celebratory list included only four new factories, all small operations, including two saddle and harness makers, hardly a growth field for the twentieth century.[14]

The city took some steps to encourage a more decorous life. In 1902, the city council banned nonprescription sales of cocaine, morphine, and opium with fines up to $100 for violations. Morphine and opium had been around for some time, but cocaine was a new drug that quickly became popular due to its relative cheapness. By 1901, Fort Worth had an estimated forty "coke fiends" who used regularly and another 300 to 400 occasional users. Officers reported that one woman had been arrested more than 100 times, largely for thefts to support her cocaine habit. One alderman actually opposed the ban on the grounds that it was better not to bother addicts; it was cheaper to let them die than to prosecute and then support them in prison.[15] The council also set an eight mile-per-hour speed limit for automobiles and required that they display an assigned number, have lights, and blow a horn before crossing intersections.[16] The municipal library, established in the 1890s, soldiered on in 1903 with expenditures of $5,424 to buy 1,494 books to support an annual circulation of 53,046 by 7,179 borrowers. In addition, a nine-hole golf course opened east of the W. G. Burton home in Arlington Heights, a precursor to Rivercrest, the city's first eighteen-hole course built in 1911 by Tom Bendelow at a cost of $125,000.[17]

The local arts scene prospered. The Greenwall Opera House became the entertainment focal point as part of the Greenwall Circuit that booked shows at over 300 Southern theaters, including Greenwall-owned houses in New Orleans, Galveston, Houston, Dallas, Savannah, and New York City. A summer theater season was added at Gruenwald Park, located at the north end of Samuels Avenue, before Joseph Z. Wheat moved the theater on May 26, 1902, to the top of the seven-story Wheat Building at Eighth and Main. Wheat, a bon vivant who also owned the Stag saloon, was rumored to have won the Wheat Building in a poker game. In addition to local productions, Fort Worthians turned out 20,000 strong in 1900 for two performances by Buffalo Bill's Wild West Show.[18]

The Acre survived but faced challenges. The city council loosened its Sunday closing ordinance to allow alcohol sales during food service, a change it rescinded when unscrupulous saloonkeepers set up "pretend restaurants." Gambling thrived in many saloons, such as the White Elephant, Two Johns, Twin Brothers, Silver Dollar, Our Friend, Gray Mule, and Board of Trade (the saloon, not the chamber). In September 1901, Tarrant

County began enforcing a new state law prohibiting slot machines, a move that led, in 1903, to the county's assumption of enforcement responsibility for all state gambling statutes. The Acre also offered "leg shows," supposed variety theaters in which women displayed more flesh than talent. At two of the more notorious saloons, the Crown at 1213 Calhoun Street and the Standard at 1301 Rusk Street, untold numbers of farmers and other visitors lost hard-earned cash to female "entertainers" pushing overpriced drinks.[19]

The Acre had several interesting habitués. One was Buck "Beau" Blake, a large man with blue eyes who worked in ranching south of Brownsville after commanding an Irish brigade in the Boer War. Blake earned his nickname for telling friends he was "Beauing up" (shaving and pulling his pants out of his boots) to visit women on neighboring ranches. Blake and Ed Armstrong, a known killer, argued over a cattle brand one night in an Acre saloon. When Armstrong pulled a pistol and ordered Blake to admit that he lied, the Irishman remained cool, looking over Armstrong's shoulder while stating "It's all right Harvey; he's only kidding,"

Fort Worth bar, circa 1900, with Sam Miller, bartender. Courtesy of University of Texas at Arlington Special Collections.

apparently talking to Blake's partner, Harvey Watson. When Armstrong turned in that direction Blake knocked him a dozen feet and continuing the beating on the floor. Another character was Lou Sanders, a tough-as-nails African American woman known for her willingness to fight, even holding her own in a struggle with a police officer that continued for two blocks until a bystander intervened on the officer's behalf.[20]

The city council tried to deal with complaints about the Acre by establishing a designated prostitution area. On February 1, 1902, a proposed council resolution complained that Rusk Street lay "wholly abandoned to houses of prostitution" and stipulated that the houses be given thirty days' notice to close. After this resolution failed, a second measure, presented in April 1902, restricted "dissolute women" to the area bounded by Rusk, Eighth, and Front, the approximate Acre boundaries—in effect creating an officially designated zone for prostitution. The adoption of this plan included an agreement between Fort Worth and Tarrant County to alternate fines so that prostitutes paid the city fine of $9.50 one month and the county fine of $10.50 the next. Many prostitutes, seeking to avoid paying, moved out of the Acre and into other neighborhoods, stirring complaints that led to suspension of all prostitution arrests within the Acre while enforcement accelerated in other areas. The willingness of the council to forego income from fines suggested a degree of financial stability that had been missing at the end of the 1890s. In 1903 the police established eight "beats" where officers were assigned for regular patrol, with Beat Two covering most of the Acre. The police's annual report, submitted in March 1903, listed 3,008 actual arrests, including 918, the largest number, for intoxication and 260 for being a "dissolute woman."[21]

Despite all the accommodations, the officially designated and sanctioned reservation succumbed to its own excesses. Many held high hopes for the program, including some aldermen who voiced optimism that the local arrangement would become a model for the nation. Those hopes soon crashed into reality when the women, now freed from threat of prosecution within the designated zone, turned brazen. The Women's Christian Temperance Union (WCTU) complained that prostitutes, who before had stayed discretely indoors, now sat openly in doorways and on porches in "flaring clothes and some even smoking cigarettes." The city administration tried to quiet critics by ordering police to ensure the observance of "proprieties," but many remained unconvinced and protested a plan to designate one block of Calhoun Street as outside city jurisdiction, making it an unrestricted red-light zone similar to one that Waco had recently established. Opposition increased after the death of Fort Worth Police Officer Andrew (Andy) J. Grimes, shot by a hack driver when he ordered the driver to move from in front of the Union Depot. Although the incident occurred outside the Acre, the death of a police officer increased demands for taking a hardline approach. The council, faced with moral outrage from those who condemned the Acre and with demands for law and order, ordered all houses of prostitution closed.[22]

The official and open reservation may have ended, but little else changed. The perseverance of prostitution was clear in continuing council debates over nonenforcement of vice laws, in which some aldermen blamed the police while others, more attuned to the economic perspective, argued that the police were simply reflecting the wishes of a divided community. This group argued that legitimate businesses formed the backbone of support for the Acre and that stringent police action would simply push Acre denizens to Dallas, where wholesale buyers would follow. This fear was not just paranoia. In 1903, a Dallas grand jury recommended creation of a sizable prostitution-protected reservation, complete with medical supervision. Neither was the concern unique to North Texas. Merchants in many other cities, including those in Chicago, openly voiced fears that customers would shop elsewhere if prostitution and/or gambling were eliminated. At this stage, financial motives still trumped Progressivism's reform agenda concerning prostitution.[23]

At the same time, evidence appeared that the Acre's survival also involved police corruption. In 1903, two officers faced charges for failing to enforce Sunday alcohol laws after a witness saw them enter Bennett's Saloon at Fifteenth and Main where they joined several men in consuming alcohol with no money exchanged. A few months later, Detective James W. (Jim) Thomason was charged with accepting bribes from William (Bill) H. Thompson, a known gambler. Thompson alleged that he paid Thomason in return for the freedom to operate, save for a mutually-agreed four arrests per year. Thomason attributed the allegation to retaliation but admitted receiving from $5 to $50 on several occasions as either loans or fines that he turned in. The Police Committee found Thomason not guilty of accepting bribes but ordered him disciplined for accepting loans from a known gambler.[24]

Other problems went unabated. A letter to the editor from "A Newcomer" complained of sickening odors from gutters, of sidewalks so covered with expectorant that women could not let their dresses touch the pavement, and of nights filled with the constant rumbling and shifting of rail cars, the bumping and crashing of switch engines, and the excessive use of warning whistles. The writer also thought little of Fort Worth's citizens, stating that parts of Main Street were covered by a "filthy lot" of women in loud wrappers with dangerously low-cut tops and that residents too readily worshiped a few long-term leaders. The complaint closed by describing Fort Worthians as small-town provincials who placed high values on the opinions of anyone bearing a title like "colonel" or "general" without regard for expertise.[25]

Fort Worth tried to attract industries but with little success. In 1900, a proposed cottonseed mill required a stock investment of $100,000, but a marketing plan offering 400 shares at $25 each with weekly payments as low as fifty cents stalled with $40,000 still needed. In 1901, a group of forty New York capitalists exploring Texas's investment opportunities spent three nights in Fort Worth and two in Dallas but left without making any concrete commitments. In 1902, wholesale merchant A. N. Evans lamented stagnant commercial growth, noting that the only new businesses were a few retail shops and manufacturers of horse collars and harnesses, sundries, and baking powder. Evans suggested that the city offer a twenty-year tax exemption for all manufacturers, an idea that never got off the ground.[26]

Despite the industrial lull, Fort Worth's leading men put on a positive face. In November 1902, Mayor Powell, speaking to Chicago investors, compared Fort Worth to the "Windy City" when it was the same size, arguing that both owed their successes to the work of a few great men. Powell also stressed the importance of Fort Worth's rail facilities, bragging of more railroad cars than Dallas, Waco, San Antonio, and Denison combined. The same month, Board of Trade President Paul Waples described an ongoing struggle for urban supremacy between Texas's four largest cities: Fort Worth, Dallas, Houston, and San Antonio. Paddock, speaking after Waples, claimed that Fort Worth enjoyed three of Texas's four largest industrial payrolls—railroads, packinghouses, and wholesale trade (lumber was the fourth)—but that it needed a hundred more small businesses to complement the large.[27]

Civic energy found an organizational center in a revived Board of Trade. The board had disappeared during the economic crises of the 1890s but resurfaced after the turn of the century. The Board appointed a committee dedicated to aiding commerce that offered three options: obtaining another packinghouse, building another Spring Palace, or holding a livestock show. The report favored a stock show but the full membership opted for another exposition, a choice Paddock supported. Paddock contended that an exposition would bring factories while a livestock show would not, and he warned that acquiring another packinghouse seemed unlikely in the short term. The grandiose plans called for a $35,000 building very similar to the original Spring Palace, with a height of 100 feet and an area of 250 feet by 100 feet. Plans expanded to include a brick or stone auditorium with spacious grounds, a racetrack, animal stalls for a stock show, and a combination baseball-football field that would be the site of an annual fall festival, similar to the State Fair in Dallas, Waco's Flower Carnival, or San Antonio's International Fair. Promoters began the project with alacrity on September 20, 1900, by offering $10 shares and receiving thirteen bids from potential sites, but by October eagerness dissolved into apathy. Only two of thirty-nine subscription committees reported donations. The board's general membership tried to revive the campaign by appropriating $1,000, which succeeded in pushing pledges to $12,000 in 1901.[28]

Shortly afterwards the idea vanished, a development that may have been the product not of apathy but of attention being diverted to other options, especially opportunities afforded by Fort Worth's massive rail facilities and its proximity to an expanding agricultural production. During the 1890s, Texas emerged as a major supplier of agricultural products with a 114.8 percent increase that accounted for more than one-fourth of the Southwest's total production.[29] Part of that spike reflected higher prices enriching the livestock trade. Since the late 1880s, grazing acreage had declined due to conversion of land into lumber production, the public domain, and forest reserves. At the same time, drought reduced the productivity of available grasslands and an 1899 blizzard destroyed up to 50 percent of the cattle in northwest Texas. These factors combined to radically decrease supply, which drove prices for beef on the hoof to six cents a pound, amounting to $30 to $40 for three-year old steers, an almost doubling in value. The rise in cattle prices was good news for the Southwest and especially Texas, which stood to benefit disproportionately. Texas, Oklahoma, and New Mexico held one-fifth of all the nation's cattle. Texas alone held 15 percent of the nation's livestock, including almost half the cattle and more than one-fifth the hogs in all the western states, and more cows, hogs, and horses than any other individual western state.[30] Despite these large herds, Texas in 1900 counted only twelve slaughter-houses capitalized at $1.23 million, minuscule compared with fifty-one slaughterhouses in Illinois worth $70.8 million or even the thirty-one in Missouri worth $7.84 million.[31]

Of all Texas cities, Fort Worth was most favorably positioned to take advantage of the potential offered by large cattle herds in an area with so few packinghouses. Fort Worth sat adjacent to a cattle kingdom that stretched from the Gulf Coast to New Mexico, an area so vast that only the Rio de la Plata of Argentina rivaled it. As early as 1901 the cattle trade was recognized as one of the two pillars of local commerce (the other be-ing the wholesale trade), and ties between Fort Worth business and agri-culture remained high. Many Texas cattlemen maintained a local resi-dence, and three-fourths of the city's shop owners were or previously had been involved in the cattle business. Fort Worth also boasted functioning stockyards that handled 403,475 head in 1900 and a small packinghouse that ran an annual profit of $50,000 despite being unable to process all the supply. The lack of slaughterhouse capacity meant that most Texas cattle were shipped elsewhere, and Fort Worth, with the state's best rail service, was a major cattle shipping center. According to 1901 railroad statistics, 97.3 percent of cattle and 99.5 percent of hogs entering Fort Worth via rail also left via rail. At the same time, businessmen locally and nationally were be-coming increasingly attracted to reduced shipping costs associated with local operations, an advantage that already had led to the rise of meat-packing in Omaha and Kansas City. From that point, Chicago's near mo-nopoly over the meatpacking industry began to weaken. At the same time, availability of supply, proximity to ports on the Gulf of Mexico, and trans-portation facilities all worked to Fort Worth's advantage, making it a strong contender for becoming a regional packinghouse.[32]

In 1901, dreams became reality. In October 1900 Greenlief Simpson re-ported that Fort Worth was involved in negotiations for a packinghouse "worthy of her possibilities as the gateway to the great cattle-producing section of the Southwest." Under the original scheme, citizens would put up $200,000, with another $400,000 coming from the stockyards, to entice one of the big four packers (Armour, Swift, Cudahy or Morris) to build and guarantee three years' operation of a facility capable of processing 1,000 hogs and 500 cattle daily. On May 26, 1901, headlines announced that the city had attained "the longing of her heart," an Armour packinghouse

"complete in every way," that would employ 500 workers to slaughter 500
cattle and 2,500 hogs daily. The actual decision had been made earlier,
but the announcement was delayed while a secret buyer bought land
around the stockyards. The massive project seemed certain to have a multiplier effect similar to that experienced at Kansas City and St. Joseph, Missouri, where new packinghouses had brought factories and explosive
population growth.[33]

The addition of Swift sweetened an already rich deal. In June 1901,
widely circulating rumors were fanned by the arrival of Swift's representatives. They had also considered other locations in Texas, including
Grand Saline, which they dismissed as not cost effective. Swift initially
demanded inducements equal to those given Armour, but the two packers compromised, agreeing to split a mere $100,000 subsidy. Headlines
pronounced "Packing House [sic] Assured" and "Marks the Beginning of
a New Era" after Swift and Armour signed contracts for plants that would
employ more than 1,000.[34]

Incredibly, collections for the subsidy did not go well. They began
quickly with $40,750 committed in just four days but then slowed to only
a trickle. Judge G. W. Armstrong, who headed the solicitation campaign,
mused that the same offer in 1890 would have been met within an hour,
especially since he believed that the packers would bring other factories,
including those not related to animal trade. As grumbling arose, rumors
spread that Dallas representatives were in Chicago offering $300,000 for
Swift and Armour to switch sites, a threat that carried some teeth because Dallas had opened its own union stockyards in April 1901. These
reports stirred the Board of Trade to organize solicitation committees
based on occupation, thus creating competition among the groups. Even
at that, the fund lay short until a mass meeting was held at city hall on
October 7, 1901, conducted by R. W. Hall of the Fort Worth and Denver
Railway. Despite his background, Hall emphasized the importance of
factories, arguing that railroads alone were insufficient for building a
city. Fort Worth could add ten rail lines, Hall said, and its population
would increase by no more than 10,000, leaving it just another overgrown
town. He asserted that the time was ripe to aggressively pursue factories
because the Beaumont oil field had eased the burden of high fuel costs;
and he warned that if the offer failed, Fort Worth would be known only as
a place where railroads changed cars, and owls would roost in its buildings and coyotes would roam its lawns. Finally, the last $15,000 was
raised, allowing the *Register* to proclaim, "Fort Worth Never Failed."[35]

Work began quickly on a wide range of projects. In January 1902, Colonel H. C. Holloway, called the father of the stockyards, marked the start of construction by cutting down a tree. Both companies laid cornerstones on March 12, 1902, and just one year later, on March 6, 1903, they held formal grand openings. Swift's seven-story slaughterhouse began with 800 workers processing 750 cattle, 1,500 sheep, and 3,000 hogs daily; and Armour's capacity and employment, while not listed, were deemed to be similar. The impact quickly moved far beyond the slaughterhouse walls. Swift's investment included $175,000 that it paid for 1,300 acres running along both sides of Main Street from the Trinity River north to the Ellis Addition. Much of the land was used for employee homes on half-acre lots. Work began simultaneously on a new Fort Worth Livestock Exchange Building costing $100,000, alleged to be the handsomest in world, and an expansion of the stockyards to 490 pens capable of holding 13,000 cattle, 10,000 hogs, 5,000 sheep, and 3,500 horses and mules. The stockyards covered an expanse one-quarter mile wide, bounded on the west by Marine Creek, and stretching one-half mile both north and south of the packinghouses. The yards used five locomotives to move livestock around immense facilities that included three hay barns holding 600 tons and two scales capable of weighing sixty cattle at once.[36]

Even during construction, the companies prepared for expansion, leaving one wall unfinished to facilitate anticipated enlargements that would push daily capacity to 1,500 cattle and 4,000 hogs. In part, these considerations were based on developing an international export trade thanks to advantageous transportation rates. The cost of transporting beef from Chicago and Kansas City to seaports ran sixty cents per 100 pounds, three times the price from Fort Worth to the Gulf. Fort Worth offered not only cheaper shipping but also ample capacity, with five railroads running to two ports: the Missouri-Kansas-Texas, the Santa Fe, the International and Great Northern, and the Houston and Texas Central running to Galveston, and the Texas and Pacific linking to New Orleans. Early expansion was also motivated in part by a desire to ward off competition from the likes of Schwarzchild and Sulzberger of New York, Chicago, and Kansas City, which in 1903 showed interest in a Texas site that many assumed would be either Fort Worth or Dallas. Dallas, which had secured the Armstrong Packing Company, was actively seeking a second facility in hope of replacing Fort Worth as the packing center of the Southwest.[37]

The packinghouses had an immediate economic impact of great proportions. More than 50 times as many cattle and almost 120 times as many

TABLE 4.3.   Livestock sold to Fort Worth packers,
             1901–1903

	Cattle	Hogs	Sheep
1901	2,000	116,629	231
1902	4,787	81,202	435
1903	274,316	143,000	51,850

Source: *Fort Worth Record*, March 8, 1904, p. 2.

TABLE 4.4.   Total livestock handled by the
             Fort Worth stockyards, 1902–1904

	Livestock*
1902	226,106
1903	732,741
1904	1,045,179

Source: Robert Harris Tallbert, *Cowtown Metropolis:
Case Study of a City's Growth and Structure* (Fort Worth:
Leo Potishman Foundation, Texas Christian University,
1956), p. 125.

* Livestock includes cows, calves, hogs, sheep, horses,
and mules. While horses and mules were not slaughtered,
they were brought to the stockyards to be bought and
sold and thus are counted among the total.

sheep were slaughtered in 1903 as in 1902, and the number of hogs processed almost doubled despite chronic supply shortages (see table 4.3).[38]

The number of animals through the stockyards also increased dramatically, more than tripling from 1902 to 1903, helping make the cattle trade
the state's largest industry in cash volume (see table 4.4).[39]

The economics of the two packinghouses dwarfed existing industries.
The value of their combined production approached $8 million in the first
year and was projected to exceed $10 million in the second. In contrast, the
nearest competitor, flour milling, produced 650,000 barrels with annual
revenues of $3 million, and the next largest single employer, Texas Brew-
ing, had a workforce of 180 compared with 800 each for Armour and Swift
(see table 4.5).[40]

The economic impact was felt both outside and inside Fort Worth.
Regional farmers and ranchers stood to benefit significantly. The

TABLE 4.5.   Estimated annual revenues of significant
Fort Worth industries, 1903

	Estimated annual revenue ($ millions)
Packinghouses	8.0
Flour milling	3.0
Texas brewing	1.5
Iron and metals	0.5
Windmills	0.25
Harnesses and saddles	0.25
Miscellaneous	0.1

Source: Fort Worth Telegram, May 17, 1903, section 4, p. 6.

packers needed 6,000 hogs daily which, at the then current rate of six
cents per pound, would put $35 million into farmers' pockets each year. In
addition, the area immediately adjacent to the packinghouses experienced a rush of residential development. Sam Rosen and a Beaumont in-
vestor paid $18,475 for 320 acres three-fourths of a mile west of the
packinghouses, where they developed Rosen Heights Addition. Construction boomed within Fort Worth as well. City officials issued more
than 500 building permits in the six months after April 1902, driving the
value of taxable property from $16.5 million in 1901 to $18.9 million in
1902, and boosting municipal tax revenues from $290,000 to $330,000.[41]

The plants also stimulated population increases. The settlement closest to the packinghouses, originally known as Marine, incorporated
as North Fort Worth. Although the packinghouses remained outside
the city limits of both, Fort Worth and North Fort Worth experienced remarkable growth surges, fueling projections that within five years North
Fort Worth would be a city of 10,000 and Fort Worth would have a population of 75,000. Some optimists envisioned Fort Worth becoming the
Kansas City of Texas while others, including the Register, believed Fort
Worth would become Texas's largest city. Even Dallas officials feared that
Fort Worth would reach population equality. Early, unofficial population
counts seemed to justify the optimism. A census conducted by the General City Directory, 1902–1903 claimed a Fort Worth population of 35,482,
an increase of 4,795 that trailed only the 1895/1896 increase of 4,854 and
the 1892/1893 increase of 5,223.[42]

The Fort Worth packinghouses also had national implications. In the late 1880s, the large packers, including Swift and Armour, dominated America's beef supply, establishing a cooperative oligopoly capable of controlling cattle prices and assimilating smaller concerns. Swift took over the Anglo-American Company, Libby, McNeil & Libby, the old Chicago Packing Company, and the St. Joseph and the Sioux City stockyards. Armour absorbed the Omaha Packing Company, which effectively reduced the number of significant producers to four. In the process, Swift and Armour developed a high level of cooperation, evident in their shared control of Fowler Brothers Packing of East St. Louis, their agreement to build at Fort Worth, and their working alliances in Chicago, Kansas City, and St. Louis. Still, J. Ogden Armour denied the existence of a conspiracy to establish a Beef Trust, although he admitted that the two had cooperated in

Fort Worth city flag, 1903, featuring railroads, livestock, cotton bales, and industries. *Fort Worth Telegram*, July 26, 1903, p. 11.

expansions at Kansas City and, especially, at Fort Worth where, he claimed, their plants had made Fort Worth a major livestock market.[43]

The impact of Swift and Armour was impressive on many levels. Most notably, they fueled significant population and commercial increases that pushed Fort Worth beyond regional status, making it a city of national importance. A case can be made that railroads had accomplished that feat years earlier, but this argument fails the test of achieving a critical mass. In the twenty-four years since the first railroad, the population of Fort Worth climbed only to 26,688, but in just seven years after 1903 it reached 73,312. The difference lay in significant job creation, the essential building block of large municipalities that was not provided by railroads, which tend to be high-capital industries with relatively few employees. Little question exists that the addition of Swift and Armour in 1903 represented a giant step in Fort Worth's transition from town to city. Not yet answered was whether or not they completed that process.[44]

5

SAVORING SUCCESS, 1904–1909

T hrough the first decade of the twentieth century, Swift and Armour proved true to their billing as great economic forces. The packinghouses spurred the local economy both directly, as the first large employers, and indirectly through attraction of ancillary businesses and stimulation of banking. However, by 1909 some felt that Fort Worth had become a victim of this success, that complacency had replaced zeal, effectively muting what had been an aggressive civic front bent on commercial expansion. For others the problem lay not in the magnitude of the packinghouses' impact but in their limitations as simply another expression of an agriculturally based, non-diverse economy incapable of overcoming Dallas's superior population and industrial output. All the while, struggles continued with perennial problems in the water supply and in Hell's Half Acre, which survived a serious setback to receive open recognition.

In the first few years after 1903, Fort Worth developed as a major packing center with no obvious negatives. National recognition seemed confirmed by a 1905 presidential visit, although Theodore Roosevelt stayed only an hour, just long enough to ride in parade through downtown, give a short speech, and plant a tree. In 1906, after just two full years of packinghouse operations, the Fort Worth stockyards ranked sixth nationally, trailing in descending order Chicago, Kansas City, Missouri, St. Louis, Omaha, Nebraska, and St. Joseph, Missouri. Fort Worth boosters seriously eyed the third spot behind Chicago and Kansas City as supply and capacities grew. In the first six months of 1906, local livestock receipts showed the greatest increases of all major markets, including Chicago, and in the first four months of 1908, Fort Worth handled 28,603 more cattle than St. Louis, indications of accelerating growth as supply increased to meet demand. What happened in North Fort Worth played the salient role in a rise of more than 300 percent in Texas meatpacking between 1899 and 1904 and its ranking by 1909 as the state's largest industry.[1]

In contrast to pre-packinghouse days, most livestock entering the Fort Worth stockyards after 1903 never left the Northside environs. In 1905 Swift and Armour bought just over 57 percent of the 1,418,156 animals

President Theodore Roosevelt planting a tree next to the Carnegie Library, 1905. Courtesy of University of Texas at Arlington Special Collections.

received, and in 1906 they took in 88 percent of all livestock arriving via trains, excluding horses and mules. In that year, some 30,969 railcars laden with livestock arrived but only 4,852 departed, most going to Kansas City, Omaha, and St. Joseph, with a very few diverted to Los Angeles and Arizona.[2]

The labor required to process such huge quantities radically changed Fort Worth's employment environment. In 1904 Swift and Armour employed 2,000 workers, more than ten times as many as Texas Brewery, and over twice as many as the next seven largest companies combined (see table 5.1).

The packinghouses and their supporting infrastructure underwent almost constant expansion. The stockyards, pushed to the limit by local and outside buyers, expanded to forty-two acres, with 200 employees earning a monthly payroll of $7,000. In November 1908, the dynamics of supply and demand stimulated a $100,000 subscription to attract a third major packinghouse. The fund, which was quickly subscribed, brought a stream of interested factory representatives but never produced a major commitment, although a small operation, the Cass Packing Company, opened at Jones and Twenty-second, just south and west of Marine Creek. The threat alone was enough to push Swift and Armour into major additions, but the two meatpackers did not announce their plans immediately, waiting until they were assured that Fort Worth's annexation of the city of North Fort

TABLE 5.1.   Fort Worth industries with more than 100 employees, 1904

Industry with number of individual businesses	Number of employees
Packinghouses (2)	2,000
Brewery (1)	180
Ice houses (2)	177
Flour mills (3)	145
Furniture makers (3)	113
Biscuit maker (1)	105
Dressmakers (43)	104
Foundries and machine works (4)	101
Total	2,925

Source: Fort Worth Record, October 16, 1904, section 3, p. 16.

Worth did not include their plants, which would have subjected them to $7,000 in annual municipal taxes. Assured of exclusion, Armour spent $500,000 to double its beef and pork production and Swift increased its overall capacity by 40 percent, making its Fort Worth operation the equal of Omaha and inferior only to Chicago and Kansas City.[3]

The period was not without major setbacks, both natural and man-made. The nineteenth century suffered natural devastation at a high rate, a byproduct of urbanization and industrialization documented by Ted Steinberg. Steinberg found that extremes of nature carried increasingly damaging consequences in the late nineteenth century as population shifted from farms to cities, especially to cities located in desirable but disaster-prone areas.[4] Urbanization also created heightened vulnerabilities independent of area risk factors simply from concentration of population. This effect was seen in May 1908, when torrential rains flooded much of Fort Worth, paralyzing railroad service and washing out the Exchange Avenue Bridge, while killing seven and leaving 5,000 homeless.[5]

Fires, which are often man-made phenomena, also posed great urban hazards. In 1908 flames destroyed the Shamrock saloon (also known as the Bucket of Blood), one of the Acre's most notorious dives, and did $250,000 in damage to the Texas and Pacific depot. The next year fire leveled a glass factory, and seven people died at the Southern Hotel on Jones Street across from the Santa Fe depot.[6] The worst fire, in April 1909, consumed a large portion of the fashionable residential district just south of the Texas and Pacific reservation. The firestorm began in Mrs. Hatcher's barn at Jennings Avenue and Peter Smith Street, the city's highest point, then spread quickly thanks to high winds and dry conditions brought on by a month-long drought. The fire burned out of control for hours despite the arrival of firefighters from Weatherford, Texas, and Dallas. (Three large fires destroyed seventy-five buildings in Dallas while its crews fought in Fort Worth.) The path of destruction in Fort Worth was one-half mile wide and a mile-and-a-half long, covering twenty square blocks, but might have been much worse if the new steel and stone Union passenger depot had not protected the wholesale district and the rest of downtown. Some 300 buildings burned, including four churches, two schools, and the Texas and Pacific repair shops and roundhouse, containing twenty locomotives. The total estimated loss reached $3 million, a huge sum for the day.[7]

Disasters such as floods and fires tended to be acute, but industrial development often created chronic unsavory problems. In July 1902, during the packinghouse construction phase, a visitor remarked that large plant piping had converted Marine Creek into a big sewer, a fact that residents quickly realized all too well. During the first year of operations, down-stream residents sued, claiming that discharged waste had rendered the creek odorous, especially during dry summer months. A group associated with the livestock trade asked forbearance from lawsuits, citing fears that court fights would jeopardize Fort Worth's industrial golden calf. A com-promise solution lay in the installation of a bacterial purification system costing $60,000 to $75,000 that became operational on May 22, 1904. Unfortunately, the system failed to keep pace with demand, leading in 1918 to four court cases against the packinghouses and the city over effluent pollution.

The first signs of the coming automobile age and its problems also ap-peared. In 1906 only eighty-three automobiles were reported, but so many people expressed fear that they were "absolutely dangerous to the public" that the city council reduced the speed limit from eight to seven miles per hour. Those early concerns may have been prompted by the first serious wreck, which occurred on June 30, 1906, on Arlington Heights Road (either West Seventh or Camp Bowie today). The crash involved a "powerful" car with an eighty-five horsepower motor driven by H. H. Derrough, who suffered fractures while his passenger broke an arm.[8]

Industrialization also brought management-labor issues that proved troublesome. Local labor relations had remained relatively quiet since the violent strike of 1886, but in July 1904 Michael Donnelly, president of the Amalgamated Meat Cutters and Butchers' Workmen of America, or-dered a national packinghouse strike seeking an increase in the hourly rate for unskilled labor from fifteen cents to eighteen-and-a-half cents. Union employees at Fort Worth's Swift Plant voted to walk out, but Ar-mour locked out workers before they had a chance to vote. Both plants continued operations using management and nonunion labor, doing so well that production suffered more from livestock shortages than from the strike. Management's success, combined with an absence of local grievances, sapped the energy from the local effort; the number of pickets dropped from 600 in July to only 250 in September. Recognizing a losing cause, the national union leadership sought a settlement but found man-agement unwilling to make even minor compromises. Particularly gall-ing, the companies refused a blanket reinstatement of strikers, insisting on reviewing each worker individually, a position the union suspected as

Early cars displayed in front of the Texas and Pacific Railway station, circa 1905. Courtesy of University of Texas at Arlington Special Collections.

a ploy to dismiss older employees. Eventually labor conceded all points, returning to work without a contract covering the unskilled.[9] The defeat must have been a severe blow, but the local labor movement survived and would continue its struggle. In 1906 a large crowd cheered and applauded Mother Jones, a prominent figure in American labor.[10]

Associated problems notwithstanding, the Armour and Swift plants spurred considerable economic and demographic development. Boardman Buckley Paddock recognized very early that a crucial aspect of the packing-house effect lay in the stimulation of other commerce. Soon, others also recognized that dimension. In 1903, before slaughtering began, the *Telegram* lamented Fort Worth's paltry two score factories, but in October 1904 the *Fort Worth Record* reported that steady growth had raised the city's manufacturing sector to some 200 factories capitalized at $7.21 million and employing 21,852 workers. The packinghouses would have accounted for most of that capital but they employed only 2,000 workers, leaving almost 20,000 employed in other concerns. That number seems high, considering that the 1900 census showed Tarrant County with a population of only 52,376, but no doubt exists that business and commercial expansion affected population growth. An informal census conducted in 1904 counted 46,290 residents in Fort Worth, an addition of 23 percent since January 1902, the largest increase in the state even without counting the 5,180 who lived around the stockyards in the city of North Fort Worth. By 1907 population estimates reached 75,000, and Fort Worth seemed destined to pass the 100,000 mark. These projections were optimistic but not without precedent. After a packinghouse opened in St. Joseph Missouri, in 1892, the population almost doubled, increasing from 52,324 in 1890 to 102,979 in 1900.[11]

Swift and Armour complemented Fort Worth's railroad industry, although most of the impact involved facility development around the plants, which did not show up in city assessments because they were located outside town limits. For example, between 1904 and 1905 the taxable value of Fort Worth's railroad property increased only 1 percent, from $1.25 million to $1.26 million. In contrast, the effect on freight and passenger traffic statistics was remarkable. Demand for freight railway cars showed steady double-digit increases from 1905 through 1907, and the number of railroad cars interchanged rose 32 percent from 1903 to 1904, from 436,556 to 575,147, and reached 827,412 by 1907. Passenger traffic showed even more impressive growth, increasing from 18 to 26 percent annually between 1903 and 1907.[12]

The growth helped Fort Worth, now with the South's largest passenger depot, solidify its position as the largest railroad center in the Southwest. In 1907, twelve companies ran ninety-eight passenger trains daily in and out of Fort Worth. The Texas and Pacific, Fort Worth's first railroad, was the clear leader with twenty-eight daily departures or arrivals, an impressive figure but no more than 29 percent of the total.[13]

Commercial expansion boomed to the extent that in 1905 lumber cost more in Fort Worth than anywhere else in Texas. During one six-month period in 1906, some 1,065 feet of Fort Worth street frontage experienced new construction, a figure unsurpassed in the Southwest, and plans were announced for a fifteen-story skyscraper at Eighth and Houston. Still, demand for commercial space exceeded supply to the point that a disinfectant company had difficulty finding a suitable building.[14] In 1908 the pace of construction slowed due to a national economic slump, but construction rebounded in 1909, creating, in the perspective of a *Record* cartoon, the threat of "rubberneckitis," or sore necks caused by looking upward to view all the construction.[15] A sense of urbanity associated with changes in the landscape may well have played a role in the adoption of a commission form of city government, in which elected commissioners served not only as a legislative body but also as executive department heads. A referendum approved the change in April 1907, and the commissioners took their new offices on May 7.[16]

Construction caused a spike in tax values and in post office receipts. In 1905, municipal tax assessments soared to $26.2 million, an increase of $2.12 million over 1904, while Tarrant County values reached $30.6 million,

Rubberneckitis, 1909. *Fort Worth Record*, May 29, 1909, p. 1.

an increase of $3.6 million, and the largest of any Texas county. An un-
named factory representative inspecting Fort Worth for possible expansion argued that post office statistics provided the most accurate measure
of an area's commercial growth. Comparing the fourth quarter of 1904 to
the same period of 1903, he found that sales of second-class postage, used
for newspapers and magazines, had almost quintupled and that total
mail volume doubled. The upward trend continued, although at a
slower pace, as total postal receipts increased almost 20 percent between
1906 and 1907.[17]

Bank transactions also grew significantly. The total deposits in Fort
Worth banks went from $5.91 million in 1903 to $8.71 million in 1904, an
increase of 47 percent, while weekly bank clearings—the total of all checks,
drafts, and notes presented for settlement—jumped 11 percent (from $168.9
million to $188.5 million), followed by a 41 percent rise in 1905 (from
$188.5 million to $265.5 million). The rate of increase, which often led all
other cities, pushed Fort Worth to twelfth nationally in 1907, a remarkable achievement for only the fifth-largest city in Texas. In the first nine
months of 1908, Fort Worth was one of only eleven cities with increased
clearings, but it finished the year down considerably, then rebounded in
1909 to almost equal 1907 (see table 5.2).[18]

Fort Worth's industrial development experienced general and steady
increases for several years following 1903. In 1906 the effect was modest,
with seven new businesses employing only 137, but even this was enough
to increase manufacturing and industrial capitalization to an estimated

TABLE 5.2.   Annual totals of Fort Worth
              bank clearings, 1903–1909

	Total funds cleared ($)
1903	168,907,738
1904	188,484,605
1905	265,506,187
1906	317,393,685
1907	395,936,584
1908	254,745,760
1909	337,782,874

Source: *Fort Worth Record*, January 3, 1908, p. 1.

$10 million, with an annual production value of $40 million. A major portion of this investment capital represented twenty-two larger firms that employed twenty-five or more workers, including eight companies in heavy industries such as steel and brass foundries, four manufacturers of furniture or construction material, three grain mills, three food and beverage producers, two cotton oil mills, one oil refiner, and one producer of consumer goods. Fort Worth's five largest employers (not counting the packinghouses outside the municipal limits) were: Texas Brewing (175), Fort Worth Furniture (150), Burrus Mills (125), Fort Worth Machine and Foundry (100), and Fort Worth Iron and Steel (90).[19] In 1907, the number of factories rose to 167 with the addition of a $50,000 glass factory scheduled to employ 250 men and 70 boys, the $100,000 Gin Manufacturing Company, the Roofing and Manufacturing Company, which was constructing a $50,000 building, and six smaller projects ranging from $10,000 to $30,000. In 1908 the Bolt Works, which had opened in 1904 at the terminus of the Hemphill Streetcar Line, expanded and added rolling mills to become Texas Rolling Mills, one of only two steel companies in the Southwest.[20]

While packinghouses remained the commercial elephant in the room, Fort Worth also developed as a significant grain and milling center. Only a few years earlier the grain trade had been inadequate to fund even one elevator, but prospects improved after Muggs and Dryden, later known as Muggs and Pemberton, built storage facilities with a capacity of 175,000 bushels. This investment provided the economic base that supported the construction of twelve elevators, but demand still exceeded capacity so greatly that hundreds of grain-filled railcars carried the excess to the Gulf. By 1908 the grain market had become so important that Paddock suggested an exposition highlighting Fort Worth's status as the Southwest's grain and milling center.[21]

Advances and improvements seemed to be happening everywhere. In 1904 F. G. McPeak received two De Forest wireless radios; in 1905 streetcar service south of the railroad reservation began with a line running down Main and west on Magnolia before returning via Henderson; and in 1906 a total of eighty-six automobiles were registered, two with "powerful" fifty-horsepower motors.[22] Between 1907 and 1909, a national banking panic that closed eleven national and forty state banks in the United States curtailed most new industrial development, but it had little effect on Fort Worth's noncommercial sector. All Saints Hospital was formally dedicated in 1906 after a decade in the making. Work had begun in 1896 with a lot purchase, but it progressed so slowly that the foundation was not laid until 1900 and the facility did not become operational until 1905. Even then, full operations were delayed pending extension of water and electric services. In addition, A. T. Byers of Arlington Heights opened the $200,000 Byers Opera House at Rusk and Seventh (entrance on Seventh); the Tarrant County Benevolent Home for Orphans, capable of housing forty boys and girls, was built at Stop Five of the Interurban; and the Kindergarten Association established a settlement house at Crump and Eighteenth run by Mrs. Margaret Grabill, a veteran of seven years in Colorado mining camps. In 1908, local Baptists succeeded in luring the Southwestern Baptist Theological Seminary away from Waco, Texas, after a two-year courtship.[23]

Fort Worth's overall development from 1899 to 1909 can be seen in a comparison of wages, salaries, and value added by manufacturing. Between 1899 and 1909, the number of manufacturers increased 116 percent, wages increased 127 percent, salaries (non-hourly, white collar workers) 269 percent, and value added by manufacturing 153 percent. The number employed grew 51 percent between 1904 and 1909. The gains were all the more impressive because they did not include Swift and Armour, still outside the Fort Worth city limits (see table 5.3).

Commercial growth offered hope for ending shortfalls in the municipal budget. According to the mayor's 1904 annual report, serious budget issues had developed in 1900 after Fort Worth spent $500,000 on streets and on what was thought to be a long-term water supply fix (the Mead system)—an outlay that drained the treasury and led to suspension of

TABLE 5.3.   Manufacturing businesses, employees, wages, salaries, and value added, Fort Worth, 1899, 1904, and 1909

	Businesses	Employees	Wages ($)	Salaries ($)	Value ($) added by manufacturing
1899	68	—	565,000	131,000	1,341,000
1904	102	1,748	843,000	213,000	2,479,000
1909	147	2,641	1,285,000	484,000	3,395,000

Sources: *Thirteenth Census of the United States*, vol. 9 (Washington, D.C.: Government Printing Office, 1913), pp. 1214–15; Robert Harris Talbert, *Cowtown Metropolis: Case Study of a City's Growth and Structure* (Fort Worth: Leo Potishman Foundation, Texas Christian University, 1956), p. 126.

interest payments. After 1904 many felt that the worst had passed as the gap between revenue and expenditures narrowed, in part due to restructuring of debt through refinancing. In 1904 the annual interest on debts of $1.82 million totaled $147,621, the city's largest budgetary item. By 1909 refinancing had lowered the interest payments to $96,550 (second to the fire department budget) even though the city's debt was not significantly reduced. In addition, Fort Worth's governmental finances benefited from property assessments that increased from $16.5 million in 1901 to $21 million in 1904, and then more than doubled to $46 million in 1909, thanks in part to annexation of suburban communities. Tarrant County's taxable assets rose similarly, to $787.7 million in 1909, Texas's third largest total behind Dallas ($94.8 million) and Harris ($89.1 million) counties.[24]

The near tripling of Fort Worth's property assessments between 1901 and 1909 was driven more by absorption than by internal growth. Increased property valuations within the city limits accounted for only $5 million of the increase, with the remainder coming from annexations. For example, the annexation of North Fort Worth added $3 million to valuations and Glenwood another $1 million. Fort Worth's expansion was overdue in light of prevailing tendencies of the period. According to Kenneth T. Jackson, American cities of the nineteenth and early twentieth centuries utilized boundary adjustments as the dominant form of population growth. Until 1909, however, Fort Worth remained confined to only seven square miles, while San Antonio had spread to thirty-six square miles, Dallas to twenty-three, and Houston to almost twenty. Aggrandizement of territories not only added population but also inspired confidence in community vitality, which spurred citizens into greater efforts.[25]

Prodded by Paddock, the Board of Trade in 1909 presented an ambitious plan to absorb eighteen square miles, including the suburbs of Arlington Heights, North Fort Worth, Rosen Heights, Sycamore Heights, Polytechnic Heights, Riverside, the Factory Place, the Van Zandt Addition, Mistletoe Heights, and Fairview Heights. The proposal met with considerable opposition in many of the intended acquisitions, including Polytechnic Heights, Riverside, and Arlington Heights. Arlington Heights's financial condition had improved after the developers sold the Arlington Heights Street Car Company for $480,000 and used some of the funds to invest $125,000 in new acreage and $50,000 in the Lake Como Pavilion. North Fort Worth was willing but demanded that Fort Worth assume its $193,000 debt and fund $200,000 in improvements. Fort Worth met North

Fort Worth's conditions but proposed a less ambitious overall scheme that excluded Arlington Heights, Rosen Heights, and parts of Riverside and Sycamore Heights. The scaled-down plan still would have added 70,000 residents and increased the city's area to sixteen square miles.[26]

Even the smaller version proved too controversial. Suburbs threatened with absorption against their will exercised their political muscle so effectively that Tarrant County's state legislative delegation led a successful opposition to the charter revisions that authorized annexations. Fort Worth reacted by immediately cutting off water, light, and sewerage connections to the recalcitrant suburbs, closing schools to their children, and refusing to respond to their police calls. The legislative defeat did not affect the mutually agreed annexation of North Fort Worth (not including the packinghouses) on March 11, 1909, and of Glenwood on June 29, 1909, which increased the urban land mass to just over fifteen square miles. A few newly-absorbed manufacturers sought exemptions, arguing that they had built based on assurances from the Board of Trade that they would remain outside city taxing limits, but the city rejected those petitions as unfair to other tax-paying concerns.[27]

After a short honeymoon period, the Mead waterworks system, begun with such hope, proved incapable of maintaining required production levels. As late as 1905 all seemed fine, and the *Record* called the system the greatest municipal improvement in Texas history. The city water department reported that pure and ample water had brought 936 new connections, increasing receipts from $53,940 in 1904 to $85,217 in 1905, while expenses decreased $5,391 and rates fell by half. Soon thereafter, well production dropped to only 2.5 million gallons daily, below the 3 million gallon contractual level. To bolster output, the city drilled fifteen new wells, called the Powell Field, four miles southwest off Benbrook Road, piping the production to the Holley Pumping Station. In addition, the city spent $21,000 for air compressors to increase water flow at existing wells. The expenditures wiped out the positive cash flow, putting the waterworks once again into deficit operations. Mead argued that the system worked properly but that dynamics had changed because new wells, including those added by the city of North Fort Worth and the packinghouses, drew 2 million gallons daily from the same water table. Fort Worth disagreed and refused to pay the contracted fee, but Mead won a $30,000 court judgment.[28]

Although assigning blame consumed considerable effort, the more serious issue lay in developing solutions to a problem that had long been a drag on finances. To make a bad situation even worse, the recent annexations had added population and thirty-nine miles of water mains, aggravating demand issues. The addition of 100 new connections each month to an already overburdened system raised serious questions about the viability of wells as a primary water source. In June 1907 Water Commissioner Lee Stephens argued that little hope existed for a system based on wells, despite considerable money spent on air compressors and efforts to revive the Mead system. Stephens suggested that maintaining a sufficient well-water system would require spending another $600,000 on a 2 billion-gallon reservoir that would function not as a direct water source but as a drainage pool supporting the underground water table. Former mayor J. T. Powell disagreed vehemently, calling Stephens's claims and proposals "dense ignorance" and insisting that enough water lay underground for all eternity. Stephens admitted that a $100,000 annual expenditure could carry the current system through another decade, but argued that a reservoir would still be required. Therefore, he contended that the greater economy lay in doing the inevitable rather than wasting money to revive a dying supply. City engineer E. C. Woodward offered a third alternative, proposing a dual system with drinking water supplied by wells but all other water pumped from a $986,000 reservoir on the Clear Fork of the Trinity River one-half mile west of the Parker County line. In March 1908, work began on converting 550 acres into a reservoir, with promises that water would flow by year's end.[29]

The projections proved overly optimistic. Lack of funding slowed reservoir construction at the same time that the existing waterworks deteriorated from poor maintenance. In September 1908 city officials abandoned three Mead wells after their flow dwindled below the point necessary to support pumps and, as the summer of 1909 approached, offered only prayers that no crisis would force widespread use of river water. In April 1909 the mayor, two city commissioners, and the city engineer toured the waterworks, finding an appalling state of disrepair. The eleven wells of the Powell field southwest of town past the old stove foundry (now Vickery Boulevard) lay almost totally dismantled, and what remained of the Mead system suffered from vandalism and poor-to-no maintenance. The city councilmen then admitted what many had charged, that one-fourth of the water supplied during the year had been pumped unfiltered from the Trinity River. Powell, who became water commissioner in 1909, still favored wells. He recommended halting work on the Parker County reservoir and expanding the well system, but the commission remained

committed to the mixed use plan, with the reservoir for non-potable supplies and a 5 million-gallon well-water reservoir for human consumption. In 1909, improvements that raised daily output to 8 million gallons
seemed to have, yet again, solved the problem. Once again, that would
prove not to be the case.[30]

The city's other perennial issue, open vice in Hell's Half Acre, earned
local law enforcement scathing criticisms. A January 1904 grand jury
report broadly attacked county and city officers, chiding beat patrol-
men for "willful negligence" that allowed gambling houses to exist and
describing the city detective force as ignorant of its duty. The report
singled out an unnamed police investigator who personally conducted
a stranger to an "assignation house," and it termed the arranged fine
system simply a form of de facto regulation. The grand jurors recommended that the unofficial agreement become official, that the city seek
state legislative authority for a vice reservation where the worst excesses could be eliminated and the rest reduced and controlled.[31] In
November 1904, Reverend Dr. Alonzo Monk, a Methodist church pastor, joined in, blasting the police from the pulpit for making a few token
arrests of nonwhites while ignoring well-known operations catering to
Anglos. In a city hall speech, Carrie Nation, a famous prohibitionist cru-
sader noted for wielding an axe against saloons, praised Monk while
urging women to "clean out this hell hole," which she described as one
of the most corrupt towns she had ever seen. She also visited a "moving
picture establishment" on lower Main Street where she chastised the
manager for the indecent images. As usual, nothing changed. In 1905, a
preacher touring the Acre expressed shock at a woman dancing for the
amusement of a mixed audience of "whites and coloreds," at the presence of girls as young as thirteen cavorting with coarse men in "wine
rooms," small areas partitioned by flimsy curtains allowing a modicum
of privacy, and at saloons in which women mingled with men soliciting
drinks and "things even worse."[32]

The pressure eventually brought a police reaction. J. H. Maddox, cam-
paigning for chief of police, promised if elected to resign if he did not
close the dives and illegal joints operating in "lower end of the city." Following election, Maddox sought a municipal ban on alcohol sales in variety theaters, a move supported by the Texas Brewing Association as part
of a multicity campaign to blunt the prohibition movement by attacking
some of the worst abuses. Variety theaters, which replaced saloons and

casinos as the source of most complaints, were not just a Fort Worth issue. Gunther Barth's study of the rise of modern cities found that most city dwellers identified variety shows with dissolute men and lewd women, and that most suspected (correctly) that salacious tastes shaped the performances. Fort Worth's variety theaters were notorious for their female "entertainers" who circulated offstage, conning gullible patrons into buying exorbitantly-priced drinks.[33]

The county sheriff also entered the enforcement picture. On November 20, 1904, sheriff's deputies began closing all gambling houses and saloons on Sundays, which made for great theater of the moment but little else. Ironically, the Sunday closures actually spurred an increase in intoxication arrests due to drinkers who overindulged in harbored liquor or illegal supplies. Those who failed to think ahead or find bootleggers simply waited for midnight when the doors reopened, then tried to make up for lost time. The raids, including one in January 1905 with sixty-eight special deputies, were effective to the extent that the average county jail inmate population declined from one hundred to seventy-five. Like all previous campaigns, the effort waned, and the county tended to leave alcohol enforcement to city officers while it concentrated on gambling. In December 1905 a newspaper article headlined "The Lid is Off in Fort Worth" recounted the ease of finding games of roulette, craps, and poker both in the northern business district and on lower Main Street. The reporter relayed his findings to County Attorney Jefferson Davis McLean, who insisted that strict enforcement was the still the order of the day. The next day deputies raided the casinos cited, claiming that they had been unaware of the locations until the article appeared, an illogical statement considering that the casinos were so blatant that a journalist had no difficulty locating them.[34]

Political connections, rather than ignorance, explained the prevalence of gambling and prostitution. Even the *Telegram* admitted that vice survived because many civic leaders believed it necessary for the city's welfare. The newspaper quoted unnamed vice purveyors who insisted that most politicians opposed eradication and would deal strongly to restrict police interference. In 1905 an assistant city attorney obliquely confirmed the unofficial existence of a "reservation" exempt from vice enforcement when he refused to prosecute women from "the district of the city known as the 'reservation'." Moreover, when the city magistrate also adopted nonenforcement, Police Chief Maddox ordered an end to prostitution arrests from "a known district not frequented by the general public."[35]

Three tragedies gave new but still transitory emphasis to vice enforcement. The first occurred in December 1906 when a policeman, Officer John Nichols, was shot and killed inside the Standard Theater. The officer's death led the *Record* to ask, "How long are we to tolerate the reproach of this noisome section of an otherwise decent city?" Speakers at mass meetings and letters to the editor railed that the Acre constituted the worst den of iniquity in the state and was responsible for three-fourths of Fort Worth's crime.[36] To "quicken the moral pulse" and help bring an end to the "unspeakable evilness of Hell's Half Acre," a *Record* columnist joined Detective Al Ray on a tour of dives and brothels where he said depravity lay "like an open sore," visible to anyone passing to or from the Union Depot. An account of their adventures appeared under the headline "Christmas Night in Hell's Half Acre." The journalist took care to avoid casting blame on the police, arguing that officers could only fight vice as hard as public sentiment demanded and that closure would have to spring from citizen demand.[37]

The two began at the Standard Theater on Thirteenth Street, just two blocks off Main Street. When they entered the theater, their ears were assaulted by the singing of a peroxide blonde wearing a low-cut dress who rambled through the audience as she sang, wheedling beers at $1.00 each or wine for $5.00. A glass of wine would gain the purchaser a few minutes with her in one of the wine rooms. The theater bill also included a motion picture and a live act in which a seven-year old girl sang while making suggestive expressions. At the bar a group of women, described en masse as without a single handsome face but "not all homely," waited to separate men from their money. One, a twenty-two-year-old English woman wearing a dress ending just below her knees, admitted receiving 20 percent commissions on drinks bought for her, including several purchased by Officer Nichols's assailant just nights before the shooting.[38]

The Standard Theater proved to be the high point of a tour that took a steady decline into seediness. The Crown, another theater, was far dirtier than the Standard, both in setting and clientele, but the Black Elephant on Rusk Street between Thirteenth and Fourteenth was the worst of the lot. The *Record* columnist lamented an insufficient vocabulary to describe the filthy, horrible, smoke-filled and foul-smelling atmosphere in which the mostly African American patrons danced lewdly in "disgusting familiarity."[39] For some reason, the adjacent Shamrock, a notorious hell hole that for twenty years was considered one of Texas's worst dives, was not mentioned. The Bucket of Blood, as the Shamrock was commonly called in deference to its frequent beatings, knifings, and shootings, occupied three stories with a saloon on the ground floor, a variety theater presenting the most repugnant shows on the second floor, and a rooming house (prostitution front) of the "lowest order" on the top floor.[40] Detective Ray included a tour of several saloons: the Do Drop In, the Redlight, the Anchor, Marion Warren's place (where blacks and whites mingled), the Arizona (which had a brothel), the Star, the Acme, Don O'Connell's, and the Cave (a gathering spot for professional beggars, many of whom were physically deformed). The article suggested that people whose sympathies had been stirred by these unfortunates would have been disgusted by the sight of the "repulsive creatures" in their nightly revel.[41]

Officer Nichols's death and the resulting publicity brought quick but temporary responses. On January 3, 1907, a *Record* political cartoon urged banishing the Acre "monster." The next day Detective Ray headed a large force that went through the Acre closing "cribs" or "box houses" as a crowd of about 1,000 followed. Arrests began at the more upscale spots employing white prostitutes, many of whom reacted with surprise and asked if it was a joke and how long the crusade would last. The march then turned south to Fourteenth Street between Rusk and Calhoun before reaching the Black Elephant and the Shamrock. Soon word spread and the officers found the lights turned off at the Do Drop Inn, another notorious hangout. The officers arrested 115 men and women, but that number could have been much larger if they had not released many "variety actresses" (prostitutes) on their promise to leave town immediately, and had not given several vagrants orders to either get a job or leave. For several days, raids and arrests continued, resulting in the closing of the Crown and Black Elephant and the Standard Theater's suspension of alcohol sales. By January 12, 1907, some $2,000 in fines had been leveled and trade reduced to the extent that 200 Acre denizens left town. The clean-up was so dramatic that men reported walking down some of the worst streets without hearing even one solicitation.[42]

The second event involved Tarrant County District Attorney Jefferson Davis McLean. McLean, who had been elected on an anti-vice platform, began fulfilling that pledge by raiding eighteen casinos on his first night

1907 cartoon urging an end to Hell's Half Acre. *Fort Worth Record,* January 3, 1907.

in office and kept at it, earning credit from the 1906 grand jury for suppressing gambling. The grand jury's high opinion was not shared by gamblers, who allegedly convinced Jorden Y. Cummings to oppose McLean's reelection in 1906. Cummings bristled at charges that he was the hand-picked choice of gamblers, maintaining that he would simply do a better enforcement job than McLean, who, he claimed, had failed to close many casinos, including one in the "very shadow of the courthouse." McLean defeated Cummings and, following Officer Nichols's death, vowed to prosecute variety theater cases in county courts that could impose heavier punishments than could the municipal courts. On March 22, 1907, Bill "One-Armed" Thompson, a flamboyant gambler whose casino was being raided, shot and killed McLean and was killed immediately afterwards in a shootout with Officer Hamil P. Scott.[43]

The ramifications of McLean's death spread across the state but were especially evident locally. Other cities ramped up enforcement. Waco officers cited McLean's death as motivation for raids that confiscated five wagonloads of gambling equipment, and the Dallas police chief ordered all gamblers arrested on sight. Many state legislators had been attending the Southwestern Exposition and Fat Stock Show the day of the shooting, and their shock and dismay contributed to the passage of a state law making gambling a state felony offense. The local reaction of deep anger spawned threats of vigilante violence against gamblers. Civic leaders took the threats so seriously that people with cooler heads walked the street urging calm. The response to McLean's death was not only aggressive but also profound, raising widespread questioning about whether the Acre was worth the bother. Speakers at mass meetings declared gambling abhorrent, and prominent citizens organized the Jefferson Davis McLean Law and Order League, with J. J. Jarvis as president. Jarvis expressed the change in attitude succinctly, proclaiming, "This is no longer a frontier city. The 'Wide-open-town fallacy' of lawlessness and immorality is no longer entertained . . . the notion that crime and vice are necessary for prosperity is a libel."[44]

Fort Worth commissioners reined in abuses. They ordered disorderly houses to close by July 12, 1907, or face arrest, and they restricted saloons to designated areas. The saloon limits ran west on Belknap to Taylor and back to Houston, then south to Seventh where it jogged over to Throckmorton before continuing south to the Texas and Pacific reservation, then south on Main to Elizabeth before turning north on Arizona, then east on Front (Lancaster) to the city limits, then north to Twelfth and over to Rusk and north back to Belknap. Many saloons within the geographical boundaries closed as habitués relocated to residential sections to avoid scrutiny. Consideration was given to moving "that undesirable element that have hitherto occupied Rusk, Calhoun and other neighboring streets" into a "vice district" north and east of Front Street (Lancaster Avenue), only a few blocks east of the Acre but off the main thoroughfare between the respectable north end and the Union Depot. That plan fell through under stiff opposition from residents of the relocation site.[45]

Support yet survived for the Acre as an economic necessity. After a few months, a petition signed by "a large portion of the representative

businessmen of the city" asked that the Acre be left undisturbed, arguing that it would die a natural death as business expansion raised property values to unsustainable levels. In June 1907, another petition called
for the resignation or removal of Police Commissioner George Mulkey on
the ground that he was "detrimental to the growth and prosperity of our
city." According to the *Record*, many respectable citizens signed "because
they believe that a 'wide open town' makes for business prosperity and
that certain laws ought to be winked at in order that prosperity may not
be interrupted." Judge William R. Booth, a large property owner involved
in both petitions, confirmed that petitioners tied the Acre to economic
development. He suggested that hundreds of thousands of dollars of
commercial property lay idle because of the crackdown and that the Acre
was necessary for Fort Worth to become a great city, although he supported
centralizing vice within restricted geographic boundaries to enhance the
maintenance of order.[46]

Mulkey survived the effort to displace him. Recall supporters held the
petition for five weeks in hopes that the commissioner would modify his
"extreme position," but when he refused, they submitted more than 1,200
signatures on August 30, 1907. The effort proved for naught after the city
secretary found only 594 qualified voters among the signers, leaving the
petition well short of the 1,044 signatures required. The rejection sparked
a celebration at city hall, during which Mulkey told the celebrants that
when he took office, Fort Worth had been the wickedest city on earth,
worse even than Paris, France, and that he knew that some financial interests would oppose its cleansing. McLean's successor as district attorney also addressed the crowd, vowing to continue the struggle, and others asserted vociferously that the time had passed when gambling and
other vices were necessary for prosperity.[47] In September, Mulkey put new
vigor into enforcement by ordering the police to clear an area bounded by
Rusk, Throckmorton, Thirteen, and Railroad. Acre evacuees had made
the area so dangerous that lone police officers refused to enter. He also
demonstrated a commitment to law and order at all levels by addressing
the obvious, that joints like the Bucket of Blood could not have operated
without official collusion. To add action to words he sought grand jury
indictments accusing five police officers of taking bribes.[48]

Once again the forces supporting the Acre had only to wait for more
propitious times. On November 1, 1908, less than two years after McLean's
death, the *Record* reported that the Acre had rebounded and was almost

as bad as ever. Liquor flowed so freely that taxes derived from its sale ranked third in the state, behind San Antonio and Houston but ahead of Dallas.[49] In 1909 Fort Worth admitted the obvious by granting the Acre official recognition. Part of the justification for reversal lay in complaints that unclad women roamed hotel corridors in the business district disturbing guests with their overtures. On June 7, 1909, city commissioners ordered all "disreputable persons" to vacate residential areas and move into a designated zone of toleration, commonly called a reservation. Located on the eastern boundaries of the Acre, the reservation ran from the north side of Fourteenth Street and north on Calhoun Street to east on the north side of Ninth Street before turning south on Grove Street and back to Fourteenth. The city commissioners promised that within those borders gamblers and prostitutes would face no interference, but outside they would be vigorously prosecuted. Many legitimate businessmen supported the arrangement as a way to retain the Acre's economic benefits, both direct and indirect, while ridding the business district of those scantily-clad women. Mulkey, who officially was still police commissioner, maintained a hard-line stance, announcing that he would never allow a reservation to exist. Mulkey's resistance proved difficult when the Fort Worth police chief accepted the plan, stating he would restrict all "unfortunate women" to the area.[50]

A major selling point for the reservation had been that concentration would allow more effective control, thereby reducing associated excesses such as robberies and thefts. This theory faced a serious challenge in August 1909 when Bob Hammond, upset over stringent enforcement, shot and killed Police Officer W. A. Campbell outside the Jockey Club saloon at Thirteenth and Rusk, and then surrendered immediately at police headquarters. Campbell had arrested Hammond several times for alcohol violations and had wounded him in the leg just one month earlier, leading Hammond to publicly threaten the officer. The threats were so taken so seriously that one night a captain and an assistant chief armed with rifles followed the officer on his rounds.[51] The killing of three law enforcement officials in less than three years reflected a violent tendency out of proportion to Fort Worth's size. According to the 1900 U.S. census, Fort Worth ranked 158th nationally in population but had thirty-eight homicide arrests in 1909, more than the nation's eighth largest city, Cleveland, Ohio. Moreover, Fort Worth recorded only 258 arrests for assault in 1909, compared with 1,597 such arrests in Cleveland. The disparity between arrests for assaults and for homicides indicated that Fort Worthians were statistically more likely to introduce firearms into disputes, a tendency which the *New York Times* blamed on the city's Western and Southern heritages.[52]

Campbell's death brought familiar and innovative reactions. A crowd of 1,300 attending a city hall meeting demanded removal of saloons from the Acre, while the county attorney said the murder would be Acre's death knell. The *Record* repeated its mantra, calling the Acre the "lowest, basest, rottenest plague spot of municipal life of the United States," but the newspaper abandoned its traditional closure recommendation to support relocation. It suggested that some place of "carnality" away from the heart of the city might be necessary.[53] The city and county decided jointly to close the reservation despite concerns that doing so would only spread, not end vice. Tarrant County set September 6, 1909, as the Acre's final day, promising after that date to prosecute any of the Acre's twenty "resorts" employing the estimated 150 prostitutes or the 450 freelancers not associated with a house. (The total of 600 was approximately one prostitute for every 100 residents of Fort Worth.)[54] On September 5, 1909, the *Fort Worth Star Telegram* headline "Acre Denizens Begin Hegira" reported moving vans busily hauling off furnishings as "For Rent" signs appeared in yards. Some effort was made to ease the transition by converting one of the best known prostitution houses into the Mildred Clifton House for fallen women. Fort Worth commissioners also tried to prohibit liquor sales in the Acre, but the courts ruled against them, and attempts to enforce a 1909 state law limiting towns to one saloon per 500 residents had little effect. Fort Worth's 178 bars (one for every 350 residents) were grandfathered.[55]

The situation for blacks remained grim, but incipient signs of organized racial resistance appeared. African Americans remained all but shut out of local politics. In 1900, Fort Worth's black population of 4,249 represented almost 16 percent of the city, but only 238 blacks, or fewer than 6 percent, were registered to vote in 1904. Blacks also faced discrimination in the workplace, including at the federal post office, where a white letter carrier was suspended for refusing to train an African American. In 1905, a petition led to unanimous passage of a city ordinance that, in the stated interest of making streetcars "safer," required separate public transit seating, with exceptions allowed for nurses and officers with prisoners. The local black community condemned the law, but a proposed boycott became meaningless and fizzled when Texas passed a state Jim Crow code requiring segregated seating. The legislation led to some resistance, including an incident in August 1906 when a black man refused to give up his seat and was struck by an off-duty police officer with a pistol, which discharged, striking two innocent bystanders. The local Federation of Women's Clubs also displayed bias, urging the establishment of African American neighborhoods in all nine wards, not for integration but to make it easier for whites seeking servants. In 1906, black leaders met at a skating rink at Third and Throckmorton to protest production of *The Clansman*, a theatrical drama that became the basis for *The Birth of a Nation*, D. W. Griffith's 1915 classic film saluting the Ku Klux Klan. Mayor W. D. Harris refused to ban the performance, noting that *The Clansman* had played the previous year with no ill effects. In 1909, the *Fort Worth Democrat* sponsored an essay contest in which school children described the value of the Klan, with the winner receiving *Clansman* tickets. One essayist called the Klan the protector of the weak from the outrages of "lawless negroes [*sic*]" while the winner credited the Klan for protecting "womanhood and girlhood from the negro [*sic*] uprising that followed the civil war [*sic*]" and blamed carpetbaggers for excesses that "the slow-witted African could not understand." As late as 1906 the *Record* continued to use base racial epithets in headlines.[56]

African Americans made some advances. William Madison "Gooseneck Bill" McDonald moved to Fort Worth around the turn of the century and helped build a black business community around Jones and Ninth and, along with mortician R. C. Houston, founded the first African American bank in Texas and only the fourth in the South. The bank operated out of the Masonic Temple on East Ninth Street, which housed several other black businesses. Plans also were announced by the Negro Texas Missionary and Educational Convention for a Negro Industrial College in the College Heights section of east Fort Worth. Intense opposition from area residents forced the college, which was the first private school in Texas for African Americans, to relocate to Arlington Heights, where an inaugural class of forty began learning industrial arts and agriculture.[57] In 1909, the council appointed "G. Smith (colored)" as special policeman for Willow Grove Park, reserved for African Americans. Smith was not the first black police officer but was one of the early few.[58]

By the end of the first decade of the twentieth century some long-term economic facts seemed evident. Following a slump in 1908, business had

rebounded in 1909, and with several projects already in the planning
stage, 1910 looked promising. By every calculation, the packinghouses
had jump-started the local economy, pushing it into regional, if not national prominence. Thanks to Swift and Armour, stockyards receipts recorded almost uninterrupted growth, and in 1909 the stockyards broke
the 2 million barrier in total livestock handled annually.[59] The Fort Worth
facilities were the major factor in the 300 percent increase in Texas's
slaughtering and meatpacking production between 1899 and 1904 and in
spurring another 172.3 percent increase between 1904 and 1909 to make
meatpacking the state's largest industry (in value of production), with
fourteen establishments producing $42.5 million.[60]

Although their effect was impressive, the packinghouses served the
ends of increasing existing commerce more than the goal of creating a
diverse economy. Swift and Armour were part of an agricultural-based
economy dominating the Southwest, Texas, and Fort Worth to the detriment of other industrial development and commercial diversity. The 1900
U.S. census noted that Texas manufacturing largely involved processing
raw materials provided by stock-raising, agriculture, and minerals and
that "they have been greatly stimulated by the rapid increase in production of these materials." This was certainly true of Fort Worth, where the
commercial base industries, packinghouses, and millers, involved production of two great food staples, meat and flour (see table 5.4), and of
Tarrant County, which in 1909 remained a major agricultural producer.

TABLE 5.4.   Annual value of Fort Worth
production by industry, 1904

	Value ($) of products
Wholesale trade	24,000,000
Packinghouses	8,000,000
Mills	3,000,000
Brewing and ice	1,600,000
Iron	500,000
Windmills	250,000
Furniture	250,000
Harnesses and saddles	200,000
Miscellaneous	200,000

Source: Fort Worth Telegram, May 17, 1903, part 4, p. 6.

In 1922, Paddock reassessed his estimation of the packinghouse effect, downgrading it to second behind that of railroads.[61]

Comparing Fort Worth's post-1903 industrial progress to Dallas's reveals only minor changes. In 1899, four years before the packinghouses opened, Dallas had 160 percent more businesses, 201 percent more wage earners, and 363 percent more salaried employees. In 1904, five years later and one year after the packinghouses opened, Dallas's lead had declined slightly to 142 percent more businesses and wage earners and 267 percent more salaried employees. In 1909, after the packinghouses had been operating for six years, Dallas still led by triple digits in every category, with 107 percent more businesses, 137 percent more wage earners, and 232 percent more salaried employees (see table 5.5). These statistics did not present a wholly accurate picture because Fort Worth's numbers did not include the packinghouses, which were still outside the city limits. Including the meatpackers would have increased the number of Fort Worth businesses by only a few, but would have presented the cities as equal in wage earners and, possibly, in salaried employees. Of course, Dallas had

TABLE 5.5. Number of businesses, wage earners, and salaried personnel in Fort Worth and Dallas, 1899, 1904, and 1909

	Fort Worth	Dallas	Percent difference (Dallas over Fort Worth)
1899			
Businesses	68	177	160
Wage earners	943	2,842	201
Salaried employees	108	500	363
1904			
Businesses	102	247	142
Wage earners	1,423	3,445	142
Salaried employees	226	830	267
1909			
Businesses	147	305	107
Wage earners	2,059	4,882	137
Salaried employees	449	1,490	232

Source: *Thirteenth Census of the United States*, vol. 9 (Washington, D.C.: Government Printing Office, 1913), pp. 1214–15.

businesses just outside its city limits as well, so the true balance between the two cities is speculative. What can be argued strongly is that as late as 1909, Swift and Armour, though important, did not raise Fort Worth's industrial output to match that of its nearest and dearest rival.

A statistically less obvious but still important packinghouse effect lay in sustaining Fort Worth's interest in railroads, the industry that had dominated its commercial affairs since the 1870s. In 1901, just after plans for the Armour packinghouse were announced, residents refused to support a subscription drive to attract the St. Louis-San Francisco Railway (also known as the Frisco) unless the company relocated its headquarters. A compromise was reached in which the Fort Worth and Rio Grande, which the St. Louis-San Francisco was buying, maintained its local offices and the company agreed to purchase 250 acres southwest of the Union Depot. Such insouciance would have been unthinkable before 1901. In 1902, the International and Great Northern Railroad bought six acres in Glenwood for machine shops and a roundhouse, becoming the first railroad not to seek or receive a subsidy before building.[62] In 1903 Paddock stated that railroad development had reached a level of saturation so that solicitations or bonuses were no longer necessary. The Board of Trade agreed, opting to redirect its energies away from transportation, which the Board termed as already all that could be desired, and into other industries. In June 1904, the new coolness toward railroads contributed to Tarrant County's significant upward adjustment of railroad property assessments. The Texas and Pacific Railroad, which topped the list at $25 million, objected strongly, arguing that it already paid $26,830, or 12 percent of all county taxes, but to no avail.[63]

The new coolness may be well understood in view of the sacrifices Fort Worth residents had made to become a rail center. The first to arrive, the Texas and Pacific, received 320 acres directly south of town that in 1901 was considered worth at least $1 million, and later arrivals often received both cash and land. In twenty-five years between 1876 and 1901, Fort Worth invested more than $2 million in railroad development (see table 5.6).

The packinghouse effect also reduced Fort Worth's willingness to make similar sacrifices to attract other industries. This happened, in part, because Swift and Armour were such a major coup that many thought no more work was needed. In 1903, soon after the plants opened, the Board of Trade complained that many members had let memberships

TABLE 5.6.   Subsidies granted to Fort Worth railroads

	Year established	Monetary subsidy ($)	Value ($) of facilities and land
Texas and Pacific	1876	[?]	1,000,000
Santa Fe	1881	120,000	340,280
Missouri-Kansas-Texas	1881	25,000	48,650
Fort Worth & Denver	1881	—	154,000
Fort Worth & New Orleans	1885	75,000	105,210
Fort Worth & Rio Grande	1887	40,000	53,600
Cotton Belt	1885	35,000	17,200
Rock Island	1894	35,000	120,000

Source: Fort Worth Register, July 14, 1901, pp. 7–10.

lapse because business was so good that they saw little need for the organization. The loss of enthusiasm was also evident in lamentations about the passing of the old guard who had sacrificed for the community good. Long-time residents recalled how John Peter Smith, who had already invested heavily, offered $5,000 more when the Santa Fe Railroad bonus seemed in danger, and even Paddock lamented the decline in broad-based business involvement in promoting Fort Worth.[64] In 1907, a $50,000 drive for a Livestock Exhibition Building began so poorly, collecting only $12,000, that work ceased and the project lay in danger of abandonment.[65] Once more, a few public-spirited citizens rallied, this time marching in groups on the streets chanting:

Rah! Rah! Rah!
Who are we?
Fort Worth Boosters!
Don't you see![66]

Their exuberance pushed the fund to success, allowing the Livestock Exchange to hold its grand opening on March 11, 1908, during the Southwestern Exposition and Fat Stock Show. That level of energy was becoming rarer and taking more effort to stimulate.[67]

After 1903, commercial promotion focused on attracting smaller businesses. The Home Factory and Industrial Association, or the Factory Club, was an example of the new boosterism. The organization, which grew rapidly to reach 250 members, elected Judge Booth (one of the organizers of the petition to remove Mulkey) as president. Booth called for an emphasis on small factories, arguing that experience had shown it was more profitable to attract small institutions and let them grow than to spend huge resources for large companies that often withered from lack of demand. In that spirit, the club successfully wooed the Plumhof Saddlery with thirty employees from Waxahachie, Texas (another business in a nongrowth field). Yet the change in focus seemed counterintuitive, given the tremendous success of 1903 and the amount still left to do. In October 1909, the *Record* noted that with only a few exceptions, all great cities became great by having factories, but that Fort Worth still was not a manufacturing center, despite having rail transportation links second to none in the South providing access to cheap fuel, raw materials, and distribution routes. In the second decade of the twentieth century, Fort Worth would recommit to industrialization, but only after facing more obstacles.[68]

6

Recession and Realization, 1910–1915

etween 1910 and 1914 the economy once again struggled. From 1903 to 1910, Fort Worth solidified and developed around Swift and Armour and their supporting infrastructure, a task so monumental and demanding that little effort went into anything else. That concentration of focus was understandable and appropriate, given the enormity of the endeavor, but it was overdone to the extent of shutting out all other concerns. The opportunity costs associated with one-dimensionalism became apparent after 1912 not because the packinghouses declined—they did not—but because Fort Worth's neglect of industrial development limited post-1910 startup businesses to small, service-oriented retail shops instead of factories. Fortunately, commercial focus reemerged just as the nation's economy boomed following the outbreak of war in Europe.

Although the level of overall growth lagged, Fort Worth made significant progress in other areas. While boosters did relatively little on the commercial front, they proved instrumental in relocating a university from Waco, Texas, and city administrators made real advances in sewage treatment, the school system, and bridge construction, all desperately needed civic accoutrements. Perennial water problems forced abandonment of the strongly-defended well system, an overdue decision that would lead, finally, to safe and plentiful water, an important and necessary commodity for metropolitan life. In addition, automobiles, a major facet of twentieth-century urbanization and industrialization, began to reach critical mass, with 959 counted in 1910. The sanctioned vice reservation that closed in 1909 received support from unlikely sources, but the Acre faced new challenges from the prohibition movement and a more diversified entertainment environment. In contrast to its other advances, Fort Worth remained violent and racist.[1]

Between 1900 and 1910, Fort Worth experienced its most remarkable population growth to that point. The 1910 U.S. census counted 73,312 people, up 175 percent from 26,688 in 1900, the largest percentage rise of all large American cities. The total increase, 46,644, exceeded that of Houston, San Antonio, and Galveston (which actually declined as a result of the massive 1900 hurricane), but slightly trailed the 49,466 that Dallas gained. As a result, Fort Worth passed Galveston to become Texas's fourth largest municipality and the South's tenth largest (San Antonio, Dallas, and Houston ranked seventh, eighth, and ninth, respectively). Tarrant County actually exceeded Dallas County in total population growth, 55,196 to 53,022, and in percentage increase, 105 to 64 percent.[2]

Fort Worth's rapid growth was all the more impressive because it occurred during a period of limited geographical expansion. Between 1900 and 1910, Fort Worth annexed North Fort Worth with six and one-half square miles, Glenwood with two and one-half square miles, and one-half square mile that became the Tenth Ward, raising its area to seventeen and one-half square miles, still considerably smaller than Dallas's twenty-five square miles or San Antonio's thirty.[3] Fort Worth's population growth without expansive territorial acquisitions was a clear statement of the packinghouse effect, but other forms of commercial activity contributed, too. Fort Worth retained its position as the Southwest's leading railroad center, with 104 passenger and 204 freight trains daily, and increased its total factories from only 20 in 1901 to 282 in 1911, a substantial rise but one dominated by smaller companies. In October 1910 a parade showcasing local industries drew 50,000 people to watch horse-drawn and automobile-powered floats. Bewley Mills's entry, one of the most elaborate, contrasted the company's 1882 beginnings, depicted by a barn, with a replica of its modern seven-story headquarters.[4] Fort Worth contributed to and was part of a statewide commercial surge between 1900 and 1912 that saw Texas increase 174 percent in the value of industrial production, 153 percent in agriculture, 105 percent in forest products, and 249 percent in mining.[5] Despite all the celebration, Dallas in 1910 remained industrially superior by wide margins. Of course the outcomes would have been much different if the packinghouses had not been excluded from Fort Worth statistics (see table 6.1).[6]

Fort Worth ranked very high in some other measures of wealth. In 1910 Winfield Scott, with a net worth of nearly $1.4 million, was the only

TABLE 6.1.   Comparison of manufacturing statistics for Fort Worth
and Dallas, 1910

	Fort Worth	Dallas	Percent difference (Dallas over Fort Worth)
Manufacturers	147	305	107
Wage earners	2,641	6,621	151
Salaries	$484,000	$1,831,000	278
Wages	$1,285,000	$2,604,000	103
Capital	$7,443,000	$17,688,000	138
Value of products	$8,661,000	$26,959,000	211

Source: *Thirteenth Census of the United States*, vol. 9 (Washington, D.C.: Government
Printing Office, 1913), pp. 1214–15.

millionaire and the richest person in town, and he grew even wealthier
in the next three years, leaving an estate worth $4 million at his death in
1913. Following Scott in 1910 was R. D. Farmer, with a net worth of
$507,550, and another eight men with fortunes ranging from $169,000 to
$400,000. From 1909 to 1910, Tarrant County's assessed property values
increased by $3.82 million to $88.5 million while its 1912 banking deposits
reached $26.1 million, an increase of $8 million over 1911. Bank clearings
reflected even more remarkable surges, rising to $337.8 million in 1910, a
15 percent increase over the 1909's $292.6 million and 647 percent more
than the 1900 total of $45.2 million. The total dipped slightly in 1911 to
$319.9 million but rebounded in the first 11 months of 1912 to $347.8 million, exceeding both prior years with one month remaining. The percentage increases were so remarkable that Fort Worth ranked fifth nationally
in growth between 1903, when the packinghouses opened, and 1913.[7]

Fort Worth's rapid financial climb following 1903 was another consequence of the arrival of Swift and Armour. The stockyards increased from
only one acre in 1902 to 120 acres by 1912, capable of accommodating
25,000 cattle, 10,000 calves, and 15,000 hogs needed to supply a system
that could process 4,500 cattle, 4,000 calves, 10,000 hogs, and 3,500 sheep
daily, a volume of trade exceeded only by Chicago and Kansas City. The
numbers were so large that Fort Worth was said to be one of only a half-
dozen sites significantly affecting the world's market basket. Such massive operations radically boosted the local job market, adding a major
stimulus to the economy. Packinghouse jobs were neither plush nor especially well-paying, but they offered steady employment with pension

plans, free medical services, and English lessons for immigrants. In macroeconomic effect they made up for low pages with sheer numbers. In 1912 Swift and Armour employed 3,800 workers with an annual payroll approaching $3 million, but the total effect was much larger due to support businesses employing approximately 6,000 people and producing trade valued at $75 million. The meatpackers also continued to boost Fort Worth's railroads. In the first eleven months of 1912, the stockyards received 3,794 railcars of livestock, enough to fill 190 trains. Fort Worth residents recognized the packinghouses' contribution, crediting them in a 1910 survey for the area's economic success.[8] In 1911, the stockyards area incorporated as Niles City and immediately became the nation's wealthiest city. Incorporation was motivated by fears that the recent annexation of North Fort Worth would become a stepping stone to Fort Worth taking in, and taxing, Swift and Armour. Niles City, named after Louisville V. Niles of Boston (who owned a large part of the stockyards), consisted of just one square mile that included both packinghouses, valued at $10 million, and only 500 residents, a radically skewed mix that created the nation's highest per capita net worth.[9]

From 1910 through 1914, the stockyards experienced steady growth, despite fire damage in March and June of 1911 and a drop in supply through much of 1911 that lasted well into 1912.[10] The decline in livestock was part of a national trend in which the seven largest markets experienced downturns in cattle receipts, especially Chicago, which saw its share of the national trade decline from 36 to 32 percent. In 1911 both Chicago and St. Louis reported fewer cattle, and Kansas City declined in both cattle and calves. The situation only worsened at the start of 1912. Fort Worth was the only major market not reporting declines in cattle, which helped make its stockyards the nation's third largest cattle market, the second in calves, and the fourth in sheep. That was made possible, at least in part, by recently opened rail access to New Mexico cattle herds, another case in which railroads and packinghouses enjoyed a symbiotic relationship. These outcomes were reversed concerning hogs. Fort Worth's hog receipts fell 30 percent, the nation's largest drop, compared with 28 percent in St. Joseph, 19 percent in Chicago, 17 percent in Kansas City, 12 percent in Omaha, and only 4 percent in St. Louis.[11]

The Fort Worth market benefited from aggressive buyers and favorable shipping rates. The local plants, like many other packinghouses, raided livestock from other markets. When the hog supply declined in

1912, Swift and Armour split the $50,000 cost for twenty-six hog-filled railcars arriving from St. Joseph. Fort Worth packers also enjoyed an advantage over Oklahoma packers because of favorable railroad rate structures that made it more expensive to ship livestock from Texas to Oklahoma than from Fort Worth to Chicago. This made it difficult for Oklahoma City competitors, like the Morris and Sulzberger packinghouses, to poach from the Fort Worth stockyards. The combination of price increases, shipping advantages, and wide-ranging livestock buyers increased hog receipts at Fort Worth to the extent that supply once again approached demand by September 1913.[12]

In 1913 and 1914, the Fort Worth market resurged, enjoying a happy coexistence of high prices and supplies while most other markets remained sluggish. In 1913, stockyards volume increased 15 percent over 1912, rising from 1.76 million to 1.97 million animals, with more than 59 percent, or 1.14 million, slaughtered locally. The increase, combined with declines in other markets, solidified Fort Worth's position as the nation's third largest livestock processor and helped fuel expansions that raised packinghouse employment to 5,000. Driven by the euphoria, some boosters even dreamed of replacing second-place Kansas City.[13]

The increases were shared by many farmers and ranchers across North Texas. In 1914, livestock providers earned an estimated $67 million based on rates of $55 for steers, $40 for cows, $18 for calves, $13 for hogs, $5 for sheep, and $140 for horses and mules. Prices for horses and mules soared after 1914, when representatives from England, France, and Russia, embroiled in World War I, flooded the United States with orders for 20,000 animals. The demand drove local prices even higher, reaching $270 per head, and made Fort Worth the world's third largest horse and mule market.[14]

As of 1910, the packinghouse effect had not sparked a corresponding boom in other industries. A comparison with 1900 showed a massive 2,472 percent increase in livestock received, 2,462 percent increase in livestock slaughtered, 2,400 percent increase in packinghouse employees, and 14,900 percent increase in annual packinghouse revenue, indubitable evidence of the effect of Swift and Armour. Growth rates for non-packinghouse industries remained remarkably lower. For the same period, Fort Worth factories increased but 35 percent, capitalization 71 percent, and non-packinghouse employees by 122 percent. None of the non-packinghouse increases reflected anything close to a 1,000 percent increase (see table 6.2).

TABLE 6.2.   Comparison of Fort Worth infrastructure and industrial
            development, 1900 and 1910

	1900	1910	Percent increase (1910 over 1900)
Property assessments	$21,000,000	$54,000,000	157
Miles of street railways	29	95	228
Miles of permanent paving	0	47	
Livestock received	89,000	2,288,700	2,472
Livestock slaughtered	65,000	1,665,000	2,62
Annual packinghouse trade	$500,000	$75,000,000	1,900
Packinghouse employees	200	5,000	2,00
Factories (other than packinghouses)	209	282	35
Factory capitalization (other than packinghouses)	$2,688,045	$4,600,000	71
Factory employees (other than packinghouses)	1,449	3,215	122
Daily water consumption (gallons)	5,500,000	16,500,000	200
Passenger trains (daily)	34	102	200
Freight trains (daily)	70	208	197

Source: Fort Worth Record, July 10, 1910, part 2, p. 1.

During and after 1910, Fort Worth experienced significant development, but much of it involved service and retail entities rather than factories. In 1910, the Westbrook Hotel opened at Third and Fourth between
Houston and Main at a cost of $1 million. Reputedly the finest hotel in
the Southwest, the Westbrook boasted 302 rooms with amenities like
toilets (200 with baths), running hot and cold water, telephones, and
air conditioners. The same year, the Board of Trade actively sought a
university, even though the city already had a small college named Fort
Worth University. Board of Trade officials first tried unsuccessfully to
draw Southwestern University away from Georgetown, Texas, then succeeded in luring Texas Christian University (TCU) from Waco. TCU, which
opened itself to offers after a fire destroyed its main building, considered
Dallas, Waco, and Gainesville, Texas, before accepting Fort Worth's offer of
$200,000 and a choice of two sites. Initially, subscriptions lagged because

of doubts that a second college would offer much advantage, but supporters emphasized that the school's faculty and other employees, plus
some 600 students, would contribute $500,000 annually to local commerce.
The cornerstone of the new TCU was laid May 9, 1911, prompting infrastructure development, including a city request for bids for sewer line to
accommodate "Texas Christing [*sic*] University." Fort Worth University
then threatened to relocate unless it received a fifty-acre campus and
$200,000 in facilities, which the university claimed were required for it to
receive a $100,000 Methodist Educational Board endowment. The request
(demand) faced tough sledding because it represented a large investment
for an institution with an existing valuation of only $50,000, and because
many considered the proposal importunate in view of the $30,000 al-
ready donated by Fort Worthians, including $15,000 just four years previ-
ously. When an adequate response failed to materialize, the university
moved to Oklahoma (eventually becoming Oklahoma City University),
but the loss was hardly felt because the addition of TCU gave Fort Worth
seven colleges enrolling 4,500.[15]

In 1911, commercial construction reached remarkable levels. Montgomery Ward, attracted by railroad distribution, erected a five-story building at Seventh and Grove, and in August Texas's largest office building
opened after fourteen months of construction. The massive four-story
structure, located at Tenth and Commerce, contained 1.65 million square
feet of floor space, with the Majestic Theatre occupying the ground floor
and the Rock Island and Frisco railroads taking much of the upper space.
Construction also began on the Fort Worth Wagon Factory, which promised to employ up to forty workers to produce 120 wagons each month,
and on the Pierce-Fordyce Refinery on seventy-five acres northwest of
Fostepco Heights. The refinery would cost $1.5 million and employ 100 to
150 workers. Its construction was deemed the industrial event of 1911,
but its real significance lay in what it portended for the future. Suburban residential growth continued with the opening of Hubbard Heights,
advertised as removed from the "unpleasant features of commerce and
industry," and Ryan Place, between College and Eighth. Ryan Place
tapped into the upscale market by offering Fort Worth's only restricted
access community, with an entrance graced by two columns of Missouri
marble. In 1911, construction permits totaled nearly $2.92 million, the sec-
ond highest total in all the Southwest, ahead of Houston's more than

Majestic Theatre, 1920s. Courtesy of University of Texas at Arlington Special Collections.

$2.19 million and San Antonio's $1.82 million, but trailing Dallas, which led the region with $5.18 million. (Local partisans groused that Dallas benefited from the $1 million Adolphus Hotel.)[16]

Through 1911, the zeal for industrial development seemed to be reviving. The Board of Trade and the city commission adopted "We're for Smoke" as their official slogan, a reference to the association between smokestacks and industries. The organization also changed its name to the Chamber of Commerce out of concern that Board of Trade implied a limited mandate focused on merchandising. The members also named Paddock honorary president for life. At an August 1911 dinner on the roof of the new Westbrook Hotel, speakers emphasized that Fort Worth must work to keep up with the manufacturing development of other cities. A proactive city commission also contributed, proposing in 1911 to offer companies ten years of free water "as a means of bringing smoke-stacks to the City [sic]."[17]

The city infrastructure reached a new level of mature development that reflected Fort Worth's loftier status. In 1910, the city commissioners contracted the electric franchise to J. R. Nutt Company of Cleveland, which took over all the facilities of Fort Worth Power and Light and the electric operations of Fort Worth Gas. As part of the agreement, Nutt promised to cut rates in half and spend $2 million building the South's and Southwest's grandest generating plant, including the tallest smokestack in the South (250 feet high). In May 1911, ground was broken on the north bank of the Trinity River just west of the streetcar bridge, with completion scheduled in one year. On September 1, 1912, a Cleburne Interurban line opened, making it possible to ride from Denison, Texas, about eighty-five miles north of Fort Worth, to Cleburne, thirty miles south of Fort Worth. The Cleburne trains ran hourly until 8:30 P.M. with a theater departure at 11:00 P.M. City streetcar service had reached a high point of development by 1912, carrying 40,000 riders daily over twenty-three routes covering sixty-six miles. Also in 1912, a major bond issue funded construction of four bridges, including structures spanning the Trinity River at Seventh Street and North Main Street. The contract for the North Main Bridge, the largest at 1,752 feet long and fifty-four feet wide, went to Hannan and Hickey Brothers Construction of St. Louis for $373,953, while Tarrant County Construction built the Seventh Street Bridge for $106,772.[18] The public school system stood on relatively equal footing

North Main Street wire bridge with courthouse in background, circa 1900. Courtesy of University of Texas at Arlington Special Collections.

with Texas's other major cities. In 1910 Fort Worth's enrollment and faculty ranked fourth in Texas, the same as its population, but the city's schools had the state's highest average attendance and length of session.[19]

The waterworks remained a glaring exception to the litany of progress. The failure of the dual system became evident in April 1910, when a typhoid outbreak was traced to river water in the system intended for human consumption, which was supposed to be supplied only by wells. City commissioners blamed pump failures for poor well production, a position seconded by J. H. Howland, a water systems inspector for the National Board of Fire Insurance Underwriters. Howland found the two pumping stations in poor states of repair and pointed to a $20,000 dam under construction near the Holley Pumping Station as a more reliable water source. In December 1910, a fire damaged the Powell Field's ten wells off the Benbrook Road, forcing the almost total abandonment of the Mead system and a reliance on river water to the extent that officials warned citizens to boil drinking water. The situation deteriorated further in 1911, when unknown vandals put emery dust in the oil of a new $25,000 air compressor, shattered a Holley Plant pipeline, and clogged pumps using rags. Water supply became so poor that Southside residents met to air grievances, particularly citing a period when they went without water flow for six hours while water department personnel repeatedly assured them that all was fine.[20]

The city finally began to turn away from wells and to construction of a large reservoir. A city engineering report issued in December 1912 found that well water could not provide a cost-effective and reliable supply and recommended a surface reservoir coupled with a filtration system as the only viable option. The report suggested three possible sites and their estimated costs: one on the Clear Fork costing $905,000 and two on the West Fork, the first at Eagle Cliff around the Ten-Mile Bridge for $995,000 and the second at Mound Dam, one and one-half miles south of Eagle Cliff, for $1.24 million. Paddock opposed using the West Fork, arguing that it was no more reliable than the Clear Fork and had poorer quality water due to decaying vegetation. Despite those concerns, voters in April 1911 approved a $1.35 million bond issue with $1 million set aside for a reservoir on the West Fork and a filtration system for the Trinity River station, and $350,000 for well improvements.[21] Progress on the filtration system went smoothly and quickly. Work began June 29, 1911, at the Holley Plant to install filters costing $70,000 that could process 10 million gallons daily. In July 1913, testing indicated that the filtered Trinity River water contained fewer bacteria and other contaminants than well water.[22]

Reservoir plans began well but ran into difficulties, most of which were related to cost overruns. Due to the project's size, the city divided contracts into general construction, masonry work, basin excavation, dam construction, and conduit laying. The original specifications called for a lake thirty feet deep covering 3,000 acres, but dimensions expanded to a forty-seven foot depth capable of holding more than 7 million cubic feet of water. These changes pumped up costs so much that one critic called the project Fort Worth's Panama Canal, a charge Mayor W. D. Davis answered by saying he would be glad if it had a similar benefit. Flippancy aside, the debate became serious, stirring such heated public reactions that commissioners closed their finance meetings to avoid confrontations, a move that probably contributed to the mayor's defeat in the 1912 Democratic primary.[23]

In November 1912, city officials assured critics that the treasury's $187,000 was sufficient to finish the reservoir, but they were wrong. In January 1913, they requested another $300,000 bond issue to increase the reservoir's capacity to 30 billion gallons instead of the originally planned 22 billion gallons. The matter became more complicated in May 1913 when the dam's contractor, Underground Construction Company, went bankrupt. Inflated costs and mismanagement may have played a role in the bankruptcy, but so did outright fraud. In 1913, Charles McCormick, former president of Underground, was arrested for allegedly inflating charges, and W. T. George, a company officer, was accused of bribing inspectors to overlook substandard concrete and other materials. (George was acquitted.) Left with a partially completed dam and a host of unpaid workers, the city opted to take over. Using the abandoned workforce camped at the construction grounds, the city commission estimated that it would take about two months and cost $29,000 to finish the dam. The commission also determined that it would take another $550,000 to complete the reservoir, on top of $300,000 added just four months earlier. A quick audit found that $935,514 of the $1 million appropriated for the reservoir had been spent, and another $428,609 had been spent on wells when only $350,000 was budgeted. Still, after four years, the reservoir was finally completed at a cost of $1.3 million and was named Lake Worth, after the commission had rejected Lake Panther, Lake Tonkeway [sic] (after an American Indian tribe), and Lake Jarvis. The finished basin covered 4,400 acres, was twenty-seven miles in circumference and would hold 25 billion gallons when filled.[24] The water still had to be delivered several miles away, which required a conduit costing $60,000 at a time (1915) when the city's general fund was overdrawn by $33,000 and only $3,800 remained from the bond issues of 1911 and 1913. By this time, the public had become so fed up with the seemingly endless drain that voters rejected two bond packages in January 1916. Once again Fort Worth was saved through the grace of some its leading citizens, who provided financing conditional on repayment from waterworks income. Thanks to their help, the last section of pipe was completed in January 1917.[25]

Safe drinking water was desperately needed in the seemingly perennial battle with disease, as epidemics or near epidemics seemed to appear with regularity. In 1912, Palo Pinto County (approximately forty-five miles west of Fort Worth) barred travelers from Fort Worth following reports of hundreds lying stricken with smallpox. The county rescinded the order after the Fort Worth health office assured it that the outbreak had been confined to only seventy-six cases, largely among "negroes [sic] and Mexicans." In January 1913, meningitis hit North Texas with 190 cases reported in Dallas, 100 in Fort Worth, and 97 in Waco. The relationship between these outbreaks and poor drinking water was suggested by repeated warnings to boil drinking water, including a 1914 Health Board directive issued after the discovery that 40 percent of the water supply contained bacilli related to typhoid.[26]

Other health issues existed besides the water supply. Only in 1910 did the city administration ban the practice of dumping sweepings in streets, and then only after many complaints, including one report of a mound on Oak Street reaching three feet high and 100 feet in length. The ban may have only shifted the problem a few yards to larger dumping grounds. In 1914, a large dump filled with all varieties of filth extended from the south bank of the Trinity River just 200 feet west of the Paddock Viaduct all the way south to Florence Street. Liquid wastes added to the foulness, especially after rains, due to property owners who shunned the sewage system because of its service fees. In 1914, commissioners found 8,000 buildings without sewer service, including homes, churches, and businesses employing significant numbers of workers. In 1916, the city finally forced a degree of compliance by demolishing all dry closets situated within 100 feet of sewer lines. The state also became involved, mandating that Fort Worth cease dumping raw sewage into the Trinity River, leading to a hurried plan to build a $1 million sewage disposal plant before Dallas, which lay downstream, enjoined further use of the river. The aldermen also announced plans to build a contagious disease hospital near the five-acre tract on South Main Street donated years before by John Peter Smith. Work also began on a sixty-bed, city-county hospital at Fourth and Jones streets costing $20,000.[27] The general poor state of health was reflected in a 1910 report that approximately one in ten local school children suffered from disease or disability such as inflamed tonsils, bad teeth, or poor eyesight. (Some children came to school wearing their grandparents' glasses.)[28]

Cocaine remained a popularly-used substance with an estimated 500 addicts, some as young as fourteen. Users obtained the drug with a doctor's prescription, bought it on the black market, or patronized unscrupulous pharmacies that illegally sold it over the counter. A police sting in October 1911 led to arrests of four druggists but had little effect because the fine ran no more than $50 for the first offense. Users either snorted the powder or injected it as a liquid. Willie Beland, a fifteen-year-old addict from Percy Street, reported that dealers commonly carried syringes of a cocaine-morphine mix, selling twenty-five cent injections. In September 1913, Chris Arnold, described as a 25 year old drug addict, accidentally started a fire while burglarizing the Metropolitan Pharmacy at 905 Main Street. Arnold's mother reported that her son was covered with needle punctures from his cocaine and morphine use.[29]

Prostitution continued to flourish, but gambling did not seem to excite much interest. In 1911, the Waco chief of police, in town for a convention, complained that he had never seen so many prostitutes flocking in the streets and hotels. Of course he may only have been expressing sour grapes over Waco's loss of TCU to Fort Worth. A 1910 police report also confirmed the vitality of the sex-for-hire trade. The "social evil" accounted for 1,153 arrests in 1910, the second-highest cause of arrest (exceeded only by intoxication, with 1,598), and approximately one-sixth of the year's total of 6,932 arrests. In contrast, gambling charges resulted in only sixty arrests, suggesting either that gambling was no longer as prevalent or that it was not viewed as a threat to order. One of the few gambling issues to reach public notice involved a 1913 complaint by the county attorney that fifty nickel slot machines with a payoff of $1.00 operated under the guise of dispensing a package of gum, rather small potatoes compared with open casinos.[30]

A clamor for reestablishment of a vice reservation arose in the courthouse, of all places. In October 1910, the forty-seventh state district court grand jury's report on city graft and corruption noted that closing the reservation had not eliminated or reduced immorality and that the number of Acre habitués had not diminished. The grand jurors added that, if a rooming house over a saloon existed that was frequented only by the decent and moral, it had escaped their notice. The report recommended returning to a set-aside section, echoing the old argument that police could better control a concentrated area. In January 1911, the court sought citizen support, suggesting that conditions allowing "houses of ill fame [to] exist on Main Street to an alarming extent" were unlikely to change until public opinion demanded it. Soon thereafter, a group petitioned for reinstatement of the reservation, arguing that closure had simply moved vice from Commerce and Calhoun to the business district on Main and Houston. The petitioners noted that Houston and Dallas had established reservations and that the Texas Court of Civil Appeals had sustained Dallas's designated area specifically for the regulation of "houses of ill-repute." Police Commissioner Bob Davis, Chief of Police O. R. Montgomery, and Sheriff William Rea supported the petition, arguing that because prostitution could not be eliminated, the better choice lay in confining it to a well-lighted and well-policed section where liquor was prohibited. The commissioners appointed the petitioners as a committee to locate a suitable area.[31] Complaints from grand juries continued, including a 1912 report complaining that police officers ignored streetwalkers and houses of prostitution, acting only if they received complaints. In 1913, the forty-seventh state district court grand jury called once again for restricting prostitutes to a defined district to end their spread into the rooming house district. The problem was aggravated after Dallas closed its recognized vice district and began a major crackdown in October 1913. An example of the dispersal effect was seen in 1913 when J. W. Renfro, a former Fort Worth chief of police, was indicted for maintaining a house of prostitution at 205 and 207 East Belknap in the north side of downtown, far removed from the Acre.[32]

Two sensational events also filled the news in 1912. First, J. Beal Snead shot and killed A. G. Boyce, Sr., the manager of Capitol Ranch, in the lobby of the Metropolitan Hotel after Boyce's son had run away with Snead's wife to Winnipeg, Canada. The younger Boyce, Snead, and Mrs. Snead had become acquainted while attending Southwestern University in Georgetown, Texas. Snead was acquitted of the father's death, then tracked the younger Boyce to Amarillo where he killed him.[33]

The second high-profile matter involved J. Frank Norris, pastor of the First Baptist Church at Third and Taylor, who had become one of the reservation's most vocal critics. Norris, described by the *New York Times* as a "saloon-fighting Baptist minister," declared that no one who allowed property to be used for immoral purposes could remain a church member. He also threatened to seek injunctions to prevent creation of a reservation and called on city commissioners to make a real cleanup, not just a whitewash, of Hell's Half Acre. Norris argued that the Acre no longer facilitated but retarded progress, and that its removal would attract residents of "the best sorts."[34]

In 1912, a series of arsons and other crimes plagued Norris. On January 10, 1912, a suspicious fire did $5,000 in damages to his church, and four days later two shots narrowly missed him as he sat in the church study. On February 4, both the church and Norris's home at 810 West Fifth Street suffered fire damage. On February 27, a man attempted to assault Norris around 913 West Second Street but was fought off by a companion, and in March Norris and a church deacon received threatening letters. The forty-eighth district court grand jury investigated, calling the pastor and others to testify before indicting Norris for perjury after forensic evidence linked the threatening letters to his parsonage. The night Norris made bond, his home suffered serious damage during an early morning fire that began in an inside closet.[35] Many stood by the embattled preacher. Church members published a statement of support, and the pastor of Waco's First Methodist Church outspokenly defended Norris as a victim of Fort Worth's immoral society, which he described as one of the worst in Texas. The Waco pastor claimed that the mayor and many Fort Worth businessmen protected the Acre because they willingly sacrificed morality in favor of urban commercial supremacy.[36]

Norris survived more indictments and two trials but continued his involvement in shady affairs. At the end of March 1912, he resigned from the pulpit, citing poor health, just as additional indictments charged him with arson at the church and his home. The perjury trial began April 9, 1912, ending April 24 with a not guilty verdict. The arson charge, which was almost dismissed, went to trial in August 1913 amid reports that $1,500 was offered for anyone willing to confess and take the heat off the preacher. Norris again won acquittal, despite testimony that placed him leaving the church just before the fire began. The narrow escapes did little to rein in the incidents. In 1916, an ardent young supporter shot himself in the hand during a church service. Subsequent investigations revealed a plot in which the man was to shoot into the ceiling, then escape, leaving Norris to claim he had survived an assassination attempt. The scheme went awry when the pistol discharged inadvertently, wounding the accomplice so that he could not complete his escape.[37]

The Acre probably faced a bigger threat from prohibition than from Norris and his ilk. The prohibition movement had gathered strength in the 1880s, especially in a stretch of states of the Upper South and West, including Texas, but died out only to be reborn in 1908. The renewed effort found so much success in rural counties that, by 1910, some 156 of Texas's 254 counties had voted dry. After 1913, after winning more impressive victories and adding converts, the movement segued into cities, the stronghold of anti-prohibitionists. A statewide rally in June 1911 brought 20,000 anti-prohibitionists to Fort Worth; a local march by prohibition supporters held the following week attracted only 1,200. Fort Worth's brewery industry also fought back by touting beer's nutritional value, noting that the British classified beer as a food and arguing that its low alcohol content made moderate consumption "absolutely harmless." A prohibition referendum in July 1911 lost statewide by less than 1 percent—226,999 to 223,748—but was rejected by a larger margin in Tarrant County, 7,295 to 5,932. With total eradication of alcohol apparently out of reach—for now—prohibitionists chipped away through legislation, including a 1913 state law mandating that saloons close at 9:30 P.M., a measure that owners warned would cost Fort Worth saloons $400 in daily sales and 200 jobs. Although those predictions may have been an exaggeration, the number of saloon licenses issued in Fort Worth did decline from 176 in 1914 to 160 in 1915.[38] Prohibition was among the Progressive Era's reform movements, alongside women's suffrage, old age pensions, and accident insurance for workers. Fort Worth was never a hotbed of radicalism but it did have a significant population who supported reform. In 1911, the Socialist Party ran a full slate of candidates in the municipal election, receiving 1,200 out of some 4,200 votes cast but losing every race.[39]

Any decline in the Acre's trade may have been more a product of a diversifying entertainment scene than moral revulsion. Nell Irvin Painter's study comparing reform in 1870 and in 1919 suggested that the more recent period differed from the earlier in the increased availability of mass entertainment accessible to working-class Americans. Prior to the 1910s, saloons played the dominant role in working-class leisure, but their influence eroded due to prohibition and temperance movements and the rise of other options such as baseball, movies, and amusement parks. The most noticeable entertainment development in Fort Worth appeared in a proliferation of cinemas after 1910. One of the earliest, the Healy Theater, opened on June 16, 1910, at 1004 Main Street with 340 seats—including 125 in the balcony for smokers. Fort Worth's morality guardians reacted quickly to control the new medium, establishing a three-person censorship board in 1911. Some of their trepidation stemmed from lurid reports of a national juvenile delinquency epidemic associated with movie houses, due not only to salacious content but also on the destabilizing effect of Sunday entertainments in general. The Law Enforcement League organized around enforcement of City Ordinance 473 forbidding most Sunday recreations, including movies. The Citizens Welfare League, supported by Paddock, successfully struck back in a three-page appeal published in two local newspapers that called for "more liberal enforcement of the Sunday law to give to the people innocent entertainment." The first Sunday following repeal of the ordinance in November 1911 saw 20,000 crowd into Fort Worth's eleven theaters, but the issue became muddled when Tarrant County, with concurrent jurisdiction, began enforcing its own ban on Sunday entertainments. The county's involvement posed a much more difficult problem because elected county officials also answered to rural constituents who tended to be more conservative and geographically less exposed to diversions. However, given the political costs associated with repeal and the improbability of total enforcement, the county commissioners opted for a traditional subterfuge, assessing limited but regular fines that allowed uninterrupted operations while maintaining appearances. County law officers even cooperated by scheduling raids between features to avoid interrupting films in progress. In any case, the spread of entertainment venues continued. Construction of a vaudeville theater on Rusk between Ninth and Tenth began in 1911. The theater would cost $300,000 and seat 1,800. Baseball increased in popularity for many reasons, not the least of which was that it allowed fans to be both spectators and participants. The Fort Worth Jobbers and Manufacturers Baseball League boasted teams representing twenty companies such as Monnig's Dry Goods, Armour, Washer Brothers, Nash Hardware, and King Candy. Morris Park, which cost $30,000 and featured a double-deck grandstand, opened in 1911 to acclaim as the finest professional baseball field in the South, rivaled only by New Orleans.[40]

The growth of other entertainment and the decrease in saloon traffic did little to make Fort Worth less violent. On January 21, 1910, a police captain shot and killed a Texas Ranger. The incident began when J. M. "Grude" Britton appeared at police headquarters to complain about Captain Tom Blanton's conduct during a raid on the Amarillo Hotel, a "well-known disorderly house" on Jennings between Twelfth and Thirteenth that happened to be owned by a woman friend of Britton. (Connections between law officers and the demimonde were not unusual; Captain Blanton owned the Senate saloon at Sixth and Main.) When Britton became irate and threatening, the desk sergeant demanded his weapon but relented after Britton displayed Texas Ranger identification. As a second captain escorted Britton down the city hall steps, Blanton, returning after hearing of the allegations, walked up and fired three shots into Britton's chest.[41]

Between 1913 and 1915, three police officers were killed in the line of duty. In 1913, Tommie Lee shot and killed Officer Tom Ogiltree and another man and wounded two others. The spree began when Lee apparently went berserk, firing at a man on the street and then running into McGar's Pool Hall, where he killed Walter Moore and shot a seventeen-year old boy, both bystanders. Lee left the pool hall fleeing east to Eighth and Grove, where he shot Ogiltree as the officer responded to the gunshots. Lee then seriously wounded a junk dealer before shooting himself in the jaw as a crowd of 2,000 surrounded him in a culvert on East Fifth Street. Afterwards, a crowd of 500 battered the door to the Tarrant County Jail, leaving only when members of the crowd were allowed inside to verify that Lee had been removed. Because Lee was African American, the mob turned its anger on the black business district around East Ninth and Calhoun, spending the night beating any hapless person found on the streets as well as breaking windows and destroying shops, all without police interference. The governor sent fifty members of the Texas National Guard to restore calm, but the troops arrived too late to prevent thousands of dollars in damage to the Moore Estate Building at Ninth and Jones and the nearby Dunbar Building. Eventually, authorities charged ten men who had been involved in the riot and fined them $25. Lee was hanged at the county jail on March 9, 1914.[42]

Two policemen were killed in 1915. Police Captain G. Frank Coffey was shot to death on June 26, 1915, in front of Buck Cooper and Sons, a saloon at North Main and Twenty-fifth in the stockyards district. Coffey had gone to the tavern to arrest Ed Cooper and was shot by Tom Cooper, Ed's brother, who was acquitted after another police officer, Henry Vaughan, testified that Coffey had drawn first. The next month, Officer Pete Howard died after he was stabbed eight times in the back and his throat was cut while he was making an arrest in Battercake Flats, a squalid area known for "bad negroes [sic]" located just west of the Tarrant County Courthouse between Weatherford and Belknap. Howard had been walking an arrestee up a hill to the city jail when the man began fighting and was joined by an accomplice. The two escaped immediate apprehension, but in 1916 Martin Flores received a life sentence and in 1918 Joe Estapanear, who did the actual stabbing, was killed by a U.S. Army sentry near Reynosa, a Mexican town across the border from McAllen, Texas. Estapanear had joined a bandit gang that operated on both sides of the border. In 1926 Governor Miriam "Ma" Ferguson granted Flores a full pardon.[43]

Battercake Flats was one of several distinctive Fort Worth neighborhoods. Just east of Jones Street lay Irish Town, known in 1923 as the bloodiest police beat, which had begun as an Irish settlement but became largely African American; "Little Mexico" was nearby around lower Calhoun and Jones near the Acre; "Little Africa" ran along East Ninth; the Cabbage Patch, near the wholesale vegetable market along Front Street, had immigrants from many nations (after 1918 it became known as the League of Nations); Hogan's Alley was a small enclave on Thirteenth Street; Bum's Bowery, a nationally known haven for "traveling gentlemen," or hoboes, was on the north side of the Texas and Pacific west yard; and Quality Grove was an African American section on the Northside. More affluent neighborhoods included Silk Stocking Lane on Main and Houston between Fourth and Eighth, named for the upper-class women who flocked to its fine shops, and two areas known as the Gold Coast, one around Summit and Pennsylvania and the other along West Third Street. The latter was home to the Fuller House at 720 West Third Street, which became an exclusive rooming and boarding house serving many of the well-to-do young marrieds and the city's most eligible bachelors, including Robert Milam, Harry Vinnedge, and Congressman Fritz Lanham. Emma and Minnie Fuller operated it with an aristocratic air from 1905 to 1915, and its kitchen was known for excellent breads. (The building was razed in 1935.) Nearby sat the homes of Dr. Carroll Peak, John Peter Smith, and Zeno Ross, and the mansion of Congressman Sam Cantey stood at Third and Lamar.[44]

Fort Worth's uneven but relentless commercial and infrastructure advances stood in contrast to its lack of progress in race relations. From 1910 to 1918, African Americans were more often victims than perpetrators of violence. On February 10, 1911, Will Knox was arrested for an attempted assault on white woman and sentenced the next day to four years confinement, but he was shot and killed by the victim's husband as deputies walked him down the courthouse steps. Despite Knox's death, the black community suffered as a crowd of 1,000 ruffians destroyed the Dixie Theater, a recently opened black cinema at Main and Eleventh, while police officers stood by idly. The police chief claimed that officers had restrained themselves to avoid injuring innocent bystanders, but Judge J. W. Swayne ordered his grand jury to investigate the "disgrace" and to indict any officers who failed to do their duty.[45] Many blacks never even made it to trial. According to the Tuskegee Institute, sixty-nine people were lynched in the United States in 1915, 90 percent of whom were black. Georgia led the list with eighteen, followed by Mississippi and Alabama with nine each and Arkansas, Florida, and Texas with five. In 1916, the total fell to fifty-four, fifty of whom were black. Georgia again led with fourteen, but Texas climbed into sole possession of second place with nine.[46]

The Knox incident was just one of many injustices meted out to blacks. In 1910, Police Commissioner George Mulkey announced the appointment of special policemen to drive out idle African Americans, and the commission voted unanimously to ban film of the Jack Johnson–Jim Jeffries championship boxing match because it involved a black man (Johnson) fighting a white man (Jeffries)—and winning. In 1911, four blacks from Dallas on a motoring jaunt were arrested twice within twenty minutes by officers who assumed the car was stolen. Also in 1911, police officers had to fight off an angry mob at the Texas and Pacific passenger depot to rescue a white woman and black man discovered to be traveling together. In 1913, the mayor's address at an African American Odd Fellows convention caused a storm of protest and a quick denial from the mayor that he had told the group he was honored to have them in Fort Worth.[47] Blacks even had difficulty finding a final resting place. Plans for a "Negro" cemetery ran into widespread opposition from whites who supported the idea but did not want it in their neighborhood.[48]

Other groups also faced injustice and segregation. In 1911, clashes between Anglos and Hispanics lasted several days, most occurring in

"Little Mexico," a largely Hispanic district around Twelfth and Calhoun. The local press claimed the confrontations began when Anglos retaliated over a series of robberies committed by Hispanics. One evening's violence began at a saloon at Thirteenth and Calhoun when a "Mexican" slashed an Anglo with straight razor and then had to be rescued from an angry mob. Thwarted in taking revenge on the attacker, the crowd turned on any Hispanic available. The police responded by raiding the neighborhood and arresting forty-eight Hispanics. Those arrested faced problems in court when the presiding municipal judge complained he could not distinguish them because all but one sported mustaches. The situation for new arrivals was little better. Many Eastern Europeans, drawn by packinghouse jobs, crowded into squalid housing around Calhoun and Commerce between Twenty-second and Twenty-third where an immigrant community numbered up to 1,000 from Greece, Bulgaria, Serbia, Rumania, Bohemia, Spain, Mexico, Poland, and Germany. In one reported case, forty Macedonians existed in eight hotel rooms while thirty-six Serbians shared just six rooms. Immigrants, welcomed at first for their cheap labor, were quickly rejected when the economy soured during the 1912 economic downturn. In that period, Fort Worth's United Charities, complaining that the city suffered under an "avalanche" of foreign labor, asked the Galveston immigration office to head off all foreigners, suggesting that "bohunks" without employment be denied entry.[49]

At times, the city government and its employees demonstrated sensibilities superior to the general public. In 1910, eight policemen resigned rather than endure taunts they received while guarding strikebreakers crossing a picket line. In May 1916, residents of 1300 New York Street petitioned for the forceful removal of three black families from the neighborhood, and in January 1917, another group sought the banishment of a "colony of Mexicans" living in the area of South Main Street around the Gulf, Colorado and Santa Fe Railway tracks, alleging that they constituted a nuisance and lowered property values. Both appeals went to the city attorney, who ruled that the city could not restrict habitations based on color or nationality.[50]

Racism may not have extended to residential codes, but it was part of Fort Worth boosterism. In 1910, the Board of Trade boasted that "Fort Worth has the most nearly all-white population of any city in the Southwest." The group based the claim on school statistics indicating that African Americans constituted only 10 percent of the student body in

Fort Worth public schools, compared with 15 to 17 percent for San Antonio, Dallas, and Houston. In addition, the Board of Trade advertised that San Antonio had a larger "Mexican" population and that Houston had more foreign-born. The converse of that boast was that Fort Worth had more Hispanics than Houston or Dallas and more foreign-born than Dallas or San Antonio, the former explained by Hispanics working as railroad labor and the latter by Eastern European immigrants employed by the packinghouses.[51]

Despite its racist rhetoric, the Board of Trade performed laudable work promoting railroad and industrial development. In 1910, Board of Trade President Newton H. Lassiter, who was also general attorney for the Rock Island and the Trinity and Brazos Valley railroads, promoted a northwest rail route through Springtown and Azle, Texas, that would run north of the Texas and Pacific and south of Fort Worth and Denver tracks. Lassiter pushed the route as necessary to prevent forfeiture of the region's trade to Kansas City and St. Louis. The idea was solid but the cost was high, exceeding the subsidies that Swift and Armour had received in 1903. The first segment, stretching thirty miles to Springtown, required a $500,000 subscription that would then serve as bond security to finance the remaining mileage. Lassiter's proposal was supplanted in 1912 by a less costly agreement that extended the Gulf, Texas and Western Railway eastward from Jacksboro, Texas, sixty miles northwest of Fort Worth, to a connection with the Texas and Pacific tracks in Palo Pinto, providing access all the way to Seymour, Texas, a distance of 135 miles.[52]

The Fort Worth economy that showed such promise in 1910 and 1911 struggled from 1912 to 1914 with few initiatives reaching completion. The big news in 1912 involved the largest real estate transaction in Fort Worth's history (to that date), the $450,000 sale of the James Building at Seventh and Main streets. In 1913, Fort Worth claimed to be the cold storage center of the Southwest, with just six fewer carloads of capacity than all the rest of Texas, and a Denton Interurban line opened, as did a Texas Power and Light plant costing $2.5 million, the Pierce-Fordyce Oil Refinery costing $1.5 million, and several smaller factories. In 1914, a new Chamber of Commerce auditorium was completed, touted as the grandest southwest of Kansas City; plans were announced for a ten-story building on Main between Ninth and Tenth; and the Fort Worth National Bank merged with the State National, creating a $10 million super bank. The merger prevented a default by State National Bank brought on by the

Throckmorton at Jennings, looking northeast, with city hall on the right and the Carnegie Library center, circa 1912. Courtesy of University of Texas at Arlington Special Collections.

embezzlement of $165,000 by M. L. Woods, State National's vice president. Although the list of 1913 accomplishments appeared impressive, all the projects except the proposed skyscraper had begun earlier, an indication that the economy was coasting rather than expanding.[53]

The economy's distress became evident in 1913 and 1914. The Chamber of Commerce displayed remarkable candor in its 1913 annual report, admitting that the year's progress had not been spectacular, that railroad traffic had sagged and building permits had dropped from $3.39 million in 1912 to $2.15 million in 1913, a loss of more than 36 percent. To make matters worse, the construction permits included only six factories, costing a mere $90,000 to build, or less than 5 percent of total permits, with residential building accounting for the rest. In 1914, permits declined another 3 percent to $2.09 million. In part, the 1914 declines were part of a temporary depression in the American economy following the outbreak of war in Europe. Fort Worth's bank clearings reflected the war's effect, falling in September 1914 at the war's start, then rebounding in December but still closing the year at $396.2 million, down almost $22 million from 1913.[54]

The war certainly exercised a limited negative effect, but the Fort Worth economy also suffered from a loss of industrial focus. The Chamber of Commerce's list of objectives for 1912—parks and boulevards beautification, road and bridge improvements, and promotion through advertising— indicated a shift to developing existing facilities rather than attracting factories. The chamber spent much of its energy on sojourns designed to increase patronage for local merchants and wholesalers. In July 1912, approximately 100 boosters traveled to Gainesville and Whitesboro, and in October a large contingent took a six-day whirlwind tour of fifty Panhandle and West Texas towns. The chamber's 1912 annual summary listed the establishment of these trade ties as a major accomplishment. Doubtless they increased wholesale and retail sales, but they also represented an opportunity cost in attention diverted from industrial development.[55]

Paddock and other supporters remained upbeat and optimistic. Paddock argued that more building occurred in 1913 than in any other single year since the packinghouses arrived, and that new residents had stimulated $5 million in construction, more than twice the official permit figure. Of course, that position tended to verify the dominance of residential over commercial construction, but Paddock may well have been correct in that Fort Worth permits did not include development outside the city limits. This possibility lay behind a *Record* editorial suggesting that Fort Worth was on its way to becoming the largest manufacturing center of the South and West (a gross exaggeration) despite perceptions of retarded growth. The editorial noted that most construction occurred away from the city center, making it less visible to the general public and visitors. Of course, that point did little to explain the drop in bank clearings.[56]

At the end of 1914, signs of revival appeared. A relaxation of financial tensions and increases in the credit supply had an uplifting effect nationally that touched the local economy. Fort Worth benefited disproportionately after 1914 from significant increases in food demand attributable to the European war, thanks to its position as a livestock and grain center. Indeed, eighty-seven of Fort Worth's 285 factories were involved in food production or processing. War-induced demands dramatically increased prices paid for most livestock, especially horses and mules, and for foodstuffs in general. The effects of that surge increased packinghouse production 26 percent and the number of rail cars inspected by 15 percent to 1.12 million. War-driven demand also made Fort Worth the largest grain market in the Southwest in 1914, with eighteen elevators holding 3.4

million bushels and two mills processing enough grain annually to fill 29,108 railcars. In addition, Fort Worth's lack of dependence on the cotton trade insulated it from the effects of a price decrease that depressed most of the South. These advantages elevated Fort Worth in 1914 to first among Texas cities in payroll, workforce, and average wage as well as in percentage of population owning homes.[57]

The war's stimulus, however, glossed over the troublesome issue of stalled commercial development plaguing Fort Worth since 1910. In 1913, Paddock blamed the stalled Fort Worth economy on the negativity of civic leadership, an unusual complaint in a town that had benefited so greatly from its citizens' sacrifices. The depths to which Fort Worth's industrialization drive had sunk was clear in the 1914 Chamber of Commerce annual report, which failed to list even one new factory. The post-1911 recession certainly played a role, but the evidence suggests that Fort Worth also suffered from a changed focus that stressed merchants over manufacturers. To a degree, Fort Worth's turn away from aggressive industrial solicitation was propelled by regional forces. In 1910, W. F. Sterling, general agent of the Fort Worth and Denver Railway, observed that Texas emphasized trade to the detriment of its industrial development, that the whole state lagged industrially because Texans had not developed an appreciation of manufacturing's importance and therefore remained content to act as wholesalers and retailers. In that context, the Fort Worth Chamber of Commerce's focus on merchandising in 1912 can be viewed as a local manifestation of a state-wide phenomenon. In the next four years, a redirection would occur at a most fortunate time.[58]

7

OTHER VOICES

Historical records of the nineteenth and twentieth centuries tell a one-sided story, largely skewed to Anglo males while almost totally ignoring the existence and contributions of non-Anglos and women of all races. The latter groups certainly played a role in Fort Worth's development, but they garnered little notice and consequently are largely lost. Women may be the most ignored category, usually only earning mention as wives or as champions of selected social causes. Their history is yet to be written, if it can be written at all. Blacks seldom appeared on the radar except as criminals or crime victims or, in a very few cases, as part of an incipient civil rights movement. Little work has been published on Fort Worth's African American community, and the potential does not seem hopeful. Hispanics have received considerable study, but the scholarship remains severely limited by the lack of resources.

Records reflect that African Americans were among the earliest settlers of North Texas. The 1850 census counted sixty-five blacks in Tarrant County, a figure that increased to 850 by 1860, dropped to 672 in the aftermath of the Civil War, and then grew rapidly to reach 5,756 in 1900 and 18,730 in 1920. The dearth of information is an effect of pervasive racism that kept African Americans in the background historically, economically, politically, and socially, blocking advancement as well as notice. Poor educational opportunities played a big role in limiting advancement. In 1920 Fort Worth Public Schools estimated they would spend $840,000 to educate 14,788 white students but only $50,000 on 1,508 blacks, a per capita difference of 71.3 percent favoring whites. In the nineteenth and early twentieth centuries, racism was not subtle or hidden; both state and local laws, such as City Code 406 defining "Negro" and "white," instituted racism as part of the legal framework. Blacks who violated racial mores, be they legal or extralegal, faced brutal reactions; African Americans constituted the overwhelming majority of an average of seventy victims lynched annually in the United States between 1900 and 1919. This number included a black man thrown from a Dallas jail window and then hanged by an angry mob in March 1910. Despite all the obstacles, a few blacks became very successful, including Dr. Trabue, who arrived in Tarrant County prior to 1865 as a slave but turned to medicine after emancipation, and William "Gooseneck Bill" McDonald, a force in Republican politics in the 1890s as well as a successful banker and millionaire. However, the great majority of black Texans existed on a thin edge of subsistence. During the 1890s, no more than 159 African American businessmen were counted in the whole state, and almost all were in small enterprises with an average investment under $3,000.[1]

Substantial demographic work has appeared on Hispanics, although the picture is far from complete. In many cases very little information is available, especially for the period before Texas entered the Union in 1845, and what exists suffers from gaps. The U.S. Census Bureau did not classify Hispanics as a separate category until 1930, which makes stratified data collection difficult. At the local level, the biggest obstacle may have been narrow cultural biases that routinely ignored those outside the mainstream. Given the limitations, researchers have been forced to rely on estimates which can vary widely. By one calculation, fewer than 4,000 Hispanics lived in Texas in 1834; a second study claimed the figure had grown to at least 20,000 by 1850, while a third suggested Texas held 75,000 persons of Mexican birth in 1845.[2] The best, earliest count is an 1887 state census, the sole published enumeration of nineteenth-century Texas Hispanics. Texas counted 79,833 Hispanics, including 78,878 classified as Mexicans, a categorization that included everyone of Mexican heritage regardless of citizenship.[3]

Despite the statistical limitations, some general conclusions can be drawn. For the first half century after Mexico won its independence from Spain in 1821, immigration into Texas remained stable and low, averaging just over 4,300 per decade. During the 1880s and 1890s, the flow slowed to a trickle, dropping to 1,082 per decade, or just 108 annually. However, the percentage of Mexicans in Texas's foreign-born population continued to increase.[4]

Nineteenth-century immigration into Texas was not only at a low level but also tended to be geographically limited. In 1887, Hispanics accounted for only 4 percent of the state's population—placing them behind African Americans (20 percent) and Germans (6 percent)—but Hispanics dominated the southwest region along the Mexican border. Of nineteen Texas counties with 500 or more Hispanics, fourteen lay either directly on the Rio Grande River or one county removed. The other five—Atascosa and Wilson (both just south of Bexar County), Bexar (county seat San Antonio), Travis (county seat and state capital Austin), and Tom Green (home to San Angelo)—were all on or south of a line running northwest and southeast through Austin. Moreover, seven of eleven counties with a Hispanic majority bordered the Rio Grande, two others (La Salle and Pecos) were one county removed, and Nueces and Duval Counties sat nearby in deep south Texas. The Rio Grande also ran alongside four of the five Texas counties with a population at least 90 percent Hispanic: Zapata (98 percent), Starr (97 percent), Cameron (91 percent), and Webb (90 percent). Only Duval (92 percent), adjacent to Webb County, did not have river access. Cameron, the southernmost Texas county, boasted the largest total Hispanic population by far, 15,437, almost twice that of second place Starr with 8,074.[5]

In the rest of Texas, Hispanics represented much lower percentages of the population, although with some seasonal variations. In 1887, only two counties north of the southwest quadrant, Dallas and Nacogdoches, were home to more than 250 Hispanics. Occasionally, evidence of mobility appeared, such as a newspaper report in 1898 from Graham, Texas, (approximately 100 miles northwest of Fort Worth) of hundreds of Mexican laborers traveling from Laredo (Webb County) to work the cotton harvest in North Central Texas around the Brazos River. That the movement received press coverage indicates novelty, that it was not common and probably not a permanent relocation. The available evidence suggests that high concentrations of Hispanics were limited to the Rio Grande region of south Texas.[6]

Mexicans arrived in the Fort Worth area soon after 1849 when the U.S. Army established a redoubt on a bluff overlooking the Trinity River, but their numbers and influence developed slowly. Company D, Ninth Texas Cavalry of the Confederate States of America, formed in 1861 in Fort Worth and commanded by Captain Jack Brison, listed "Antone" in its muster with the sole notation "Mexican who went through the war." Although later records reflect more Hispanic presence, they tend to do so in a cursory and biased manner. An 1895 collection of biographies of important persons in

Tarrant and Parker counties failed to list even one person with a Hispanic surname, and as late as 1960 a directory of approximately 200 North Fort Worth businessmen listed only two Hispanics: Louis Ayala, owner since 1924 of a barbershop at 1537B North Main, and Raul Jimenez, owner of Jimenez Tortilla Factory at 2140 North Commerce Street.[7]

Given the paucity of resources, the closest to a comprehensive treatment is Carlos Cuellar's doctoral dissertation and his book *Stories from the Barrio*, remarkable efforts considering the serious difficulties involved. Using population schedules from the 1880 census, Cuellar found fourteen Fort Worth residents who either had been born in Mexico or had Mexican-born parents. He noted that they were rather homogenous: all were males; all but one were unmarried; most were young, three were forty or over, the rest under thirty-five; ten had been born in Mexico, the rest in Texas; all except one had two Mexican parents (the lone exception was the son of a Mexican mother and a French father); and they worked at unskilled jobs, eight as common laborers, two as harvesters, and one each as a cook, barkeeper, dishwasher, and herder. Home addresses were listed for only three, two at the local jail and the third simply on First Street with no notation of direction or block number.[8]

Cuellar's study drew much of its nineteenth-century data from city directories, a common publication of the period that generally listed every resident, often including home and business addresses as well as occupations. The 1883–84 edition included two Hispanic surnames: Riley Gonzáles and Antonio Peña. Gonzáles, a laborer at the original municipal stock pens (located near where East Lancaster and Interstate 35W now intersect), lived on Seventeenth Street between Elm and Brewer in a small Hispanic community, *El Paplote*. Peña resided on Nineteenth Street between Adamson and Lawrence, probably in the same neighborhood. (Lawrence ran north and south seven blocks east of Main Street.) In the 1885–86 *City Directory*, the number of residents with Hispanic surnames increased to nine, but home addresses were listed for only three, all in a boarding house at Twelfth and Pecan. Three worked as tamale peddlers and one female was listed as an actress, but three others had risen to occupations with more status, two as tailors and one, Manuel Canapa, as manager of a grocery at Twelfth and Rusk. An analysis of home addresses from both editions revealed that most lived either just east of town, adjacent to the city's first stock pens, or on the near south side, an area now located just east of Interstate 35 and north of Elizabeth Boulevard. Only

three of the nine in the 1885–86 directory appeared in print the following year.[9]

From the limited records, Cuellar developed some logical generaliza-
tions. He found it no coincidence that Hispanics began appearing during
the early 1880s, just a few years after the arrival of railroads. Although
many early immigrants toiled as service personnel at food stands and
barbershops, or as cooks and waiters in hotels and restaurants, the majority
worked as laborers, most likely at the city's rail yards. Cuellar surmised
from the low level of employment status and nonlocal backgrounds that
most had arrived rather recently, while the reappearance of only three
names suggested that they remained rather transient. Low employment
status and lack of residential tenure, coupled with indications of tran-
sience and the relative absence of female listings, led Cuellar to speculate
that immigrants tended to be adventurers seeking financial opportunity
and/or an escape from acute deprivation, rather than stable settlers committed to long-term residence.[10]

Certainly some Hispanics did remain, although their numbers remained
rather small. The prosperity of the 1880s spurred growth and development important for the city's future while also facilitating individual economic advancement. Some immigrants prospered, often by making hum-
ble lunch stands into restaurants or by practicing trades, most notably as
tailors. Their success brought others, especially their relatives. Although
the population effect never reached statistical significance, it did contribute to the formation of the first ethnic communities.[11]

The location of the first Hispanic neighborhood remains in doubt.
Some point to *La Corte,* a barrio of makeshift homes erected near Belknap
Street where Ripley Arnold Housing stood, while others identify "Little
Mexico," a blighted region adjacent to Hell's Half Acre, providing proximity to menial service jobs in bars and bordellos as well as to the south
side rail yards and eastside stock pens. This geographic advantage probably weighed heavily in the development of a Hispanic commercial section around Thirteenth and Rusk featuring barbershops, groceries, "chile
stands," and cantinas.[12] In 1923, the *Fort Worth Star Telegram* described
"Little Mexico" as a "romantic beat" for police officers because of its
"dreamy, dark-eyed senoritas with gay mantillas who haunted the beer
cantinas."[13] Growth eventually pushed the borders south to Seventeenth
Street, giving rise to an adjoining community known as *La Diez-y-siete.*[14]

After 1900, Mexican immigration changed dramatically. Throughout
the nineteenth century, immigration had involved low numbers of largely

agricultural workers concentrated along the Texas-Mexico border or in adjacent counties. By 1900 only 71,062 Mexicans lived in Texas, but the first decade of the twentieth century witnessed a remarkable numerical increase, as 49,642 immigrated into Texas, more than fifty times the total from the 1890s. The surge came as a consequence of several "pull" forces that drew Mexicans into Texas, the most significant being an expansive economy that accelerated urban demand for Mexican labor, especially since Mexican immigrants worked hard for low wages. Movement north of the Rio Grande was facilitated by the 1901 completion of a St. Louis to Brownsville railroad line that made relocation away from the border much easier and quicker.[15]

Railroad development within Mexico complemented the forces encouraging immigration. Expansion of Mexican industry in the late nineteenth and early twentieth centuries, especially its railroads, gave many Mexicans work experience needed by Texas industries and, at the same time, made internal movement easier. The effect of new skills and new mobility put many Mexican immigrants on road crews building new tracks and repairing the old along Texas rights-of-way. The interplay of effects not only increased the number of immigrants but also changed their nature, making them more urban, more industrial, and more likely to settle outside the border region, which reduced the tendency to concentrate regionally.[16]

The development of a Mexican rail industry, along with the workforce to maintain it, was particularly important in drawing immigrants to Fort Worth. The populous south-central states that were served by Mexico's railroads included Michoacán, Jalisco, Guanajuato, and San Luis Potosí, all of which sent substantial numbers to Fort Worth in the twentieth century. The juxtaposition of easier transit and marketable skill sets led many immigrants to Fort Worth, the rail center of the American Southwest, with the most lines of service and the most tons of shipping south of St. Louis. In 1910 the *Star Telegram* complained about the large "Mexican" population enticed to the area by railroad jobs.[17]

The convergence of qualified workers and a large, dispersed railroad industry distinctively shaped Fort Worth's Hispanic settlement. Although passenger stations remained centralized at the south end of town (near what is now Lancaster and South Main), maintenance and repair yards, where most immigrants worked, cropped up in many sectors. The diffusion of those facilities, combined with tendencies to live close to employment, dispersed rather than concentrated Fort Worth Hispanics. Northeast of downtown, around Runnels Street and Terminal Road, workers on the

St. Louis Southwestern (also known as the Cotton Belt Railroad) formed *La Yarda* while *La Rock Isla,* around East Peach and Live Oak, became home to employees of the Rock Island and of smaller lines such as the Trinity and Brazos. Several railroad shops sprang up just south of the Lancaster Avenue depot, dominated by the Texas and Pacific yards at Main Street and Railroad Avenue, where the community of *El TP* began and later expanded, along with company shops, west to Vickery Boulevard and Montgomery Street. The Missouri, Kansas and Texas (popularly known at the Katy) and the International and Great Northern also had shops in the short Southside. On the Northside, the Gulf, Colorado and Santa Fe facilities on Decatur Avenue employed many Mexicans who settled in *La Loma,* bordered by Clinton, Ellis, Long, and Thirty-sixth.[18]

Railroads figured significantly but were not the only industries attracting and dispersing Mexican immigrants. The Armour and Swift packinghouses attracted large numbers of immigrants from Austria, Turkey, Russia, and various Eastern European countries, and eventually substantial numbers of Hispanics, especially those with ranching backgrounds, became a major part of the workforce. The 1905–1906 *City Directory* listed forty-four people with Hispanic surnames, many with home addresses just east of North Main Street in a polyglot community featuring immigrants from Greece, Russia, Bulgaria, Serbia, Rumania, Hungary, Poland, and Spain. From that melting pot, Mexicans established one square block (bounded on the east and west by Calhoun and Commerce and on the north and south by Twenty-Second and Twenty-Third) that grew to take in all of the area east of Main Street and south to what is now Northside Drive, making *La Empaka* the largest Hispanic community in the city.[19]

Another major industrial influence drew workers to the far Southside. The Bolt Works, a manufacturer of small nuts and bolts, opened in 1904 on Hemphill Street. In 1908, after adding rolling mill equipment, it became Texas Steel, the first facility of its kind in the Southwest. George W. Armstrong, who served decades both as owner and manager, was traditional in preferring a docile work force to an organized union shop. Armstrong even resorted to peonage, loaning his workers money and then using the debt as a means to restrain them from leaving. Consequently, he hired many Mexican immigrants who were vulnerable and therefore less likely to join unions or strike. Some of these workers lived in the sixteen company houses, *Las Casitas Amarillas,* located on Alice, May, and Pafford.

These became the seed from which sprang *La Fundición,* a largely Hispanic neighborhood east of Hemphill between Ripy and Bolt.[20]

The increase in immigrants escaped the notice of the 1910 census but not that of local sources. Fort Worth grew from a population of 26,688 in 1900 to 73,312 in 1910, a nation-leading 174 percent increase.[21] Despite that tremendous growth, only 406 "Mexicans" were listed, an undercount of major proportions made obvious by Fort Worth Police arrest statistics. For the year ending March 31, 1903, city police officers made 3,008 custodial arrests, broken down to 1,523 "Americans," 953 "Negroes," and 532 "foreigners," including 36 "Mexicans" (compared with 334 Irish, 46 Germans, and 34 "Hebrews"). In 1910, total arrests increased to 6,932, or 130 percent, approaching but slightly short of the city's overall population increase. In contrast, the number of "Mexicans" arrested rose to 412 (now ahead of Germans and Irish but still behind "Americans" and "Negroes"), an increase of 1,044 percent over the thirty-six arrested in 1903. This far outdistanced the overall population growth and suggested strongly that the actual Hispanic population had to have been much higher than recorded. For the 1910 census figure of 406 "Mexicans" to have been accurate, the police would have had to have arrested all 406 at least once and some more than once, a hardly likely event.[22]

Further, civic boasting in 1910 provided latent evidence of the size of the Hispanic population. The claim that San Antonio had more "Mexicans" constituted a thinly-veiled admission that Fort Worth had a larger Hispanic population than Dallas or Houston. San Antonio's proximity and historical ties to Mexico explain its higher percentages, but neither condition explains Fort Worth's higher numbers than Dallas and Houston. Fort Worth's large Hispanic population was an effect of its employment characteristics, its attraction for immigrants in search of jobs.[23]

The increase in immigration during the first ten years of the twentieth century paled in comparison to that of the next decade. Average annual movement from Mexico into Texas increased from approximately 4,000 immigrants in 1905 to 1909 to more than 18,000 in 1915 to 1919. Overall, 219,004 Mexicans entered Texas from 1911 to 1920, more than twice as many as had been recorded in all the years since 1820. The flow that had been a trickle in the 1880s and 1890s became a flood after 1910, largely due to the appearance of "push" factors, events internal to Mexico that drove out as much as 10 percent of the population. Although "pull" forces survived, the upheavals, abuses, and terrors of the 1910 Mexican revolution eclipsed them in significance. The rise of Victoriano Huerta in 1913 accelerated the exodus; on October 13, 1913, alone, some 10,000 Mexicans crossed the international bridge at Piedras Negras into Eagle Pass, Texas.[24]

The post-1910 "push" immigration continued the urbanization trend, the effects of which became evident in shifting demographics. Texas counties bordering the Rio Grande or with strong historical ties to Mexico retained their ethnicity to the degree that 40 percent of Texas Hispanics still lived in Hidalgo, Bexar, El Paso, and Cameron counties. But another 40 percent now lived in the state's urban counties—Harris, Bexar, Dallas, Tarrant, El Paso, Nueces and Travis. Besides differing from earlier immigrants in numbers and where they settled, the newer arrivals also tended to be poorer, unschooled—as many as 85 percent were illiterate—and less likely to repatriate, an effect of tougher immigration restrictions brought on by the Red Scare and Pancho Villa's raids on American soil. The number of Texas residents born in Mexico increased from 43,161 in 1880 to 249,652 in 1920, when they accounted for 73.7 percent of the total foreign-born population.[25]

The timing of those post-1913 immigrants was propitious in that they arrived just as worker shortages reached record levels. The demand so exceeded supply that private Hispanic labor bureaus opened at Fifth and Calhoun (operated by Juan Flores), at 215 East Fourteenth Street, and at 210 East Twelfth Street. Immigrant labor was so important that the *Fort Worth Telegram* held rallies to calm Mexican concerns over a possible second Mexican-American War. Rumors that Mexicans would be forced to fight against their homeland had spread following Villa's raids and the publication of the Zimmermann Telegram—a 1917 German diplomatic document offering Mexico U.S. territory if it joined the war on Germany's side. The local business community feared that Mexicans would flee to avoid this dilemma and aggravate an already serious labor shortage. The labor crisis intensified following America's entry into World War I, leading Texas in 1918 to establish free Hispanic employment agencies in Fort Worth, Dallas, San Antonio, El Paso, Waco, and Amarillo, a move that had little to do with altruism but quite a lot to do with fears that private agencies would channel cheap labor to other states. In 1917, the *Fort Worth Record* lamented that 2,000 "Mexicans" had recently shipped out for industries in Pennsylvania.[26]

Although the tremendous surge in Mexican immigration after 1910 certainly reached North Texas, it posited no significant change in Fort Worth's settlement pattern. The "pull" forces of attraction and dispersal had already established several Mexican American communities before "push" factors and World War I brought the local population to new plateaus. Those arriving after 1910 settled in the existing neighborhoods, extending their borders and often providing the critical mass to support ethnic businesses, but the newcomers did not create significant new communities. No evidence exists of a new Hispanic community arising during the decade.

Clearly, influences indigenous to Mexico, or "push" factors, were salient issues for increased immigration to Texas after 1910. But the primacy of earlier local "pull" factors—the city's numerous rail yards, the Armour and Swift packinghouses, and Texas Steel—proved more critical in Fort Worth's attracting a larger Hispanic population than the more populous cities of Dallas and Houston. Moreover, local employment patterns were key factors in decentralizing Hispanics into ten communities: *El Paplote, La Corte, La Diez-y-siete, La Loma, La Yarda, El TP, La Rock Isla, La Empaka, La Fundición,* and "Little Mexico." In a wider perspective, the local dispersal effect in Fort Worth can be seen as a microcosm of the broader post-1900 experience, when significant numbers first began settling outside the Rio Grande basin.

Although census figures of the period have limitations and blind spots, they reflect the arrival of a disproportionate number of Hispanic immigrants, an effect best demonstrated by comparisons to Dallas, Fort Worth's larger sister city just thirty miles east. Fort Worth's superior Hispanic numbers developed after 1887, when the state census showed Dallas County with 250 to 499 Hispanics but Tarrant County (Fort Worth) with fewer than 100. This changed dramatically in 1910 when the U.S. census listed Fort Worth's population at 73,312, only 80 percent of Dallas's 92,104, but with 406 residents born in Mexico, more than three times Dallas's 127. By 1920, Fort Worth's population of 106,482 was only 67 percent of Dallas's 158,976, but it included 3,831 people born in Mexico, 167 percent more than Dallas's 2,295. (Although underreporting of Hispanics plagued demographics, it probably was similar in both cities.) Based on the 1920 statistics, 3.6 percent of Fort Worth's population was Mexican-born, compared to 1.4 percent for Dallas. By 1930, Dallas would pass Fort Worth in absolute numbers of Mexican immigrants or their descendants, but Fort Worth's percentage of Hispanics remained slightly higher, 2.4 to 2.3 percent.[27]

The survival of the dispersal effect is still evident in contemporary demographics. In the 2000 U.S. census, Dallas had approximately twice the population of Fort Worth, but the two cities' average percentages

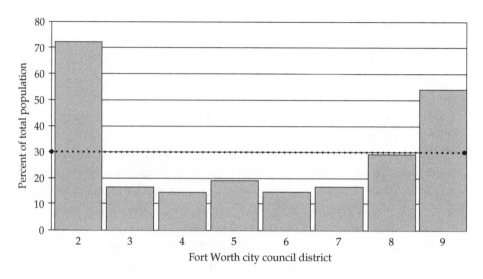

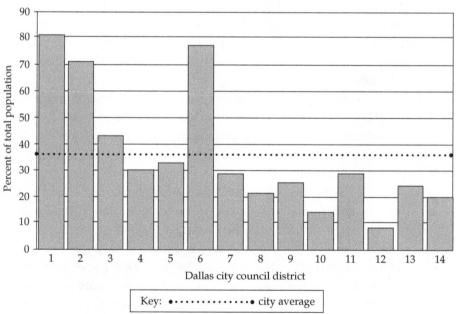

Key: •················• city average

Chart illustrating Hispanics as percent of total population in Fort Worth and Dallas city council districts, 2000.

of Hispanic population were much closer, 35.6 percent for Dallas and 30 percent for Fort Worth (see chart 7.1). An analysis of these population statistics reveals interesting trends. Variations and vagaries, especially economic conditions, work against completely even population dispersal

in which all areas share similar ethnic demographics, but differences between two similar urban areas suggest disproportionate forces. Such an
effect appears in council redistricting plans filed for both Fort Worth and
Dallas. These plans, using data from the 2000 census to identify ethnic
composition by council district, revealed that three of Dallas's twelve
council districts were more than 50 percent Hispanic: the First (80.43 percent), the Second (70.58 percent), and the Sixth (77.1 percent). Two of Fort
Worth's eight council districts were more than 50 percent Hispanic: the
Second (72.32 percent) and the Ninth (54.63 percent), giving Fort Worth a
greater percentage of districts with a Hispanic majority (25 percent ver-
sus 21 percent). One third of Dallas's districts (First, Second, Third, and
Sixth) had a higher percentage of Hispanics than the city total, while Fort
Worth counted only two (Second and Ninth).[28]

The dispersal effect becomes much clearer when comparing the degree
of population concentrations, especially in the difference between the two
cities' high- and low-percentage districts. Although the numbers can become overwhelming, Fort Worth Hispanics clearly live in less segregated
circumstances than those in Dallas. This outcome is a product of Fort
Worth's past, a relic of dispersed Hispanic settlement engendered by a historical process begun more than one hundred years ago. At the time of the
2000 census, the highest percentage of Hispanics in any Fort Worth district
was 72.32, while Dallas had two districts with higher concentrations, 80.43
and 77.1. Fort Worth's second-highest Hispanic-majority district had a
much lower percentage of Hispanics (54.63) than all three Dallas districts
(77.1, 72.32, and 70.58). The existence of three districts with extremely high
Hispanic majorities reflected a historical trend: Dallas Hispanics tended
to settle in fewer areas, to concentrate rather than disperse. The analysis
of districts with low Hispanic concentrations is also consistent. Dallas's
Twelfth Council District was only 8.27 percent Hispanic, while the Fort
Worth district with the lowest Hispanic concentration, the Fourth, was
14.4 percent Hispanic, suggesting more continuity in settlement patterns
and less segregation. The difference between the Dallas districts with the
highest and lowest percentages of Hispanics was 72.16 percentage points
(80.43 minus 8.27 equals 72.16), while the difference in Fort Worth was
only 57.92 percentage points (72.32 minus 14.1 equals 57.92), or almost 20
percent lower than in Dallas. The average deviation from citywide percentage of Hispanics for Dallas was 18 percentage points, 5.3 percent larger
than Fort Worth's average deviation of 17.1 percentage points. The difference becomes marked if each city's most Hispanic district is removed from

the calculation. Eliminating District Two in Fort Worth lowers the average deviation to 13.49, 2.41 points or 17.9 percent less than Dallas's average deviation of 15.9 with District One removed.[29]

Although neither intended nor conscious, the result has been salutary, making Fort Worth a more mixed community than its neighbor to the east, a residual effect created by early industrial and commercial developments. This pattern was established in the last quarter of the nineteenth century and then expanded and entrenched during the first two decades of the twentieth century, when Fort Worth's booming economy attracted many immigrants forced out by conditions in Mexico. Many cities recorded similar immigration, but Fort Worth's experience was unique among Texas cities because of its geographically diverse employment opportunities. The stockyards north of town, the rolling mills on the Southside, and, most importantly, the railroad infrastructure created several ethnic communities that became twentieth-century neighborhoods, a decentralizing process that defined and defines Fort Worth's Hispanic population as more dispersed, and therefore less segregated, than Hispanics in Dallas, its neighbor to the east.

8

MILITARY-INDUSTRIAL SYNERGISM, 1916–1918

After 1915 Fort Worth bloomed, thanks to a remarkably successful economy driven by multiple stimuli. The packinghouses, straining to meet insatiable war demands, were part of an equation that included military bases and a rapidly developing oil trade. Fort Worth's ability to pull out of its post-1903 complacency played a critical role in the establishment of Camp Bowie, a major army training base, and three military airfields. In contrast, the rise of the oil business was more a product of fortunate geography. The vast Ranger fields lay only ninety miles west, with little but open prairies between them and Fort Worth (although the local railroad network also played an important role). These forces combined to create an effect greater than the sum of their parts and to propel Fort Worth to regional economic supremacy, a long-cherished dream.

World War I and the army's local presence, so important economically, also became a salient force in ending official recognition and sanction of the Acre. Attacks on Hell's Half Acre had waxed and waned throughout Fort Worth's history, but in 1917 that historically sporadic opposition drew strength and permanence from a patriotic fervor linking abstinence and clean living to military preparedness. This conjunction of patriotism and morality changed the power balance, creating a force too strong for the Acre's supporters to overcome. Afterwards, alcohol, gambling, and sex for hire still existed in and around the geographic area of the Acre, but they did so without official acceptance.

Fort Worth entered 1915 already on the way out of the sluggishness that had marked 1912 through 1914 and with growing confidence that the economy was on its way up. Banking statistics supported that optimism.

Fort Worth banks held $23.8 million on deposit on December 31, 1915, a 40 percent increase over the same date in 1914. Bank clearings, which had sagged in 1914, rose 10 percent in 1915. The improved commercial situation extended to Dallas, where bank clearings grew at an even higher percentage rate but still trailed Fort Worth by almost $78 million.[1] Population figures also reflected healthy increases as Fort Worth outperformed Texas's other large cities. Between 1910 and July 1915, the estimated population reached almost 100,000, an addition of more than 26,000 or almost 36 percent, the largest total and percentage increases of Texas's four largest cities. As a result, Fort Worth briefly passed Houston to become the state's third largest city.[2]

Population growth and the expansion of Fort Worth's bank business continued to owe a lot to the packinghouses. In the course of the fourteen years from the arrival of Swift and Armour to 1916, the Fort Worth stockyards handled $1 billion in livestock transactions, a substantial sum driving local banking and the general economy. After 1914, that historical effect was complemented by war-driven demands for American foodstuffs that increased prices and profits to new levels. In 1916, the *Record* called the country's effort to meet both domestic and foreign markets a great sacrifice requiring the depletion of 50 million animals annually. While the war's effect benefited many sections of the American economy, Fort Worth, as a grain and livestock center, enjoyed a disproportionate share. By 1916, the packinghouses' capital investment, including a small Libby, McNeil & Libby packinghouse, rose to $10 million and their workforce to 3,800, with a $3 million annual payroll. The packinghouses alone produced goods valued at more than the total manufacturing and wholesale trade of either San Antonio or Dallas.[3]

The packinghouse effect touched much more than Swift and Armour. Around the two giants, a $5 million infrastructure arose, including subsidiary plants, rail facilities, and commission houses, which employed another 900 workers. About 250 people worked at the stockyards and the beltline rail line that served them, another 400 at the nearby Southwestern Mechanical Company, and 200 at seventeen commission houses. In 1915, a network of eighty buyers representing ten packinghouses outside the stockyards bought 382,263 cattle, 144,637 calves, 70,694 hogs, 94,455 sheep, and 47,242 horses and mules (more than 88 percent of the 53,640 horses and mules received), all in a year when livestock supplies declined sharply.

Most of the $1 billion spent on livestock from 1903 to 1916 went into the pockets of area ranchers and farmers who supplied many of the 23,261,716 animals purchased at an average price of $43.42. Swift and Armour and a few small local packers bought many of those, including approximately 84 percent of the hogs and more than 77 percent of the calves, but more than half the cattle and substantial percentages of other animals were processed elsewhere, creating transportation demands that contributed to the establishment of a new Missouri-Kansas-Texas Railroad line to Kansas City, giving Fort Worth eighteen railways running over twelve trunk lines that interchanged 75 percent of all Texas rail traffic. The large percentage of livestock not processed locally, especially in cattle and sheep, reflected a high level of supply that exceeded the capabilities of local plants, a remarkable change from the early days when packinghouses failed due to poor supply.[4]

Obviously, supply problems that had plagued earlier slaughterhouses had been solved, but disruptions did occur. In 1915, stockyard receipts fell in every category except horses and mules because of a hoof-and-mouth quarantine against cattle in Mexico, New Mexico, and Oklahoma. Supplies rebounded in 1916, allowing both Swift and Armour to increase capacity dramatically at the same time that the hog supply increased by 139.2 percent. The abundance of hogs fueled rumors that Cudahy Packing would build a plant between the stockyards and the beltline rail line, but nothing came of the speculation. Sales of horses and mules also increased, with many becoming part of 425,000 shipped to Europe from the United States by September 1915. Most of these were sent to England, but a few landed in France and Italy. The boom did wonders for profit margins, allowing Armour in April 1917 to announce a bonus for 1,200 employees equal to 5 percent of annual salaries. Prior to 1917, packinghouses remained the single most important player in Fort Worth's economy with an annual value of production greater than that of the next ten largest businesses combined (see table 8.1).[5]

Initially, the European war constricted capital, which limited new construction, but domestic financing eventually expanded. At the end of 1915, the Ford Motor Company opened an assembly plant on Commerce Street, and the Burdett Oxygen Company of Chicago, manufacturers of welding gases, announced construction of a $250,000 plant at Jones and Twenty-third, financed in part by local investors who bought $100,000 in stock. In 1916, easier credit brought city building permits to $2.13 million, almost $1 million above the 1915 level. Most of the permits involved small-scale projects, including 300 new homes averaging $2,500 each for a total of $750,000, or more than 35 percent of all permits. The only big-ticket

TABLE 8.1.   Estimated annual value of production
of Fort Worth's packers compared with
the next ten largest industries, 1916

	Annual production ($1,000)
Packers	**50,000**
Grain milling	12,500
Oil refining	10,000
Creamery	3,500
Metal working	2,750
Furniture	2,500
Cotton seed mills	2,087
Silos	1,500
Clothing	1,250
Printing	850
Bakeries	500
Total	**37,437**

Source: *Fort Worth Record*, September 29, 1916, Booster Edition, p. 11.

items, two new creameries and two commercial additions, amounted to only $100,000. The most important economic news of 1916 occurred outside the city limits (and, therefore, outside the record of permits) at 2600 West Seventh, where work began on a Chevrolet assembly plant costing $350,000 and capable of producing 150 cars daily. Production began so well, with more than 1,100 cars delivered by September, that Chevrolet expanded the plant, increasing its capital investment to $900,000 and raising employment to 1,500. The demand for steel, much of it needed for oil pipelines, put Fort Worth's Texas Rolling Mills on a twenty-four hour shift and necessitated a $300,000 expansion that increased employment to 300.[6]

Other industries also thrived. In 1917 the printing trades, which had long been a staple of the local economy, boasted that their annual payroll was sufficient to build a ten-story building. Fort Worth, with seventeen grain elevators capable of holding 4.89 million bushels and three flour mills producing 3,000 barrels daily, became Texas's largest and the nation's fourteenth largest storage center for wheat, corn, and oats. The grain trade facilitated construction of a $250,000 Purina Mills plant, with half the capital provided by local investors who received preferred stock returning 6 percent interest. The combined effect was important, but the grain trade accounted for only $45 million in 1917, a pittance compared with livestock's $250 million, which represented more than half of the value of all agricultural products processed in Fort Worth. Fort Worth also continued as a leading wholesale center, thanks largely to access provided through its extensive rail transport network. In the fiscal year ending August 31, 1916, jobbers reported a trade of $200 million, a 160 percent increase since 1913. Wholesalers put up impressive dollar sales but, as before, by simply merchandising goods overwhelmingly pro- duced elsewhere they created few jobs and accounted for very little in value-added transactions.[7] The wholesale trade existed and grew thanks to Fort Worth's location as the nearest major city and principal supplier to much of West Texas, a vast area stretching hundreds of miles served by an army of roving jobbers representing Fort Worth merchants. Dallas merchants enjoyed a similar dominance in East Texas, but Fort Worth boosters thought they had the better of the split. This belief appeared to be buttressed by a 1913 federal study calculating that West Texans en- joyed a per capita wealth of $1,146, much larger than the $507 ascribed to their counterparts in East Texas and exceeded by only four states. The differences between East and West Texas—and between West Texas and most of the rest of the United States—seemed impressive but may have been skewed by the presence of a few extremely rich ranchers and oil- men in a relatively small West Texas population.[8]

Fort Worth's economic success was most clearly evident on Main Street, the city's commercial thoroughfare. In 1916, a total of 710 busi- nesses engaged in ninety-two fields crowded the street's expanse from the Tarrant County Courthouse on the north to the railroad tracks south of Front Street. The list included 101 law offices, eighty doctor's clinics, forty-two bars, twenty-nine cafes, eight banks, seven picture shows and pool halls, five hamburger stands, four department stores, three military recruiting offices, and one bowling alley. Clear divisions marked the street's three major sections. Law and professional offices congregated around the courthouse, department stores occupied the middle, and businesses serving a more transient trade grouped close to the railroad terminals.[9]

After 1914, economic growth seemed to occur without much encour- agement. Fort Worth investors bought stock in the Burdett Oxygen Com- pany and the Purina Mills Plant, and some new businesses such as the

View looking west on Seventh at Main, circa 1912. Courtesy of University of Texas at Arlington Special Collections.

Chevrolet assembly plant received donated land, but direct subsidies seemed to be a thing of the past. In 1916, S. B. Ricaby, secretary of the Chamber of Commerce, suggested foregoing taxes on industries building in the undeveloped area between the stockyards and downtown. Ricaby put forth the initiative as a way to bring new businesses to fill the large void, reasoning that the lost commercial tax revenue would be offset by residential property taxes paid by new employees. The idea foundered under the weight of disinterest and questions over legality.[10]

Fort Worth's location played an important role in raising commercial hopes in 1916, when conflicts along the Rio Grande fueled rumors of a second Mexican-American War. Many were quick to see an opportunity that Fort Worth, only 300 miles north of the border, could exploit to great advantage. Local boosters, reacting with alacrity, bragged that Fort Worth was certain to receive the "lion's share" of government contracts in North Texas. Early signs of that effect appeared in a noticeable but measured increase in packinghouse demand and in an army appropriation request of $15 million for the purchase of 75,000 horses and 25,000 mules. In July 1916, the army ordered 13,950 horses and mules through the Fort Worth stockyards, further stimulating a market already overheated by European demand. In time, speculation assumed grander proportions, suggesting that mobilization would bring an army base that would "pour gold" into the city, much of it to be spent on food. This optimism surged after the War Department named Fort Worth the supply point for southern armies if a conflict developed between the United States and Mexico, a designation that promised to pump $10 million into the economy. These dreams fell victim to peace when the crisis was resolved short of war.[11]

In the spring of 1917, the focus switched to Europe, where American involvement loomed. The U.S. declaration of war on April 6, 1917, had major local consequences, most deeply in the ninety-nine Tarrant County lives lost through military service and the scores of others who suffered wounds and dislocation. Many others trained and served, and many mustered for lunch-hour and evening military drills as a home guard. Most found ways to show their support, even if only by cheering or participating in a massive patriotic parade in April 1917 that featured 35,000 marchers. City government facilitated the war effort by guaranteeing the jobs of workers entering the military; purchasing $80,000 in Liberty Bonds, then reselling $50,000 to 384 employees with payments stretched over ten months; joining much of the nation in adopting daylight savings time; and registering Fort Worth's 360 German residents.[12] War fervor left little room for diversity. In July 1917, William J. Lee of the International Workers of the World was arrested at Twelfth and Main after urging the poor to stay out of the conflict, which he termed a rich man's war.[13]

Beyond the cost and sacrifice lay economic opportunities that Fort Worth worked to develop. Ben E. Keith, president of the Chamber of Commerce, traveled to Washington after learning that the War Department planned several Texas bases. In the nation's capital he presented the secretary of war with site proposals and inducements that included more than 2,000 acres with free water, sewer, electric, and telephone connections. An army inspection team viewed several sites before choosing, in June 1917, an area between White Settlement Road, the Arlington Heights Boulevard streetcar line, and Stove Foundry Road (Vickery Boulevard) for the divisional mobilization of the Texas and Oklahoma National Guards. From that point events moved rapidly, with Dallas contractor J. S. Thompson beginning construction on July 18, 1917, using 5,500 workers. Camp

Bowie began as a rather moderate facility costing only $250,000, designed for 27,000 trainees (with a monthly payroll of $750,000), but it grew to a $2.24 million complex that held as many as 35,000 trainees in seventy buildings spread over sixty acres, including a large military hospital with 1,000 beds.[14] Implementation was so rushed that 5,000 troops of the First Texas Cavalry arrived while construction was still apace on August 22, 1917. Many of these early arrivals were from the Texas National Guard's 36th Division, fresh from the Mexican expedition searching for Pancho Villa. New trainees soon followed, including Tarrant County's first draftee, S. G. Menkler, a dairyman, and Second Lieutenant J. Frank Dobie. Actual training began on September 4, 1917, and just over six months later, in April 1918, a downtown crowd of 400,000 watched 27,000 soldiers of the Panther Division parade before departing for France, where they would lose 1,300 killed and earn two Medals of Honor.[15]

Chamber of Commerce President Keith was also instrumental in obtaining three army airfields. Through General Benjamin Foulois of the U.S. Army Air Service, he obtained access to General Cuthbert G. Hoare of the Canadian Royal Flying Corps, the officer in charge of selecting air training sites. Keith stressed advantages of weather, open spaces, and

CAMP BAKE OVENS, CAMP BOWIE. ' FORT WORTH, TEXAS.

Bake ovens at Camp Bowie, 1917 or 1918. Courtesy of University of Texas at Arlington Special Collections.

readily available lumber and laborers to secure approval. The three airfields, covering a combined 1,227 acres, became Carruthers Field near Benbrook, Barron Field near Everman, both used largely for flight training, and Taliaferro Field, also known as Hicks Field, located in the countryside ten miles north of Fort Worth and used mostly for gunnery practice. Work began in August 1917 on facilities costing between $3 million and $4 million to support approximately 200 aircraft. Three hundred Canadian Royal Flying Corps cadets, most of whom were Americans who had joined the Canadian air force before U.S. entry into the war, began relocating from Toronto at the end of October 1917. All three fields opened between October and November 1917, with 1,500 to 2,000 personnel at each. The U.S. Army Air Service gradually took over and by May 1, 1918, all three airfields were exclusively American. Other American training operations were established at Dallas, Waco, Houston, Wichita Falls, and San Antonio. During the war, 1,960 pilots earned wings at Fort Worth, graduating with 200 minutes' flying time (fewer than four hours), mostly in Curtiss JN-4s (or Jennies), with a maximum speed of seventy-five mph.[16]

Air training proved extremely deadly. Nationally, some 5,233 pilots received their wings by July 1918, but 205 died in various accidents. Fort Worth's mortality rates ran much higher. Fatalities were first reported in local papers as early as December 1917 and continued to appear frequently. As of February 19, 1918, after less than six months' operation, Fort Worth's three fields had experienced thirty-one of the forty-five air-related deaths at Texas bases, compared with only seven at Houston, three at San Antonio, two at Wichita Falls, and one each at Dallas and Waco. The high rate was attributed to British and Canadian trainees who accounted for twenty of the thirty-one dead, largely because the British pressed more demanding training, requiring their pilots to solo earlier and perform trickier maneuvers. Through the course of training, between 101 and 106 men died locally, including Vernon Castle, a famous British dancer who became a flight instructor after serving in France with the Royal Air Force. Castle was killed on February 15, 1918, at Carruthers Field.[17]

Camp Bowie was a segregated base, and its lack of black soldiers probably explained Fort Worth's ability to avoid major racial incidents similar to those that struck Waco and Houston. In July 1917, fighting between black soldiers and whites outside a Waco "colored" cinema spread after other soldiers rushed to aid their comrades. The brawl grew so intense that both local and military police fired on the crowd. Shortly thereafter, the sight

of four black soldiers walking through downtown Fort Worth caused considerable alarm among the populace until it was determined that the men
were delayed in transit by a late train. In August, a riot began in Houston
when a black soldier objected to a police officer slapping a black woman
and was pistol whipped and arrested. A corporal seeking the man's release
was also beaten and arrested. In response, 156 African American soldiers,
ignoring orders to stay on base, grabbed weapons and marched to town
where they exchanged shots with police and armed citizens, killing approximately twenty, including four soldiers and four police officers. In the
aftermath, up to twenty soldiers were executed and more than forty received life sentences. Fort Worth certainly did not escape because of enlightened racial attitudes. The city remained rigidly segregated, even with
separate parks, a condition made obvious by the city council's purchase in
1918 of land on North Main Street from Tom Mason, an African American, to create Douglas Park, to be set aside for blacks.[18]

All segregation rested ultimately on political segregation, and in most
of the South, including Fort Worth, the process of disenfranchisement
began at the local level. Concerned that the women's suffrage movement
might foster an idea that black women could participate, the local Democratic Executive Committee specifically prohibited "negro [sic] women"
from voting in primaries. The party of Lincoln was no better; the Republican Council posted "For white people only" signs at its meetings. At times
rigid segregation caused problems for the military. When the army tried to
transport a black prisoner from Camp Bowie, guarded by white military
police officers, it ran afoul of state Jim Crow statutes that required separate
railcars for blacks and whites. After considerable discussion the matter
was resolved by granting the military an exemption.[19]

The army arrived in Fort Worth just as another local morality movement gained momentum. The latest campaign began traditionally in 1916
as a church-based movement opposed to the permissive policing of the
reservation, that area east of Main and south of Ninth where vice was
tolerated. The new campaign, however, also sought the defeat of a plebi-
scite to allow motion pictures and other amusements on Sundays. Despite
warnings that desecration of the Sabbath would create a "wide open" town
and bring "a San Francisco Sunday with all of its fearful evils," the measure permitting Sunday entertainments was approved on April 1, 1916, by
893 votes, 3,812 to 2,919. In addition, 1916 witnessed yet another county prohibition referendum. The Business Men's [sic] Anti-Prohibition Committee

ran large advertisements in opposition, arguing that the question was not whether people would drink (they would), but whether drinkers would pay taxes and wages or make bootleggers rich. Although prohibitionists dominated the county's rural areas, most of which were already dry, the urban vote proved decisive. The outcome was rather close, however, with the ban failing 7,997 to 7,113, a victory by only 884 votes.[20] A delegation representing women's clubs also attacked public indecency, petitioning for ordinances requiring that women bathers at Lake Worth wear knee-length skirts and hose and prohibiting men from diving under water to grab women by the ankles. The clubs also asked that a separate beach section be set aside for unescorted women, a suggestion the city commission took under advisement.[21]

The reservation also faced challenges from former supporters. A major supporting argument had been that geographic concentration offered control advantages, but evidence suggested that the assumed effect was lacking. Opponents argued the opposite, noting that the Acre routinely accounted for 60 to 80 percent of all arrests and suggesting that its removal would eliminate most of those. Another faction supported the reservation as necessary to maintain public decorum by hiding prostitution from open view. That effect also seemed questionable. Police Commissioner Hugh Jamieson complained that Saturday nights would find women on the streets, on porches, and in windows acting in ways that "would make a self-respecting white man ashamed." Jamieson also questioned the deterrent effect of tolerance, noting that two girls, ages fifteen and sixteen, had applied for abode permits in the Acre, essentially licenses to engage in prostitution.[22]

An important issue moving Jamieson and others from support to opposition was the rampant exploitation of prostitutes by unscrupulous property owners and rooming house operators. The profitability of prostitution and its limitation to a rather small area brought usurious rents that reached as high as $200 to $350 monthly for small rooming houses, an inflated cost that middlemen passed along by charging prostitutes as much as $14 weekly for one-room "cribs" crammed into each building. The high cost forced many women to choose between spending a major portion of their income on rent or risking arrest by openly soliciting, which was banned, or moving out of the reservation. The last proved to be critical in building umbrage over exploitation. Attacks over exploitation rested not so much on altruism as on practicalities; exorbitant rents drove prostitutes into other sections of the city, putting them into view of complaining residents, an outcome that obviated one of the Acre's major supporting arguments. In March 1916 the police demanded a 25 percent reduction in rooming house rents in the area of Calhoun and Jones streets "known as the segregated district," warning that failure to comply would lead to complete closure. Owners and operators agreed, at least publicly.[23]

The agreement may have been more public than real. By February 1917, Commissioner Jamieson called for an end to the reservation after determining that vice lords had taken over. The two most notorious purveyors, Mack Smith and Charles Rotsky, owned ninety-seven of the district's 127 rooming houses and cribs. Rotsky alone held two rooming houses and thirty-five cribs employing more than forty working women, while Smith counted several houses and sixty cribs with more than seventy-five women. Rotsky's lawyer admitted his client owned $200,000 in Acre property but noted that he had never rented a house for immoral purposes without written authorization from the chief of police.[24]

Commissioner Jamieson's position reflected a degree of enlightenment about conditions associated with prostitution. He admitted that women from all over Texas came to Fort Worth because of its reputation as a wide-open town offering easy money, and he regretted that most had fallen because of the deceit of men whose reputations remained unspoiled. Affidavits filed by Fort Worth prostitutes in 1917 supported this view, stating that many had been deserted by husbands or seduced by boyfriends and then abandoned. Jamieson argued that exorbitant rents constituted a second victimization by unscrupulous men, this time by those controlling rooming houses and cribs. He cited an unnamed property owner with a $25,000 annual income derived from those rents and a rooming house operator who paid $50 monthly for a building that he subdivided into fourteen "cribs" renting for $14 weekly, bringing in approximately $840 monthly. Jamieson proposed some innovative efforts to help the downtrodden, such as utilizing the Relief Association to help them find other employment and offering free railroad tickets to any wishing to return home.[25]

Jamieson's distress at the exploitation and his empathy for the plight of the lowly led him to see the Acre as a disgraceful anachronism that should be closed. He faced stiff opposition from many high-placed supporters, including some fellow commissioners and the police chief, all of whom still believed that vice complemented business interests and general prosperity and that concentration controlled what could not be eliminated. The pro-Acre faction prevented direct intervention, so Jamieson used existing city ordinances, especially building and health codes, to force questionable operations to comply or close, preferably the latter. Jamieson even joined the city physician on inspection tours of shady operators in "Chinatown" and the Acre. In March 1917, Mayor Tyra joined Jamieson in support of general closure, serving notice that, pending the plan's implementation, the city would not prosecute prostitutes but would file against property owners and operators. Acre supporters put up one last attempt, organizing as the Fort Worth Rationalists to call for a referendum on whether or not to close the reservation.[26]

Implementation was not delayed long. Rumors circulated that the official closing would occur on March 19, 1917, but the mayor's absence delayed it until March 20. The assault began with an injunction issued by Judge R. E. I. Roy that forbade renting, leasing, or operating property in the reservation area for immoral purposes. Strict adherence to the directive would effectively put out of business more than 300 known prostitutes, sixty-seven renting individual "crib" houses and 240 working at sixty parlor houses. The police ordered all the houses closed but, in what reflected Jamieson's influence, did not order the women to leave town, as had been the common practice. Instead, the police allowed the women to remain on condition of seeking other employment. That evening a reporter noted that, for the first time in five years, the Acre was quiet with shades drawn and no "gaudy kimonas [sic]" in sight or ragtime pianos to be heard. Jamieson confirmed the report by walking through the district on a Saturday night without finding a single working prostitute. He promised that the Acre was gone and would not return, arguing that "legalized vice is no more a right than is a safeblower's union." The courts added further support in November 1917 by declaring Houston's segregated district unconstitutional.[27]

Jamieson's declaration may have been a little premature, as evidence suggested that prostitution had simply changed addresses or become more covert. The police chief reported that none of the prostitutes had sought relocation assistance, suggesting that they had not gone far, and seven were arrested in a residential district soon afterward. In addition, the city commissioners considered requiring rooming houses to maintain lists of lodgers and female employees, reasoning that such a requirement would help control the spread of prostitution into the rooming house district. Other evidence that the prostitutes had not left town appeared in the proliferation of suits filed against property owners and landlords for operating immoral houses, which would not have been necessary in the absence of prostitution. In addition, it was suggestive that the city attorney had to deny complaints of selective enforcement favoring prominent but unnamed property owners.[28]

The renewal of reform may have been attributable to a spike in more violent crimes. In 1916, nine murders occurred within Fort Worth: six victims were shot, two stabbed, and one beaten, and four of the murders occurred during domestic incidents. The victims included five Anglo men and an Anglo woman, an African American man and woman, and a Hispanic man. By November 1917, the toll for the year almost tripled to twenty-five, with twenty-one shot, two beaten, one stabbed, and one dying as the result of a botched abortion. The victims included thirteen Anglo men, seven African American men (four killed by sheriff's deputies or private detectives), three Anglo women, one African American woman and one Hispanic man. Fifteen of the murders, or 60 percent, took place in the Acre.[29] The Acre was the most violent section, but the most sensational incident occurred at city hall. J. K. Yates, who had resigned from the police after being reassigned to patrol, entered asking for the mayor but went into the office of Commissioner C. Ed Parsley and opened fire, killing Parsley before being killed by officers. Yates had a violent history that included killing a man who made advances to his daughter.[30]

Reform in 1917 mixed elements opposing the Acre with a rising prohibition agenda and patriotism to find energetic support among businessmen, although ulterior motives may have lain underneath that change. Robert Wiebe's seminal study argued that prohibition's popularity among the urban-industrial leadership owed a great deal to its effectiveness as a means of mass control. The assumption was that enforced temperance would create peaceful workmen who came to work regularly and minded their own business. In this view, the passion of war contributed an important chapter in a campaign designed to discipline society. By tying foreign threats to alcohol consumption, commercial barons advanced a form of patriotism that also promoted a controlled, more docile working class, adding much to the emergence during the war years of a new middle class that shared common assumptions across a wide spectrum of issues, particularly those associated with strict standards of proper conduct.[31]

The military's presence very quickly became an important part of the forces seeking control or, preferably, elimination of the Acre. Local reformers realized early on the dangers and opportunities presented by the presence of thousands of young, single men. In July 1917, the Fort Worth Equal Suffrage Association organized a committee dedicated to combating vice in and around the army camps. The suffragists, as well as other groups, arranged alternative entertainment, including a weekly dance at the Hebrew Center sponsored by the Jewish Soldiers and Sailors League. Those efforts were bolstered by federal authorities and statutes. In 1917 Congress passed and sent to the states the Prohibition amendment (the Eighteenth Amendment), which would be ratified in 1919 and would take effect in 1920. The measure's success was due to many factors. One was the tying of prohibition to the war effort, arguing that enforced abstention made soldiers more fit and put grains into food production that would have gone into liquor. The legal threat seemed so imminent that every saloon in the reservation and Irish Town failed to renew its license, leading the *Record* to cite July 11, 1917, as the Acre's final passing. Still, many other liquor dealers remained in business, including saloons on Fifteenth between Main and the Santa Fe Depot and most on the north end of downtown.

In August 1917, President Woodrow Wilson established a one-half mile dry zone around military camps, which closed 376 saloons in Kansas City and fifty in San Antonio, and in September the army prohibited alcohol and prostitution around military camps. Neither action seriously affected Fort Worth because Camp Bowie lay too far removed from downtown and the reservation. Despite the camp's remoteness, the military introduced its physical presence downtown. Six National Guard Military Policemen began patrolling in July 1917, joined in August by forty members of the provost guard who walked downtown streets until midnight. In September, city commissioners, perhaps motivated by the military's influence, forced all non-exempted businesses, including saloons, to close on Sundays.[32]

Dallas went further, implementing local prohibition on October 20, 1917. Tarrant County activists attempted to build on that triumph, arguing that Dallas undesirables would flood the Acre if Fort Worth remained wet. Instead, the most noticeable impact was a rise in liquor sold in taverns along Front Street east of the railroad viaduct, most likely to Dallasites arriving by train. The city commission reacted in January 1918 by removing Front Street from the saloon district and giving the establishments but five days to close. The combined military-reform effort compromised liquor's availability to the extent that visitors to the March 1918

"When a Fellow Needs a Friend." *Fort Worth Record,* November 24, 1917, p. 4.

Southwestern Exposition and Fat Stock Show were advised that they would find vastly changed moral conditions with joints rarer and farther between.[33]

State action accomplished a finality that reformers had not. In March 1918 Texas made liquor sales to the military a felony, and Fort Worth police began enforcing the new statute with a series of raids that arrested more than 100 men and women, indicting thirty-seven, including several rent-car drivers who procured not only liquor but also prostitutes. On April 16, 1918, Texas ordered ten-mile dry zones around military bases, backing the measure with harsh penalties of two to five years' imprisonment without parole. The bar against selling liquor to servicemen and the dry zones closed 1,800 saloons and covered not only all of Fort Worth, but also much of the state that had not already voted dry. The closings greatly reduced the police workload; in the first week following implementation, Fort Worth officers made only five arrests for drunkenness, including just one on Saturday night, compared with up to 100 on typical Saturdays. The downward trend continued, with only 470 arrests in the first three weeks after enactment, compared with 1,200 in the three weeks before. The remaining 750 Texas saloons shuttered their doors on June 26, 1918, when statewide prohibition became effective. Of course bootlegging experienced a sharp growth curve. The going rate for a gallon of liquor reached $40, making it so scarce and valuable that home burglaries soared as thieves sought stored alcohol.[34]

The military also played a major role in combating prostitution. As Camp Bowie opened, the railroads reported an influx of "immoral women" arriving from all over Texas and out of state, many from cities that had recently closed vice districts. The new arrivals plied their trade in hotels, rooming houses, and even in public parks. Like prohibition, the military's involvement in prostitution eradication began early and rested on its threat to the welfare of soldiers, in this case from sexually transmitted diseases. The medical justification carried some real weight. An army report issued January 18, 1918, stated that Camp Bowie had forty-two new venereal disease cases for the week, the seventh largest total of the thirty camps listed. The base's per capita rate of venereal infections stood at 83.0 per 1,000, almost twice the national rate of 46.6 for National Guard bases and virtually equal to the 90.3 average rate for regular army bases. These figures meant that nearly one in ten men stationed at Camp Bowie contracted a sexually transmitted disease.[35]

The military backed a demand for strict enforcement of the laws with serious consequences for noncompliance. When local liquor dealers proposed a constitutional challenge to Texas's ten-mile dry zone, the army warned that repeal would mean the loss of Camp Bowie and the airfields, and it also threatened to relocate or confine soldiers to base if prostitution was not eradicated. Dr. Frank Boyd, president of the Tarrant

County Board of Health, agreed that immediate steps were needed to end the "loathsome diseases" that had stricken hundreds at Camp Bowie. Base officials began questioning infected soldiers to learn the names and locations of prostitutes, forwarding the information to city police, who followed up with a raid on a house on East Seventeenth. The raiding officers arrested nineteen "negroes [sic]," three "mexicans [sic]," and one "American" for vagrancy, a common charge used in prostitution arrests. The military's hard line on prostitution was part of a successful national campaign. In October 1917, the *New York Times* reported that military involvement had been instrumental in closing many red-light districts situated adjacent to army camps, including the three camps near Fort Worth. The *Times* overstated the effort's success, but it was true that the military-driven campaign waxed rather than waned. In November 1917, a discussion between Fort Worth city, county, military, and federal authorities was followed by raids arresting scores and closing three cabarets and one dance hall. In December 1917, Mayor William Davis traveled to Washington seeking to counteract negative reports about Fort Worth's moral conditions. Davis assured the War Department of the city's commitment to a healthy and wholesome moral atmosphere, including ending the "unhappy conditions" regarding sickness at Camp Bowie, which he blamed on issues beyond the city's control.[36]

Medical issues led to expansions of arrest and confinement powers. In March 1918 the city announced a reinvigorated anti-vice campaign to protect soldiers from the ills of prostitution. The effort began with a raid on the "Forty-Niner Show" at the Stock Show that arrested twelve women found dancing with soldiers. Although dancing was not illegal, the arrests were part of a new mandate set forth by the War Department's law enforcement division that authorized prostitution arrests on mere suspicion. The revised military standards also provided for forced medical examinations. Eight of the women arrested at the Southwestern Exposition and Fat Stock Show, and 75 percent of all women subsequently arrested in Fort Worth, were examined at a newly established medical detention facility operated by the city but staffed by federal officers, the first of its type in the nation.[37]

Prostitution survived despite the remarkable efforts of the city and the army. In April 1918 two women running disorderly houses were convicted under military statutes barring such establishments within five miles of bases. Some lone prostitutes evaded prosecution by working in automobiles rather than houses, which led to an August 1918 state law banning "pandering" in automobiles within ten miles of Camp Bowie and the airfields. The new law reflected a more enlightened perspective in that its penalties applied equally to men and women, a timely reminder that prostitution involved the active participation of two parties, that men were accomplices and instigators. For example, an African American woman employed by a state legislator reported that several soldiers accosted her while she walked through a local park.[38]

The concentration of population in military camps adjacent to an urban area posed other health hazards that became obvious during the 1918 Spanish Flu epidemic. A serious national influenza outbreak struck at the end of 1915 but passed quickly, only to return at the end of 1917. It hit Fort Worth military installations so hard that the Camp Bowie base hospital strained to care for hundreds of stricken soldiers. Again, the danger peaked and declined quickly, so that on January 1, 1918, the brass lifted a quarantine imposed on Camp Bowie and the three air bases.[39] That autumn, Spanish Flu returned with a vengeance. The base reported no cases in early September but on October 3, 1918, the hospital held 1,500 soldiers, with as many as seventeen dying in a single day. The army again quarantined the bases and postponed inductions, but those actions were too late. Fort Worth's first civilian cases appeared in September and spread rapidly, leading to closure of some schools in early October. On October 10, 1918, city commissioners established a thirty-five bed emergency hospital at Fourteenth and Calhoun in "Little Mexico," where epidemic proportions first developed, probably due to the area's endemic overcrowding and poor sanitation associated with poverty. On October 15, 1918, the city physician reported 487 cases and forty-four deaths, but the official numbers represented only a fraction of the sick. In just one week, 1,400 packinghouse employees missed work due to flu symptoms, and Mayor Davis closed all public places including schools, cinemas, and theaters. He also asked churches to forego services or restrict meetings and citizens to stay home unless absolutely necessary. The threat proved very serious, with 699 reported civilian deaths and 106 dead at the three airfields during the autumn of 1918.[40]

Sickness and death aggravated an already serious labor shortage. In November 1918, the gap between labor demand and supply became so acute that Fort Worth commissioners sent questionnaires to nonessential businesses seeking to identify male employees who could be replaced with women and reassigned to war work. The city also cracked down on idlers with a "Work or Fight" campaign in which the police rounded up men found in pool halls and other recreation centers and turned them over to employers with warnings to go to work or face jail. The labor picture was aggravated by strikes in 1918 at the stockyards and at Miller Manufacturing, a maker of overalls, both of which ended after federal intervention.[41]

Scarcity of workers became especially acute for the packinghouses. Stockyards receipts increased almost 39 percent, from 2.55 million animals in 1916 to 3.54 million in 1917, due in part to drought-diminished grasslands that forced ranchers to sell herds. The increase in sales netted suppliers up to $250 million and required 100,000 cattle cars and refrigerated cars, cementing Fort Worth as the nation's third largest livestock market. Projections for the future were even rosier. A. B. Case, general manager of Armour of Texas, claimed that the company in 1918 would spend $30 million for livestock, another $8 million for materials, and $3 million in wages. However, supply problems continued to be an issue. Demand for pork so overwhelmed supply that city commissioners rescinded a ban on hog farming within the city limits, and receipts declined in every livestock category in 1918 and again in 1919, except for sheep, which increased dramatically. Supplies of livestock rose and fell, but labor remained constantly scarce. Armour executives complained that production suffered because they could not hire enough people to push the workforce above 2,400.[42]

The year 1917 may have been the most prosperous in the city's history, encompassing not only the huge military bases and impressive gains at the slaughterhouses but also the beginnings of an oil boom. Robert Mc-Cart, an active local booster, spoke in early 1917 about oil's tremendous profit potential, noting that it would bring up to sixty cents a barrel. Oil had reached significant status locally as early as 1915, but the discovery of vast supplies in the Ranger field in October 1917 accelerated and intensified its importance. Fort Worth, the nearest large city at just ninety miles east, became the field's base of operations, with most commercial and financial activity centered at the Westbrook Hotel. The discovery of large Texas oil fields was complemented by and benefited from a fortuitous confluence of increased demand stemming from the war, growing numbers of automobiles, and expanding industrial applications. Texas industries alone more than doubled their fuel expenditures between 1914 and 1919, from $10.7 million to $22.9 million. The potential amount of money involved quickly reached huge proportions, with $250 million already invested in Texas oil by November 1918. Other Texas cities, as well as Tulsa, Oklahoma, and Shreveport, Louisiana, shared in the prosperity, but Fort Worth, blessed by an advantageous location, had reasonable expectations of becoming the West's oil center. In December 1918 the *Fort Worth Star Telegram* gushed that Fort Worth was the leading oil center of the South, with 60 percent of Texas's oil trunk line mileage and more pipelines than any other North Texas city. Location explained part of that success, but Fort Worth's oil commerce, like its livestock and wholesaling trades, also benefited from its rail transport network. Railroads were critical in providing access and the means to move large equipment. Paddock cited the oil trade as a rationale justifying his proposal for a new rail line from Fort Worth to Jack County, and the Chamber of Commerce bragged that it was "next to impossible" to access Texas's new oil fields without traveling through Fort Worth.[43]

Oil shared another similarity with the packinghouses in its stimulation of large infrastructure development that compounded economic impacts. The proliferation of oil-producing fields in North Central Texas required miles of piping, much of which ran to Fort Worth refineries. One of the first large pipelines, covering 200 miles from Moran to Fort Worth, was built by the Texas Pipeline Company based on the company's belief that Fort Worth would be the Southwest's oil center. In 1918 that seemed likely, with construction beginning on four refineries, including the Evans-Thwing Company's $750,000 facility, capable of processing 3,500 barrels a day, and the Gulf Well Machinery Manufacturing Company, employing seventy, that relocated from Houston. Existing businesses also became involved, spending $1 million on equipment to serve the oil trade while indirect development included a $1 million argon gas plant to supply the army and navy and a $3.5 million helium plant completed in March 1919 on the north edge of town. The effects lasted into the century's third decade. By 1920, some 300 oil companies carried Fort Worth addresses, many little more than one-room offices supporting acres of hopes, and nine refineries processed 55,000 barrels daily, a significant part of Texas's annual production of 72 million barrels worth $250 million (representing about $3.50 per barrel). That year the *New York Times* reported that Fort Worth streets and businesses were filled even at 8:00 A.M. on Sundays with men talking oil as stenographers and typists toiled.[44]

The combined economic impact stimulated tremendous construction. An estimated 5,000 new residents arrived each month, sparking residential building that included, in December 1918, ten apartment houses and 500 homes scheduled for completion in ninety days. In 1918 Fort Worth issued $2.3 million in building permits, ranking twelfth nationally and overshadowing Dallas's $893,100 and Houston's $609,193. In addition, Fort Worth's downtown area experienced considerable expansion tied to the oil trade, although a petroleum executive's claim that it would take ten new skyscrapers to hold all Fort Worth's oil businesses was probably an exaggeration. Wartime restrictions had discouraged new skyscraper construction, but additions flourished. The W. T. Waggoner Building added six floors to its existing four, and the Texas State Building added two. In 1918, the dollar value of Fort Worth construction was the nation's seventh largest, a remarkable achievement for a city striving for the 100,000 population level.[45]

Driven by military bases, an insatiable demand at the packinghouses, and a growing oil industry, Fort Worth enjoyed prosperity with far-reaching effects. In 1917, exaggerated estimates claimed that 50,000 new residents were added, an impossible rate of growth that would have pushed the total population to 130,000. However, little doubt existed of substantial growth. Also in 1917, the public school system staggered under the weight of 1,000 new students, creating crowded conditions and forcing employment of thirty-five additional teachers. Banks did well, recording a $21.1 million increase in deposits in 1918, the fourth largest behind only New York City, Houston, and Richmond, Virginia. A comparison of bank statistics in 1908 and 1918 reveals increases in resources and deposits of almost 400 percent and increases in clearings of almost 200 percent. In 1919, clearings would continue to increase but at a lower rate, reaching $900.1 million, 29.6 percent above 1918.[46]

Population and financial increases owed much to a significant industrial expansion that began in late 1917 involving the automobile trade. In December 1917 the Texas Motorcar Association announced plans for a $2 million plant employing up to 500 workers. By June 30, 1918 the plant, built on land donated by the Chamber of Commerce and the Young Men's Business League, began turning out trucks with a workforce that included more than sixty overall-clad women, (Women were hired due to a shortage of male workers.) In the spring of 1918 the Southern Tire Company, swayed by Fort Worth's progress in becoming an industrial center (and by donated land), announced plans for a $500,000 plant adjacent to Texas Motorcar. Before the year's end the two businesses combined under W. H. Vernon, who boasted that they would eventually employ 2,000 and become Fort Worth's second industry, trailing only the packinghouses. In April 1918, the Bridges Motor and Rubber Company announced plans to build on 280 acres off Cleburne Cardinal Road, giving Fort Worth three automobile plants and delusions of becoming the "Detroit of the South." Grand ideas were understandable but represented more hope than substance. The *Fort Worth Record* understood the difference and credited Camp Bowie for the great industrial successes of 1917 and 1918 that made Fort Worth the "metropolis of the Southwest."[47]

Camp Bowie was important but ephemeral. The war ended in November 1918, and demobilization orders mustering out thousands began being issued the following month. Fort Worth tried to turn the closure into opportunity by soliciting discharged soldiers as workers, particularly for the growing oil industry. The effectiveness of that effort was clearly

Allen-Vernon Motor Company at Eleventh and Commerce, with Pete Vernon (*left*), the first franchised dealer in Fort Worth, 1912. Courtesy of University of Texas at Arlington Special Collections.

reflected in 18,000 new bank accounts opened in January 1919. Still, jobs continued to exceed the supply of workers. Employment agencies reported placing all ex-servicemen who registered, and area farmers faced tough sledding getting crops harvested, with 5,600 openings for farm laborers and only twenty applicants registered at the local United States Employment Bureau. In desperation, the growers searched jails where Fort Worth police offered vagrants a work option in lieu of jail time.[48]

Construction continued and expanded as the war's close brought an end to restraints. In 1919, building permits soared, giving Fort Worth an incredible total of $29 million of work under way, including a twenty-story W. T. Waggoner Building and a $2 million hotel at Eighth and Main, and a twenty-four story bank building at Seventh and Main that would the tallest in Texas. From November 1, 1919, to November 1, 1920, Fort Worth added 442 businesses, including six bakeries, twelve cafes, 147 groceries and 104 automobile-related shops, such as dealers, supply houses, and garages.[49]

The good times put city finances in the black. In February 1918, Fort Worth accounts showed a $160,000 reserve and every department, including the water works, reported positive cash flows for the previous twenty-four months, quite a contrast to the century's first years, when the city could not meet its interest payments and the water department hemorrhaged money. The new prosperity produced water department receipts sufficient to pay cash for $355,745 in improvements, including a new $147,745 filtration system that increased the daily capacity at the Holley Pumping Station from 5 million to 12 million gallons. In 1918, taxable assessments rose $14.4 million, the largest one-year increase ever (to that point), pushing the total to $82.2 million, followed by another $3.42 million jump in 1919. The growth in valuations increased city revenue without a tax increase.[50]

The magnitude of Fort Worth's post-1914 advance was clearly displayed in other statistics, especially those of 1919 that reflected the full effect of the war years. In 1919, bank deposits climbed to $85 million and bank clearings to $900.1 million, both records. Building permits reached $18.7 million, the largest of any Texas city. Fort Worth remained the Southwest's grain center, boasting elevator space for 4.26 million bushels and a daily milling capacity of 2,200 barrels for both flour and corn, as well as a rail infrastructure with ten trunk lines and seventeen outlets, plus a beltline serving the stockyards and two Interurbans. The railroads employed 5,000 and paid $636,000 in wages each month, while the $116 million local livestock industry added a monthly payroll of $619,000 for another 5,000 workers. In addition, some 200 assorted factories employed 10,964 with a monthly payroll of $1.3 million. Taken in total, Fort Worth's annual production reached $450 million. The new oil industry's contribution grew larger as North Texas fields increased daily production by 1919 to $700,000, much of which flowed into Fort Worth's eight oil refineries processing 54,500 barrels (with another four refineries under construction). The refineries were part of a conglomerate that included 500 oil companies and fifty-two oil field supply houses that, along with packinghouses and railroads, made Fort Worth a major player in three of Texas's top four industries, missing out only in lumber. In 1919, oil was already Texas's largest industry in value of production, accounting for 24.2 percent of the total and in value added, with 16.4 percent of the state total. Oil ranked third in number of wage earners (automobiles and lumber employed more). Slaughterhouses remained important but slipped to second in value of production (12.5 percent) and fourth in value added (6.2 percent).[51]

The war years accomplished what previous decades had not, driving Fort Worth's manufacturing output above that of its eastern neighbor. That outcome cannot be seen in a city-to-city comparison because Dallas in 1919 remained superior in all manufacturing categories. However, the statistics show that Tarrant County exceeded Dallas County in wage earners, wages, value of products, and value added, despite having 48 percent fewer companies. The location outside city limits of much of Fort Worth's manufacturing, especially large establishments like Swift and Armour, Chevrolet, Texas Motorcar Company, and Southern Tire Company, created the radical difference between city and county statistics (see table 8.2).[52]

Tarrant County not only bested Dallas County but also the other two metropolitan counties, Harris (Houston) and Bexar (San Antonio). Tarrant County trailed both Houston and Bexar in number of factories (as it did Dallas) and had fewer wage earners than Houston, but it had the greatest value of production, exceeding that of Harris by 48 percent and Bexar by a whopping 319 percent (see table 8.3).

Tarrant County not only led Texas in value added by manufacturers but also led all counties south of Kansas City in production value. Fort Worth's dominance was all the more remarkable because it did not come as a result of declines elsewhere. Dallas's value of production, $116.2 million, or $39.1 million less than that of Tarrant County, was the second largest in the region southwest of Kansas City. Houston trailed close behind with $105.8 million. The statistics lent enormous credence to claims that Fort Worth was becoming the manufacturing center of the Southwest.[53]

TABLE 8.2. Comparison of 1919 manufacturing statistics at the city and county levels for Fort Worth and Dallas

	Tarrant County	Fort Worth	Dallas County	Dallas (city)
Establishments	257	229	492	457
Wage earners	9,196	4,452	8,708	7,913
Wages ($)	10,563,246	—	8,752,026	—
Value ($) of products	155,299,159	38,160,092	116,160,150	$93,649,654
Value ($) added	33,706,354	12,502,858	32,671,541	$28,146,461

Sources: Fourteenth Census of the United States, vol. 9 (Washington, D.C.: Government Printing Office, 1922), pp. 1449–50, 1460–61; Robert Harris Talbert, Cowtown Metropolis: Case Study of a City's Growth and Structure (Fort Worth: Leo Potishman Foundation, Texas Christian University, 1956), p. 126.

TABLE 8.3. Comparison of manufacturing in Fort Worth, Houston, and San Antonio and each of their counties, 1919

	City	County	Percent difference county over city
	Fort Worth	Tarrant County	
Factories	229	257	12.2
Wage earners	4,452	9,196	106.6
Value ($) of products	38,160,000	155,299,159	228.5
	Houston	Harris County	
Factories	383	422	10.2
Wage earners	9,860	11,411	15.7
Value ($) of products	86,874,000	104,776,719	20.6
	San Antonio	Bexar County	
Factories	318	328	3.1
Wage earners	6,614	6,860	3.7
Value ($) of products	$35,456,000	37,045,244	4.5

Source: Fourteenth Census of the United States, vol. 9 (Washington, D.C.: Government Printing Office, 1922), pp. 1463, 1449–50.

The effect was muted somewhat due to Fort Worth's population rising more slowly than its economy. In the 1920 U.S. census, Fort Worth broke the symbolically important 100,000 barrier with a population of 106,482, an increase of 33,170 or 45.2 percent since 1910. This was substantial but ranked Fort Worth only as the nation's sixty-fifth largest city, with slower growth than the rest of urban Texas. All three other large cities and their counties experienced superior increases. The city of Dallas increased 72.6 percent, adding 66,872 to reach 158,976, the state's second largest population. San Antonio retained its position as Texas's largest city with an increase of 67.1 percent, and Houston added 75.5 percent to remain third. Many blamed Fort Worth's poor showing on its failure to annex suburbs after 1910, arguing that aggressive expansion would have pushed the population past Houston and almost equal to Dallas. That argument would have been true only if Fort Worth had annexed all of Tarrant County (an impossible scenario), which would have made its population 152,800, still smaller than the city of Dallas's 158,976. A better argument would have been that labor shortages had slowed Fort Worth's growth, and that if a workforce sufficient to meet demands had been available, these population differences might well have diminished or disappeared. Paddock admitted that Dallas retained its superiority in population but argued that Fort Worth was the leading city in North Texas thanks to its larger bank clearings and rail traffic—measures that he called the two best indicators of business activity. He also claimed that the rivalry had benefited both cities by making both more active.[54]

Despite slower than expected population growth, Fort Worth clearly turned a significant corner during the period from 1915 to 1918. In 1880, a serious effort began to put Fort Worth on the economic map. That effort first manifested itself in railroad expansion, succeeding to the extent that Fort Worth became the Southwest's rail center. By the end of the 1880s, many realized that more than railroads was required, that factories were needed. This realization suffered through the stagnation of the 1890s before finding expression in 1903. Swift and Armour were so important that Fort Worth rested on its laurels, neglecting the battle for new industry until boosters recovered their zeal just in time to attract a large military complex as World War I stimulated existing industries and oil created a whole new industry. This confluence of economic developments brought Fort Worth closer than ever to its dreams.

CONCLUSION

$\mathbf{B}$etween 1880 and 1918, Fort Worth transformed itself from town to city. To some extent, that transition was part of a national phenomenon, identified by Nell Irvin Painter, in which the United States underwent fundamental changes between 1877 and 1919 from a rural, agricultural nation to an industrial society dominated by great cities.[1] Fort Worth's experience, while part of that larger trend, was unique in its degree. According to decennial reports, Fort Worth's population rose from 6,663 in 1880 to 106,482 in 1920, an increase of 99,819 or 1,498 percent, a remarkable rate of growth. The largest percentage rise for any decade, 246.3 percent, occurred between 1880 and 1890 but amounted to an absolute increase of only 16,413. The decade showing the smallest population gain, 15.7 percent, was the 1890s, when the national depression hit Fort Worth harder and longer than Texas's other large cities. The aberration of the nineties was followed by the largest percentage increase of any large American city, 174.7 percent, which added 46,624 residents to Fort Worth between 1900 and 1910. Although the rate slowed in the decade between 1910 and 1920, Fort Worth still registered a healthy 45.2 percent rise, a population increase of 33,170. In fact, 80 percent of Fort Worth's growth from 1880 to 1920 occurred during the twenty-year period from 1900 to 1920 (see table C.1).

Fort Worth's population increases were clearly linked to its economic development. The remarkable growth of the 1880s coincided with Fort Worth's rise to become the Southwest's railroad center, followed by smaller increases during the depression of the 1890s. In 1903, the Swift and Armour packinghouses provided the second major industrial surge, turning Fort Worth into the nation's third largest livestock market and spurring

206

TABLE C.1.   Fort Worth population increases, 1880–1920

	Population	Increase in population over previous decade	Percent increase over previous decade
1880	6,663	—	—
1890	23,076	16,413	246.3
1900	26,688	3,612	15.7
1910	73,312	46,624	174.7
1920	106,482	33,170	45.2

Source: *Fort Worth Star Telegram*, August 27, 1920, p. 9.

the city's largest population spike. After initial sluggishness, the Fort Worth economy closed the 1910–1920 decade with unprecedented production statistics, thanks to multifaceted stimuli from World War I, the establishment of large military bases, and the oil fields in nearby Ranger, Texas. These factors added 33,170 residents, more than Fort Worth's total population in 1900.

Financial statistics also reveal the importance of the post-1914 period. The packinghouse effect appears clearly in comparisons between 1898 and 1905, when bank resources increased 195.3 percent (from $3.2 million to $9.5 million) and bank deposits rose 198.9 percent (from $2.9 million to $8.6 million). Both measures represented average annual rates of more than 28 percent. However, from 1905 to 1908, bank resources increased only 29.4 percent (averaging 9.8 percent per year), deposits increased only 3.8 percent (averaging 1.3 percent per year), and clearings actually declined by just over 4 percent. The slower rate of economic growth from 1905 to 1908 reflects a coasting effect, when Fort Worth leaders stopped promoting new industry after the immense success of 1903. Double-digit annual increases returned between 1908 and 1918: bank resources rose 475.5 percent (averaging 47.6 percent per year), deposits rose 393.5 percent (averaging 39.4 percent per year), and clearings rose 172.8 percent (averaging 17.3 percent per year). Large increases in the financial growth rate from 1908 to 1918 are retained even when statistics from 1898 to 1905 and 1905 to 1908 are combined to reduce the impact of slower growth from 1905 to 1908. In this analysis, the decade after 1908 still reflects average annual increases that are 40 percent larger than those of the decade from 1898 to 1908 (see table C.2). Clearly, Fort Worth's largest economic

TABLE C.2. Comparison of Fort Worth bank statistics ($), 1898, 1905, 1908, 1918, and 1920

	1898	1905	1908	1918	1920
Assets	3,200,000	9,450,000	12,226,841	59,361,100	69,826,920
Deposits	2,888,256	8,634,042	8,962,093	44,224,300	73,500,000
Clearings	—	265,506,187	254,475,760	694,451,202	891,000,000

Sources: Fort Worth Star Telegram, February 25, 1919, p. 1; October 30, 1949, Commerce Section, p. 18; Fort Worth City Directory, 1920 (Dallas: R. L. Polk, 1920), pp. 2–3; Fort Worth in Brief (n.p.: n.d.).

TABLE C.3. Fort Worth annual bank clearings ($), 1908–1919

	Funds cleared		Funds cleared		Funds cleared
1908	254,745,760	1912	386,933,676	1916	487,328,982
1909	337,782,874	1913	418,619,829	1917	668,322,418
1910	342,899,564	1914	356,453,387	1918	694,451,202
1911	349,983,382	1915	435,289,425	1919	900,098,820

Sources: Fort Worth Star Telegram, February 25, 1919, p. 1; October 30, 1949, Commerce Section, p. 18; Fort Worth Record, January 3, 1908, p. 1; Fort Worth in Brief (n.p.: n.d.).

advances occurred after 1908, well after the packinghouse effect had been established.

Moreover, most of the growth after 1908 actually occurred after 1914. Bank clearings increased $439.7 million between 1908 and 1918. But of that increase, only $101.7 million or 23.1 percent (an average of 3.9 percent per year) came between 1908 and 1914. During those six years, Fort Worth reeled under the effects of lost initiative, a national banking crisis, and the initial depressive effect of war in Europe. The slump at the war's outbreak can be clearly seen in the drop in bank clearings from $418.6 million in 1913 to $356.5 million in 1914. In contrast, dramatic growth reappeared during the four years from 1914 to 1918. Total clearings in 1918 were $338 million, above 1914, a 76.9 percent rise, or an average of 19.2 percent per year. In 1919 clearings would soar to $900 million, a 29.6 percent rise in just one year (see table C.3).

The Fort Worth experience paralleled that of Texas's statewide manufacturing growth. From 1914 to 1919, Texas experienced average annual increases of 8.7 percent in number of persons engaged in manufacturing, 21.3 percent in capital invested, and 35.3 percent in value added. These were all higher than the corresponding increases from 1904 to 1914, although the increase in establishments was higher in 1904–1914—an average rise of 6.1 percent compared with 2.6 percent in 1914–1919 (see tables C.4, C.5, and C.6). The similarity between Fort Worth and statewide figures suggests the pervasiveness of stronger commercial growth during 1914 to 1918 and clearly demonstrates that more was at work than simply a packinghouse effect peculiar to Fort Worth. The relative primacy of the

TABLE C.4. Texas manufacturing statistics, 1899, 1904, 1914, and 1919

	1919	1914	1904	1899
No. of establishments	5,724	5,084	3,158	3,107
Persons employed	130,931	91,114	57,892	—
Capital ($)	585,776,451	283,543,820	115,664,871	63,655,616
Value ($) added	298,824,898	108,135,042	58,924,759	38,506,130

Source: Fourteenth Census of the United States, vol. 9 (Washington, D.C.: Government Printing Office, 1922), p. 1448.

TABLE C.5. Percentage increases in Texas manufacturing for selected time spans

	1914–1919	1904–1914	1899–1904
No. of establishments	12.9	61.0	1.6
Persons employed	43.7	57.4	—
Capital	106.6	145.1	81.7
Value added	176.3	83.5	53.0

Source: Fourteenth Census of the United States, vol. 9 (Washington, D.C.: Government Printing Office, 1922), p. 1448.

TABLE C.6. Average per annum percentage increase in Texas manufacturing, 1904–1914 and 1914–1919

	1904–1914	1914–1919
No. of establishments	6.1	2.6
Persons employed	5.7	8.7
Capital	14.5	21.3
Value added	8.4	35.3

Source: Fourteenth Census of the United States, vol. 9 (Washington, D.C.: Government Printing Office, 1922), p. 1448.

1914–19 period's industrialization also becomes clear in statistics showing that the largest percentage production increase occurred not in
packinghouses but in foundry and machine shop products, which grew
932.3 percent.[2]

Historians have not recognized the importance of the post-1914 period,
when Fort Worth's economy reached its highest relative plateau, producing more than Dallas or any other Southwestern city. They have long ac-
knowledged linkages between Fort Worth's growth and its commerce,
specifically the railroads and packinghouses. In 1922, Fort Worth's railroads employed 5,700 workers and its packinghouses employed 5,200,
making them the two largest industrial groups southwest of Kansas City.
But the railroads and the packinghouses had been around a long time
without creating production levels to rival those of Dallas, a condition
scholars have failed to acknowledge. For example, Jill Jackson and Leta
Scheon cited railroads as the most important stimulus driving Fort Worth
development until World War II, but railroads, while continuing to play
important roles, no longer were the central economic force after the nineteenth century. A few historians and others have touched on the significance of World War I. Schoen credited military training facilities for providing a needed lift; Robert Talbert recognized that World War I expanded
Fort Worth's meatpacking industry as well as its flour milling and grain
storage facilities; and Paddock paid passing notice to the military's impact
on economic growth. However, none devoted more than a few pages to
the discussion or realized the degree of the war's contribution.[3]

Scholars with wider perspectives have developed themes congruent
with the Fort Worth experience. Walter Buenger's argument that Northeast Texas underwent important economic changes after 1914 is particularly applicable, but many others have developed closely related points.
Richard Dyskatra's emphasis on boosterism and interurban competition,
Lawrence Larsen's capitalistic imperatives behind urbanization, and
Timothy Mahoney's expansion of these ideas constitute an obvious but
not totally inclusive list. In addition, the connection between Fort Worth's
economic flowering and the military presence carries more than a passing
resemblance to Patricia Nelson Limerick's focus on the role of the federal
government in development of the U.S. West.[4]

Of course, more happened than just the building of factories. Fort Worth
made important progress in developing a local transportation network
of bridges and streets, but its most significant civic advance occurred in

waterworks development. Long-term resolution of the extended disaster that constituted the Fort Worth Water Department began to take shape in 1911, when work began on Lake Worth. Completion of the reservoir in 1913 still left quality and financial issues that were resolved only after the system achieved financial stability following 1916. Fort Worth also took a giant step toward municipal respectability by closing Hell's Half Acre. The vice district had endured since the end of the Civil War, despite periodic reform initiatives, thanks largely to a widely-assumed connection between the Acre and general economic health. Other arguments also contributed to the Acre's longevity, including supposed advantages in isolation and control derived from concentration of vice. After 1914, the national prohibition movement stimulated the local reform faction, but the salient force bringing closure arrived with the soldiers at Camp Bowie and the airfields. The military added real teeth to law enforcement and exerted economic leverage through threats of relocation to force meaningful changes in attitude and practice. This effort was strengthened by patriotic fervor that identified dissoluteness as inimical to the war effort. Together, the forces of control made possible the passage of state legislation that assured the Acre could not continue. Of course, prostitution and gambling did not end. A 1920 grand jury report suggested that police payoffs lay behind "appalling conditions" involving prostitution in Irish Town and "Little Mexico." This did not detract from what was accomplished in 1918. The closing of the Acre was not so much about ending vice as it was about ending the community's official toleration, if not sanction, of illegality in support of general commerce, a significant step on the road to modern city status.[5]

None of the changes would have happened without the work of some dedicated residents. Citizen involvement played defining roles in making Fort Worth a railroad giant, a major meatpacker, and a World War I training center. Flexibility was critical to that process. The ability of boosters to recognize in the late 1880s that Fort Worth needed more than railroads, and to realize after 1914 that the packinghouse effect had limitations, made a multidimensional economy possible. Had that not happened, Fort Worth would have been a much different place. William C. Burton, an early settler, recalled that in 1876, Fort Worthians had used a large rope to pull the city's first locomotive across an unfinished, wobbly bridge, an apt metaphor for the effort of many boosters who repeatedly pulled Fort Worth forward.[6]

Fort Worth's military connections during World War I not only had palpable economic impacts at the time but also hinted at an important legacy for later development. Rational supposition suggests that the foundations laid in 1917 contributed significantly to the development of Fort Worth's vast defense and aerospace industry. This process accelerated during World War II with construction of the Consolidated Vultee Aircraft plant, a major reason that Fort Worth firms won 22 percent of Texas's World War II defense contracts, compared with just 12 percent for Dallas. This effect continues into the twenty-first century. The Fort Worth-Dallas region received $26.4 billion in military contracts between 1998 and 2002, the third largest regional total in the nation, behind only Washington-Baltimore and Los Angeles-Riverside-Orange County. Many of those dollars fund aircraft manufacturing. In 2002, Texas boasted 184,000 aerospace jobs (second only to California), of which 62,088, or 33.7 percent, were in Fort Worth. The link between Fort Worth's World War I experience and defense spending is suggestive but needs study.[7]

In a very real sense, Fort Worth became a city between 1914 and 1918. The post-1914 period did not solely determine Fort Worth's standing in the twenty-first century; Fort Worth would experience many other triumphs and tribulations over the next ninety years. Still, the evidence suggests that between 1914 and 1918, Fort Worth became a very different place. That transformation had begun forty years earlier, when men like Paddock and Smith committed their energy and much of their wealth to building more than a county seat and more than just an overgrown country town. That they succeeded depended in equal measures on work, luck, and guile. Had any element been lacking, the outcome would have been far less impressive and far removed from the metropolitan area that developed where an outpost once stood.

EPILOGUE

Fort Worth has an unpaid debt. Boardman Buckley Paddock and John Peter Smith were Fort Worth's two biggest boosters. Both arrived when Fort Worth was still a raw village, Smith in the early 1850s, Paddock in the early 1870s, and both devoted much of their energy, money, and time to civic promotion. Smith's memory is preserved in dramatic fashion thanks to John Peter Smith Hospital and a downtown statue. In contrast, Paddock is largely forgotten and uncredited. Only the North Main Street Bridge and a small park adjacent to the county courthouse carry his name, neither widely known. The difference in levels of recognition probably stems from Smith's donation of the land for the hospital and his untimely demise in 1901 while Paddock lived into old age, dying in 1922. Paddock's contemporaries recognized his worth. In 1918 he was named the city's most distinguished man, and in 1922 the publishers of *History of Texas: Fort Worth and the Texas Northwest* dedicated all four volumes to him, stating, "No Citizen of Athens in Her Greatness Surpassed Him in Loyalty and Devotion to City and State." It is time that Fort Worth honor Paddock in a manner commensurate with his contributions.

Notes

Introduction

1. Hendricks, "Cattle and Oil," p. 3; Schoen, "Immigrant to Capitalist," p. 21; Thompson, "Factors Contributing to the Growth of Fort Worth," pp. 56–68, 71–76. Fort Worth's geography is some fifty miles east of the 98th meridian cited as a natural barrier to progress. See Webb, *The Great Plains*.

2. *Fort Worth Gazette*, May 29, 1887, p. 3.

3. Craig, *Fort Worth Stockyards and National Historic District*, pp. 2–3; Hooks, "Struggle for Dominance," pp. 3–4.

4. Talbert, *Cowtown-Metropolis*, p. 117; Hooks, "Struggle for Dominance," pp. 1, 9–11, 90, 139, 156, 184, 243–44, 248.

5. Hooks, "Struggle for Dominance," p. 2. For a historiographical discussion see Harold Rich, "Beyond Outpost," pp. 3–21.

6. Selcer, *Hell's Half Acre*, pp. 110–11, 269–79; Wilson, "Moments That Changed Our City" (2004), p. 61.

7. Larsen, *Urban West at the End of the Frontier*, pp. 116–17.

8. Cronon, *Nature's Metropolis*, p. 224; Rich, "Beyond Outpost," pp. 3–21.

9. *Fort Worth Gazette*, August 16, 1887, p. 2; March 30, 1890, p. 7; June 28, 1890, p. 1; Schoen, "Immigrant to Capitalist," p. 22; Hooks, "Struggle for Dominance," pp. 37–81; Boorstin, *The Americans*, p. 3.

10. Knight, *Outpost on the Trinity*, p. 214; Roark, *Fort Worth Then and Now*, pp. 2–9; Wilson, "Moments That Changed Our City" (2004), pp. 54–61; Wilson, "Moments That Changed Our City" (2005), pp. 36–41; Talbert, *Cowtown Metropolis*, pp. 22–23; Schoen, "Immigrant to Capitalist," p. 22.

11. Patricia Nelson Limerick, *The Legacy of Conquest*, pp. 27–30; Wilson, "Moments That Changed Our City," p. 61.

Chapter 1

1. Baker and Cagle, *Indians in the History of Tarrant County*, p. 23; *Fort Worth Star Telegram*, March 23, 1933, p. 3; *Fort Worth Star Telegram*, April 23, 1931; *Fort Worth Democrat*, February 22, 1873, p. 2; July 7, 1880, p. 4; August 20, 1880, p. 1; August 27, 1880, p. 1; January 4, 1881, p. 2; *General Directory of the City of Fort Worth for 1882*, pp. 154–55; *Fort Worth Democrat*, August 20, 1880, p. 1; September 23, 1881, p. 3; April 10, 1881, p. 4; March 5, 1881, p. 4; April 26, 1881, p. 4; March 29, 1881, p. 4; April 2, 1881, p. 3; *Fort Worth Gazette*, November 4, 1883, p. 6; February 28, 1886, p. 8; June 26, 1886, p. 8.

2. *Fort Worth Democrat*, April 20, 1881, p. 4, April 24, 1881, p. 3; April 27, 1881, p. 4; April 26, 1881, p. 4.

3. *Fort Worth Democrat*, July 12, 1881, p. 3; July 9, 1881, p. 4; December 21, 1881, p. 4.

4. *Fort Worth Gazette*, July 7, 1883, p. 4; July 11, 1883, p. 4; September 19, 1883, p. 4; November 4, 1883, p. 6; Rich, "Twenty-Five Years of Struggle and Progress," pp. 90–92; *Fort Worth Democrat*, April 18, 1879, p. 4; April 25, 1879 p. 4; April 26, 1879, p. 4; April 27, 1879, p. 4; April 28, 1897, p. 4; April 29, 1879, p. 4; April 2, 1881, p. 3; April 10, 1881, p. 4.

5. *Fort Worth Democrat*, February 5, 1881, p. 4; February 8, 1881, p. 4; February 11, 1881, p. 4; February 15, 1881, p. 4; February 16, 1881, p. 4; March 3, 1881, p. 4; March 30, 1881, p. 4; May 6, 1881, p. 4.

6. *Fort Worth Democrat*, January 8, 1880, p. 4; January 9, 1880, p. 4; March 17, 1881, p. 4; March 18, 1881, p. 4; March 19, 1881, p. 4, March 20, 1881, pp. 3–4. Many African Americans fought to overcome the overt racism and to improve their community. In 1881, two African American men petitioned the city council for appointment as Third Ward special policemen to deal with shootings and other disturbances detracting from church attendance. The aldermen tabled the motion. Dr. Trabue, a medical doctor who came to Fort Worth as a slave but turned to medicine, was cited by the *Democrat* as "a shining example of what hard work could do for his race." See *Fort Worth Democrat*, November 16, 1881, p. 4; April 20, 1882, p. 4; September 9, 1881, p. 4; March 15, 1882, p. 4.

7. *Fort Worth Democrat*, July 29, 1880, p. 4; August 16, 1880, p. 4; October 28, 1880, p. 2; December 2, 1879, p. 2; December 3, 1879, p. 3; Knight, *Outpost on the Trinity*, pp. 56–58; Duncan, "Paddock, Buckley Burton." Paddock's given names appear in various forms, but he is listed as Boardman Buckley Paddock in "Family Register of Boardman Paddock," drafted by Aaron Rolfe on June 1, 1854, in Paddock Papers, Special Collections of the University of Texas at Arlington Library.

8. Lane, "History of the Fort Worth Theater," pp. 1–2, 21–23; *Fort Worth Democrat*, March 15, 1881, p. 3; Shannon, "Theater in Fort Worth," pp. 2–3; *Fort Worth Gazette*, January 3, 1883, p. 4.

9. *Fort Worth Gazette*, January 5, 1883, p. 5; August 4, 1883, p. 4; September 28, 1883, p. 6; December 3, 1883, p. 6.

10. Garrett and Lake, eds. *Down Historic Trails*, pp. 29–30; Arnold, *History of the Fort Worth Legal Community*, pp. 17–23; *Fort Worth Democrat*, August 5, 1881, p. 4; September 18, 1881, p. 2; December 5, 1881, p. 4; *Fort Worth Gazette*, September 2, 1883, p. 8.

11. *Fort Worth City Council Minutes*, vol. B, August 2, 1881; *Fort Worth Democrat*, June 8, 1881, p. 1; August 27, 1881, p. 4; *General Directory*, 1882, p. 6; *Fort Worth Democrat*, January 2, 1880, p. 4; December 10, 1881, p. 4.

12. *Fort Worth Democrat*, September 3, 1881, p. 4; January 2, 1880, p. 4; January 4, 1880, p. 3; January 28, 1880, p. 3; November 24, 1880, p. 4; December 18, 1880, p. 4.

13. *Fort Worth Democrat*, October 28, 1880, p. 2; July 8, 1881, p. 2; April 12, 1882, p. 2; *Tenth Census*, pp. 77, 79, 342, 348, 424, 455, 1534.

14. *Fort Worth Democrat*, July 8, 1881, p. 2; September 3, 1881, p. 4; June 3, 1882, p. 4; *Tenth Census*, p. 1534; *City Directory*, 1882, pp. 6–9; Hammond, *History of the Municipal Departments*.

15. *Tenth Census*, pp. 1017, 1020; *Fort Worth Democrat*, June 3, 1882, p. 4.

16. Melosi, *Garbage in the Cities*, p. 16.

17. The first railroad in 1876, the Texas and Pacific, running between Dallas and Fort Worth, was hastily laid on inadequate foundations. Shortly after its completion a flood wiped out a bridge over Village Creek and the next locomotive fell into the creek. In 1934, the Waples Platter farm dug a channel into the creek bed and found the locomotive still there after fifty-eight years. See *Fort Worth Star Telegram*, September 28, 1934, p. 8.

18. *Fort Worth Record*, July 19, 1899, p. 5.

19. Talbert, *Cowtown Metropolis*, pp. 121–22.

20. Van Zandt, *Force Without Fanfare*, pp. 165–69; *Fort Worth Democrat*, January 2, 1880, p. 4; July 14, 1880, p. 3; September 23, 1881, p. 3; September 25, 1880, p. 4; February 8, 1880, p. 4; *City Directory*, 1882, pp. 6–9; *Fort Worth Gazette*, January 3, 1883, p. 8; January 24, 1884, p. 6; August 14, 1883, p. 6; November 3, 1883, p. 6; *Fort Worth Democrat*, April 5, 1882, p. 4; *Fort Worth Record*, August 27, 1905, p. 7; *The Bohemian* 1 (November, 1899), p. 57; Knight, *Outpost on the Trinity*, p. 139.

21. *Fort Worth Gazette*, August 14, 1883, p. 6; November 3, 1883, p. 6; *Fort Worth Star Telegram*, July 15, 1936, n.p.

22. *Fort Worth Democrat*, September 21, 1880, p. 4; September 22, 1880, p. 4; September 24, 1880, p. 3; September 28, 1880, p. 4; October 5, 1880, p. 2; *General Directory*, 1882, pp. 6–9.

23. *Fort Worth Democrat*, January 20, 1881, p. 4; January 21, 1881, p. 4; January 22, 1881, p. 4; January 25, 1881, p. 4.

24. White, "Information, Markets, and Corruptions," pp. 23, 36, 43.

25. *Fort Worth Democrat*, April 2, 1881, p. 4; April 5, 1881, p. 4; April 9, 1881, p. 4; May 8, 1881, p. 4; May 10, 1881, p. 3; June 10, 1881, p. 4; April 30, 1881, p. 2.

26. *Fort Worth Democrat*, June 24, 1881, p. 4; June 25, 1881, p. 4, June 26, 1881, p. 4; November 30, 1881, p. 4; December 23, 1881, p. 4; July 7, 1881, p. 2; July 12, 1881, p. 4; July 14, 1881, p. 4; June 27, 1882, p. 4; August 22, 1881, p. 4.

27. *Fort Worth Democrat*, February 11, 1882, p. 4; July 11, 1882, p. 4; May 3, 1881, p. 3; May 28, 1881, p. 1; April 9, 1881, p. 3; May 8, 1881, p. 4.

28. *Fort Worth Democrat*, September 24, 1880, p. 2; October 1, 1880, p. 3; September 23, 1881, p. 2; May 1, 1881, p. 3.

29. *Fort Worth Democrat*, May 10, 1881, p. 3; May 13, 1881, p. 4; January 5, 1882, p. 4; February 7, 1882, p. 4; *Fort Worth Gazette*, January 3, 1883, p. 6.

30. *Fort Worth Democrat*, September 23, 1881, p. 3; September 28, 1881, p. 3; April 25, 1882, p. 4; *Fort Worth Gazette*, July 11, 1883, p. 4; July 25, 1883, p. 8; August 1, 1883, p. 6; February 25, 1884. p. 6.

31. *Fort Worth Democrat*, May 6, 1881, p. 3; September 21, 1881, p. 2; September 23, 1881, p. 3; May 24, 1881, p. 3; July 7, 1881, p. 1; November 22, 1881, p. 4; August 8, 1881, p. 4; *Fort Worth Gazette*, January 3, 1883, p. 6.

32. *Tenth Census*, p. 1186; Ward, "Fort Worth, A Cowtown Success," p. 86, *Fort Worth Democrat*, July 17, 1880, p. 4; January 2, 1880, p. 3; August 8, 1881, p. 4; September 21, 1881, p. 2; October 30, 1881, p. 3.

33. *Fort Worth Gazette*, August 11, 1883, p. 4; August 15, 1883, p. 8; August 17, 1883, p. 4; Hendricks, "Cattle and Oil," pp. 15–16; Pate, *Livestock Legacy*, pp. 13–14.

34. Hendricks, "Cattle and Oil," pp. 16–18; *Research Data*, pp. 549–51; *Fort Worth Gazette*, March 31, 1884, p. 6; Paddock, ed., *History of Texas*, pp. 657–59.

35. *Fort Worth Democrat*, January 4, 1880, p. 1; July 13, 1880, p. 2; January 12, 1880, p. 4; January 24, 1880, p. 4; September 24, 1880, p. 2; July 7, 1880, p. 4.

36. *Fort Worth Democrat*, September 23, 1881, p. 3; July 4, 1880, p. 4; July 11, 1880, p. 4; July 16, 1880, p. 4; July 20, 1880, p. 3; July 23, 1880, p. 4; September 22, 1880, p. 4; September 19, 1880, p. 1; March 23, 1881, p. 4; September 23, 1881, p. 3.

37. Smith, *Things I Remember*, p. 5; *Fort Worth Democrat*, April 16, 1881, p. 4; May 18, 1881, p. 4; July 10, 1881, p. 3; April 28, 1881, p. 4; May 4, 1881, p. 4; May 6, 1881, p. 4; June 11, 1881, p. 4; May 29, 1881, p. 3; August 6, 1881, p. 4; July 10, 1881, p. 3.

38. *Fort Worth Democrat*, June 16, 1881, p. 4; July 10, 1881, p. 3; August 20, 1881, p. 4; September 23, 1881, p. 4; September 28, 1881, p. 4; October 8, 1881, p. 4; *Fort Worth Gazette*, February 28, 1883, p. 5.

39. *Fort Worth Democrat*, October 9, 1881, p. 4; October 27, 1881, p. 4; October 28, 1881, p. 4; November 3, 1881, p. 4; December 10, 1881, p. 4; February 11, 1882, p. 2; February 22, 1882, p. 4; March 8, 1882, p. 4.

40. *Fort Worth Democrat*, May 24, 1882, p. 4; May 30, 1882, pp. 2, 4; Harkins, "A History of Municipal Government of Fort Worth," p. 21.

41. *Fort Worth Gazette*, February 28, 1883, p. 5; March 13, 1883, p. 5; September 10, 1883, p. 5; *Fort Worth Star Telegram*, February 4, 1945, sec. 1, p. 2; Knight; *Outpost on the Trinity*, pp. 141–42; Paddock, ed., *History of Texas*, pp. 623–24.

42. *Fort Worth Democrat*, February 4, 1882, p. 4; February 8, 1882, p. 4; February 11, 1882, p. 4; March 1, 1882, p. 4; January 2, 1882, p. 6; *Fort Worth Gazette*, January 2, 1883, p. 5; January 14, 1883 p. 5; January 16, 1883, p. 5; January 23, 1883, p. 6; January 25, 1883, p. 4; August 23, 1883, p. 8.

43. Blumberg and Gottlieb, *War on Waste*, pp. 6–8; Melosi, *Garbage in the Cities*, pp. 16–19, 41–42, 89, 166, 171.

44. *Fort Worth Democrat*, February 8, 1882, p. 4; February 25, 1882, p. 4; May 10, 1882, p. 4; April 30, 1882, p. 4; May 6, 1882, p. 4; May 11, 1882, p. 4; *Fort Worth Gazette*, March 28, 1883, p. 5; February 12, 1884, p. 6; September 25, 1883, p. 6.

45. *Fort Worth Gazette*, January 28, 1883, p. 5; July 7, 1883, p. 4; January 24, 1883, p. 4.

46. *Fort Worth Gazette*, January 3, 1883, p. 7; September 25, 1883, p. 6; December 13, 1883, p. 6; August 1, 1883, p. 1; December 3, 1883, p. 6; May 2, 1886, p. 3.

47. *Fort Worth Gazette*, January 18, 1883, p. 8; March 7, 1883, p. 5; Garrett and Luke, *Historic Trails*, pp. 6, 18–21.

48. *Fort Worth Gazette*, July 10, 1883, p. 4; September 28, 1883, p. 5; November 5, 1883, p. 6; *Fort Worth Democrat*, July 14, 1881, p. 3; Garrett and Luke, *Historic Trails*, pp. 6, 18–21.

49. *Fort Worth Gazette*, January 1, 1884, p. 6; January 20, 1884, p. 1; January 24, 1884, p. 6; January 30, 1884, p. 6; February 12, 1884, p. 6; February 25, 1884, p. 6; March 31, 1884, p. 6; July 7, 1883, p. 4; July 11, 1883, p. 4.

50. *Fort Worth Gazette*, January 3, 1883, p. 8; January 24, 1884, p. 6; August 14, 1883, p. 6; November 3, 1883, p. 6; *Fort Worth Democrat*, April 5, 1882, p. 4; *Fort Worth Record*, August 27, 1905, p. 7; *The Bohemian* 1 (November, 1899), p. 57; Knight, *Outpost on the Trinity*, p. 139.

Chapter 2

1. *Tenth Census*, p. 28; *Fourteenth Census*, vol. 2, p. 20.

2. *General Directory of the City of Fort Worth for 1885–1886*, pp. 44–46; Hammond, *History of the Municipal Departments*, pp. 267–69; Farman, *The Fort Worth Club*, p. 19; *Fort Worth Gazette*, October 16, 1885, p. 8; *Fort Worth Daily Mail*, November 10, 1885, p. 4.

3. *Fort Worth Gazette*, August 12, 1887, pp. 4–5; September 16, 1887, p. 1; June 26, 1886, p. 8; February 28, 1886, p.8; September 7, 1886, p. 8; November 20, 1886, p. 8; February 8, 1887, p. 1; February 9, 1887, p. 8; February 11, 1887, p. 8; March 17, 1887, p. 8; April 15, 1887, p. 8; December 1, 1887, p. 2; December 2, 1887, p. 2; October 11, 1886, p. 8; *New York Times*, December 25, 1890, p. 2; *Fort Worth Star Telegram*, May 16, 1962, n.p.

4. Rich, "Fort Worth Police, 1873–1897" pp. 43–60; Selcer, *Hell's Half Acre*, p. 83; Knight, *Outpost on the Trinity*, pp. 81–82. Various accounts list Courtright's year of birth from 1844 to 1848 and his birthplace in Iowa and Illinois. For more on the life of Courtright, see Stanley, *Longhair Jim Courtright*.

5. For the life of Timothy Courtright, see Stanley, *Two Gun Marshal*, p. 5; *Fort Worth Council Minutes*, vol. D, April 9, 1883; Shirley, *Heck Thomas Frontier Marshal*, pp. 28–29; Speer, *Portrait of a Lawman*, p. 31; *Fort Worth Democrat*, May 6, 1879, p. 4; April 20, 1881, p. 4.

6. For the importance of Courtright to Fort Worth Law Enforcement, see Rich, "Twenty-five Years of Struggle and Progress," pp. 20–60.

7. For a general history of the development of Fort Worth local government, see Knight, *Outpost on the Trinity;* Selcer, *Hell's Half Acre.*

8. Rich, "Fort Worth Police, 1873–1897," pp. 1–20.

9. Roberts, "Was Built by Mayor Day," p. 7; Selcer, *Hell's Half Acre,* p. 68; Rich, "Fort Worth Police, 1873–1897," pp. 1–20; *Fort Worth Democrat,* February 19, 1876, pp. 3–4, February 26, 1876, p. 3, April 8, 1876, p. 3; "Fort Worth City Council Minutes," vol. A, February 8, 1876; *Fort Worth Standard,* February 10, 1876, p. 4.

10. *Fort Worth Standard,* February 10, 1876, p. 4. The political aspect of Courtright's election in 1876 first appeared in Rich, "Strange Bedfellows," pp. 27–32.

11. *Fort Worth Democrat,* "The Pistol," December 18, 1875, p. 3; *Fort Worth Standard,* "Pistols and Police," December 23, 1875, p. 3; Swasey and Melton, *Directory of the City of Fort Worth,* pp. 51, 62.

12. *Fort Worth Democrat,* December 18, 1875, p. 3; December 25, 1875, p. 3; *Fort Worth Standard,* December 23, 1875, p. 3.

13. Roberts, "Mayor Day," *Fort Worth Telegram,* August 20, 1907, p. 8; Swasey and Melton, *City Directory,* p. 51.

14. Roberts, "Mayor Day," *Fort Worth Telegram,* August 20, 1907, p. 8.

15. *Fort Worth Democrat,* April 8, 1876, p. 3; *Fort Worth Standard,* November 18, 1875, p. 1.

16. Stanley, *Two Gun Marshal,* p. 226.

17. *Fort Worth Standard,* January 27, 1876, p. 3.

18. *Fort Worth Democrat,* "The Pistol," December 18, 1875, p. 3; December 25, 1875, p. 3.

19. *Fort Worth Democrat,* "The Pistol," December 18, 1875, p. 3; December 25, 1875, p. 3; *Fort Worth Standard,* "Pistols and Police," December 23, 1875, p.3.

20. Swasey and Melton, *City Directory,* pp. 49, 51, 55, 62, 67; *Fort Worth Democrat,* December 11, 1875, p. 1, January 15, 1876, p. 1; *Fort Worth Standard,* November 18, 1875, p. 1.

21. *Fort Worth Weekly Gazette,* July 11, 1889, p. 1; *New York Times,* June 27, 1890, p. 1; July 30, 1891, p. 1; *Fort Worth Gazette,* August 7, 1890, p. 1.

22. *New York Times,* August 22, 1885, p. 2; August 23, 1885, p. 1; August 25, 1885, p. 1; August 28, 1885, p. 2; October 9, 1885, p. 3; *Fort Worth Gazette,* November 29, 1888, p. 8.

23. *Fort Worth Gazette,* January 15, 1886, p. 8; August 18, 1886, 8; August 19, 1886, p. 8; August 20, 1886, p. 8; September 14, 1886, p. 8; September 16, 1886, p. 8; September 22, 1886, p. 8; *Fort Worth Daily Mail,* January 21, 1886, p. 2; Hammond, *History of Municipal Departments,* pp. 267–69.

24. *Fort Worth Gazette,* October 18, 1885, p. 5; January 15, 1886, p. 8; February 3, 1886, pp. 3–8; February 4, 1886, p. 3; October 18, 1885, p. 5; January 15, 1886, p. 8; June 23, 1886, p. 3; December 4, 1885, p. 8; August 18, 1886, p. 8; August 19, 1886, p. 8; August 20, 1886, p. 8; September 14, 1886, p. 8; September 22, 1886, p. 8; *Fort Worth City Council Minutes,* vol. E, April 25, 1886.

25. *Fort Worth Gazette,* August 21, 1889, pp. 1–2; September 14, 1889, p. 8.

26. *Fort Worth Gazette*, October 31, 1885, p. 8; December 4, 1885, p. 8; March 13, 1886, p. 8; Knight, *Outpost on the Trinity*, pp. 141–42; *Fort Worth Star Telegram*, February 4, 1945, section 1, p. 2; *Fort Worth Daily Mail*, January 21, 1886, p. 2.

27. *Fort Worth Gazette*, February 4, 1886, pp. 4, 8; February 10, 1886, p. 8; February 19, 1886, p. 8; February 23, 1886, p. 8; February 25, 1886, p. 3; February 26, 1886, pp. 2, 8; *Fort Worth Daily Mail*, February 24, 1886, p. 4.

28. *Fort Worth Gazette*, January 3, 1887, p. 8; March 2, 1887, p. 8; August 3, 1887, p. 8; August 4, 1887, p. 8; *Fort Worth Daily Mail*, December 16, 1885, p. 4.

29. *Fort Worth Gazette*, May 12, 1887, p. 8; July 6, 1887, p. 8; July 10, 1887, p. 8; November 2, 1887, p. 8; *Fort Worth Star Telegram*, March 27, 2002, p. 6B; Melosi, *Garbage in the Cities*, p. 241. Unfortunately, Melosi's study focused on the East and Midwest with little attention devoted to the South and West.

30. *Fort Worth Gazette*, October 13, 1885, p. 5; October 16, 1885, p. 8; December 3, 1885, p. 8; December 6, 1885, p. 8; December 25, 1885, p. 8; October 14, 1888, p. 8.

31. *Fort Worth Gazette*, October 7, 1885, p. 5; October 16, 1885, p. 5; January 10, 1888, p. 6; February 1, 1888, p. 8; June 5, 1888, p. 5; November 28, 1888, p. 8.

32. *Fort Worth Gazette*, October 22, 1885, p. 8; March 6, 1885, p. 8; January 27, 1886, p. 8.

33. *Fort Worth Gazette*, December 23, 1885, p. 8; August 1, 1886, p. 8; October 28, 1886, p. 1; May 6, 1887, p. 8; Paddock to wife, March 29, 1886, Paddock Papers, Box GA 194, Folder 8; W. W. H. Lawrence to Paddock, December 2, 1885, File 2F172, Letters 1865–1899, Buckley Burton Paddock Papers; W. B. Cunningham to Paddock, March 30, 1901, File 2F173, Letters 1901, Buckley Burton Paddock Papers; Paddock to L. E. Bromeisler, January 29, 1902, File 2F176, Letters 1900–1910, Buckley Burton Paddock Papers.

34. *Fort Worth Gazette*, April 14, 1886, p. 1; April 15, 1886, p. 2; May 7, 1886, p. 2; May 13, 1887, p. 8; May 16, 1887, p. 8; May 20, 1887, p. 2; *General Directory of the City of Fort Worth for 1888–1889*, pp. 1–3.

35. *Fort Worth Weekly Gazette*, July 25, 1889, p. 2; October 24, 1889, p. 8; *Fort Worth Gazette*, January 25, 1889, p. 5; July 21, 1889, p. 5.

36. *Fort Worth Gazette*, October 11, 1885, p. 5; July 16, 1886, p. 3; July 17, 1886, p. 1; July 18, 1886, p. 2; March 11, 1888, p. 2; *City Directory, 1888–1889*, pp. 1–3.

37. David, *History of the Haymarket Affair*, pp. 3–4, 12–13, 161.

38. *Fort Worth Gazette*, March 8, 1886, p. 1; March 13, 1886, p. 8; March 24, 1886, p. 8; April 14, 1886, p. 1; April 15, 1886, p. 2; *Fort Worth Daily Mail*, March 9, 1886, p. 5; March 17, 1886, p. 8; Painter, *Standing at Armageddon*, pp. 40–42; *New York Times*, April 7, 1886, p. 1.

39. *Fort Worth Gazette*, April 1, 1886, p. 3; April 2, 1886, p. 1; April 3, 1886, p. 3; *New York Times*, April 3, 1886, p. 1; Smith, *Things I Remember*, p. 8.

40. *Fort Worth Gazette*, March 10, 1886, p. 1; April 4, 1886, p. 1; April 5, 1886, p. 1; May 1, 1886, p. 8; January 18, 1887, p. 8; June 19, 1887, p. 5; *New York Times*, April 4, 1886, p. 1; Harkins, "History of Municipal Government," pp. 23–24. Ironically, when Luke Short mortally wounded Courtright less than a year later, Officer Fulford was one of the first on the scene.

41. *Fort Worth Gazette*, April 5, 1886, p. 1.

42. *New York Times*, April 3, 1886, p. 1; April 5, 1886, p. 1; April 7, 1886, p. 1; July 10, 1894, p. 2; *Fort Worth Gazette*, October 1, 1894, p. 6; April 7, 1886, p. 1; April 6, 1886, p. 1; April 9, 1886, pp. 1, 8; April 13, 1886, p. 8; May 4, 1886, p. 1; May 5, 1886, p. 1; May 12, 1886, p. 8; May 13, 1886, p. 1; June 13, 1886, p. 8; July 26, 1886, p. 8. Merriner, *Grafters and Goo Goos,* pp. 48–49. An interesting postscript: Martin Irons, the Tyler employee whose firing began the strike, was arrested in 1894 for attempted sexual assault of a six-year old girl occurring at his grocery on Main near Fourteenth Street. See *Fort Worth Gazette,* October 1, 1894, p. 6.

43. *Fort Worth Gazette*, October 1, 1894, p. 6; October 8, 1885, p. 8; December 9, 1885, p. 8; May 1, 1886, p. 8; March 22, 1887, p. 8; May 12, 1886, p. 8; July 26, 1886, p. 8; April 25, 1887, p. 8; May 10, 1887, p. 8; June 17, 1887, p. 8; August 15, 1887, p. 2; Licht, *Industrializing America*, p. 168.

44. *Fort Worth Gazette*, May 19, 1887, p. 2; True, "Development of the Cattle," pp. 10–12; Graham, "Investment Boom," pp. 431–32, 440–44.

45. *Fort Worth Gazette*, March 11, 1887, p. 2; May 19, 1887, p. 2; Wright, "Study of Ranching Activities," pp. 67–69; Graham, "Investment Boom," pp. 443–44; True, "Development of the Cattle Industry," pp. 10–12, 15, 19–20.

46. *Fort Worth Gazette*, January 4, 1887, p. 8; January 12, 1887, p. 2; May 19, 1887, p. 2; December 1, 1886, p. 8.

47. *Fort Worth Gazette*, January 12, 1887, p. 2; November 11, 1887, p. 2; December 4, 1887, p. 8; December 23, 1887, p. 8; December 24, 1887, p. 8; March 6, 1888, p. 8; Craig, *Fort Worth Stockyards*, pp. 18–19; *General City Directory, 1888–1889*, pp. 3–4. Cold Springs, named for actual springs, was an early landmark adjacent to the stockyards area known as a picnic popular gathering spot. Its appeal ended when the springs dried, and years later its location became a source of debate. See *Fort Worth Star Telegram,* June 10, 1935, p. 7, and November 19, 1935, p. 1.

48. *Fort Worth Gazette*, March 6, 1888, p. 8; February 23, 1890, p. 7; April 24, 1890, p. 7; September 30, 1891, p. 8; Craig, *Fort Worth Stockyards*, pp. 18–19; *General City Directory, 1888–1889*, pp. 3–4.

49. *Fort Worth Gazette*, September 4,1887, p. 4; January 9, 1888, p. 8; March 7, 1888, p. 8; March 28, 1888, p. 8; May 4, 1888, p. 8.

50. Brogdon, "Political, Economic, and Social Aspects," pp. 85–86; *Fort Worth Gazette*, January 22,1 890, p. 2; May 27, 1887, p. 5; October 28, 1887, p. 1; October 29, 1887, pp. 1, 8; *Fort Worth Daily Mail*, May 26, 1887, p. 1; Jackson, *Crabgrass Frontier,* pp. 114–15; *Fort Worth Star Telegram*, August 12, 1935, p. 3.

51. Odom, "The Cats are King," pp.1–9; *Fort Worth Gazette*, April 8, 1888, p. 5.

52. *Fort Worth Gazette*, January 5, 1887, p. 8; January 3, 1887, p. 2; April 29, 1888, p. 8; July 10, 1887, p. 8; October 29, 1887, p. 2; September 18, 1887, p. 8; September 19, 1887, p. 8; February 21, 1888, p. 8; March 7, 1888, p. 8; May 2, 1888, p. 8; May 5, 1888, p. 8; May 9, 1888, p. 8.

53. *Fort Worth Gazette*, May 3, 1888, p. 8.

54. *Fort Worth Gazette*, November 1, 1886, p. 2; August 3,1887, p. 8; August 21, 1887, p. 8; August 22, 1887, pp. 7, 8; August 25, 1887, p. 8; September 1, 1887, p. 8; September 7, 1887, p. 8; September 21, 1887, p. 8.

55. *Fort Worth Gazette*, December 8, 1887, p. 8; October 17, 1888, p. 5; October 18, 1888, p. 8; October 1, 1888, p. 8; November 8, 1887, p. 8; November 25, 1887, p. 4; November 15, 1887, p. 2.

56. *Fort Worth Gazette*, November 26, 1888, p. 2; March 18, 1893, p. 10; January 1, 1889, p. 14; August 3, 1889, p. 8; June 17, 1888, p. 8; October 15, 1888, p. 8; October 23, 1888, p. 8; *Fort Worth Weekly Gazette*, November 14, 1889, p. 2; January 1, 1889, p. 1; February 1, 1889, p. 2.

57. Smith, *The Capitalist*, pp. 9, 12–14, 24.

58. *Fort Worth Gazette*, April 23, 1887, p. 5; July 11, 1889, p. 8; May 25, 1887, p. 5.

59. *General City Directory, 1885–1886*, p. 8; Farman, *Fort Worth Club*, pp. 17–18; *Fort Worth Gazette*, May 25, 1887, pp. 2–3; March 18, 1887, p. 8; March 27, 1887, p. 8; November 25, 1887, p. 4; July 21, 1889, p. 5.

60. *Fort Worth Daily Mail*, January 12, 1886, p. 2; *Fort Worth Gazette*, March 18, 1887, p. 8.

61. Duncan, "Buckley Paddock," p. 258; *Fort Worth Gazette*, July 21, 1889, p. 5; July 23, 1889, p. 8; July 30, 1889, p. 8; August 1, 1889, p. 8; Paddock to wife, 1889, Paddock Papers, Box GA 194 Folder 13.

62. Farman, *Fort Worth Club*, pp. 17–18; *Fort Worth Gazette*, April 23, 1887, p. 5; May 25, 1887, pp. 1–3; November 25, 1887, p. 4; July 21, 1889, p. 5; July 11, 1889, p. 8; *Fort Worth Weekly Gazette*, January 1, 1889, p. 1; July 21, 1889, p. 5; Licht, *Industrializing America*, p. 110.

63. *Fort Worth Gazette*, January 31, 1889, p. 5; May 16, 1889, p. 4; January 15, 1889, p. 2; March 21, 1889, p. 4; April 18, 1889, p. 8; Allen, *Texas Spring Palace*, pp. 4–10; Charter of Texas Spring Palace, 1889, File 2F172, Letters 1865–1899, Buckley Burton Paddock Papers.

64. *Fort Worth Gazette*, January 15, 1889, p. 2; January 17, 1889, p. 5; January 18, 1889, p. 8; January 31, 1889, p. 5; February 9, 1889, p. 8; *New York Times*, January 19, 1889, p.; Allen, *Texas Spring Palace*, pp. 4–10.

65. *Fort Worth Weekly Gazette*, February 15, 1889, p. 2; March 7, 1889, p. 5; March 21, 1889, p. 4; March 22, 1889, p. 3; May 16, 1889, p. 2; *Fort Worth Gazette*, February 21, 1889, p. 5; Allen, *Texas Spring Palace*, pp. 4–10.

66. *New York Times*, May 30, 1889, p. 1; June 28, 1889, p. 1; *Fort Worth Weekly Gazette*, June 6, 1889, pp. 1–3, 7; May 2, 1889, p. 6; May 23, 1889, p. 4; July 4, 1889, p. 3; Contract between Texas Spring Palace and Elgin Factory Band Trust, 1889, File 2F172, Letters 1865–1899, Buckley Burton Paddock Papers.

67. *Fort Worth Weekly Gazette*, November 28, 1889, p. 8; December 26, 1889, p. 8; January 30, 1890, p. 4; February 13,1890, p. 4; September 30, 1891, p. 8.

Chapter 3

1. Paddock, *Central and Western Texas*, pp. 262–63, 267; Knight, *Outpost on the Trinity*, pp. 123–25; Pate, *Livestock Legacy*, pp. 21–23, 123–25. Fort Worth, as the most westward Texas city north of Austin, was the center of West Texas commerce, from which its merchants benefited.

2. *Fort Worth Democrat*, December 11, 1880, p. 2; *General Directory of Inhabitants, Manufacturing Establishments, Institutions, Business Firms, etc., in the City of Fort Worth, 1890*, pp. 1–3; Clarke, "The New South," pp. 538–39; "Fort Worth, Gateway to the Panhandle," pp. 6–13; *New York Times*, September 1, 1890, p. 4; *Twelfth Census*, vol. 3, pt. 1, pp. 41–42, 279–88; *Fort Worth Gazette*, November 19, 1890, p. 6.

3. *Fort Worth Gazette*, September 28, 1890, p. 3; February 20, 1890, p. 3; May 29, 1890, p. 4. Fort Worth began as an army fort. See Garret, *Fort Worth*.

4. *Fort Worth Gazette*, April 9, 1890, p. 8; Clarke, "The New South," p. 541.

5. *Fort Worth Gazette*, March 14, 1894, p. 8; January 1, 1895, p. 6; February 2, 1895, p. 6; March 28, 1896, p. 2; *New York Times*, March 14, 1894, p. 1; January 1, 1895, p. 5; December 7, 1894, p. 1; December 10, 1894, p. 1.

6. *Fort Worth Gazette*, January 11, 1889, p. 4; May 29, 1890, p. 4; September 28, 1890, p. 3; September 5, 1894, p. 6; April 10, 1892, p. 2.

7. *New York Times*, July 12, 1890, p. 1; July 15, 1890, p. 5; July 20, 1890, p. 5; December 23, 1890, p. 9; December 25, 1890, p. 2; December 27, 1890, p. 2; January 1, 1895, p. 5; *Fort Worth Gazette*, August 1, 1890, p. 2; August 3, 1890, p. 2; August 5, 1890, p. 1; August 13, 1890, p. 2; November 14, 1893, p. 6; January 1, 1895, p. 6; February 2, 1895, p. 6; March 28, 1896, p. 2; *City Council Minutes*, vol. L, August 5, 1890.

8. *Fort Worth Gazette*, September 27, 1893, p. 4; September 28, 1893, p. 4; October 4, 1892, p. 4.

9. *New York Times*, July 16, 1890, p. 5; July 17, 1890, p. 5; January 30, 1891, p. 5.

10. *New York Times*, April 4, 1891, p. 5; September 27, 1899, p. 5; November 20, 1899, p. 3; July 15, 1903, p. 3; July 16, 1903, p. 3; March 14, 1894, p. 1; *Fort Worth Record*, December 20, 1905, p. 2; January 7, 1906, p. 9; *Fort Worth Gazette*, March 14, 1894, p. 8.

11. Clarke, "The New South," pp. 540–43; "Fort Worth, Gateway to the Panhandle," p. 6; Brogdon, "Political, Economic, and Social Aspects," p. 63; Hammond, "History of the Municipal Departments," pp. 267–69; Dexter, *Fort Worth Trade Review's Second Annual Review*, p. 29, at Amon Carter Museum of Western Art, Fort Worth.

12. *General City Directory 1890*, pp. 297–98; "Fort Worth, Gateway to the Panhandle," pp. 7–13; *Fort Worth Gazette*, October 9, 1890, p. 8; April 21, 1891, p. 5; June 14, 1891, p. 8; September 4, 1890, p. 4; Clarke, "The New South," p. 544; Talbert, *Cowtown Metropolis*, pp. 120–22; *Twelfth Census*, vol. 8, p. 994.

13. *Fort Worth Gazette*, April 15, 1890, p. 8; May 29, 1890, p. 4; September 20, 1890, p. 2; May 21, 1891, p. 8; November 6, 1891, p. 3; December 8, 1892, p. 8; Clarke, "The New South," p. 542.

14. *Fort Worth Gazette*, April 12, 1891, p. 5; April 17, 1890, p. 8; March 18, 1893, p. 17; *New York Times*, September 5, 1890, p. 1; *Fort Worth Record*, September 29, 1916, p. 4; Paddock, *Fort Worth and the Texas Northwest*, pp. 657–59. For the history of the stockyards and packinghouses, see Pate, *Livestock Legacy*, and Pate, *North of the River*.

15. *Fort Worth Gazette*, June 15, 1888, p. 8; June 22, 1888, p. 8; June 5, 1888, p. 5; April 17, 1890, p. 8; June 24, 1890, p. 7; May 5, 1891, p. 3; March 18, 1893, p. 17; April

14, 1893, section 2, pp. 1–2; April 24, 1890, p. 7; *The Fort Worth Weekly Gazette*, April 18, 1889, p. 7; *Fort Worth Record*, March 8, 1904, p. 2; *Southern Mercury*, November 19, 1891, p. 5; *New York Times*, March 10, 1890, p. 5; December 31, 1890, p. 1; Hendricks, "Cattle and Oil," p. 19; Clarke, "The New South," p. 542; Brogdon, "Political, Economic, and Social Aspects," p. 74; Pate, *Livestock Legacy*, pp. 13–21.

16. *Fort Worth Gazette*, June 3, 1893, p. 5; June 27, 1893, p. 8; September 6, 1893, p. 6; December 4,1 893, p. 6; December 17, 1893, p. 2; January 1, 1894, p. 2; November 2, 1895, p. 6; November 5, 1895, p. 6; April 2, 1896, p. 4; November 19, 1895, p. 6; December 26, 1895, p. 6; Hooks, "Struggle for Dominance" pp. 166–70; Pate, *Livestock Legacy*, pp. 19–32; *Fort Worth Register*, December 17, 1899, pp. 3, 8; Gorman and Leclerc, "Past and Present,," p. 67; *General Directory 1892–1893*, p. 40.

17. Clarke, "The New South," pp. 542, 547; *Fort Worth Gazette*, February 26, 1890, p. 5; June 16, 1890, p. 8; April 12, 1891, p. 5; September 7, 1890, p. 3; May 11, 1890, p. 24; May 25, 1890, p. 6; *Fort Worth Record*, May 19, 1907, p. 20. Title to the 320 acres, left to heirs of Fort Worth pioneer Ephraim Daggett, was challenged by claims that predated Texas independence.

18. *Fort Worth Gazette*, May 12, 1887, p. 8; June 2, 1887, p. 8; June 10, 1887, p. 8; July 13, 1887, p. 8; May 6, 1891, p. 2; March 11, 1888, p. 8; February 12, 1890, p. 8; March 6, 1890, p. 2; November 19, 1890, p. 6; April 10, 1891, p. 2; May 6, 1891, p. 2; March 2, 1892, p. 2; March 5, 1892, p. 5; September 10, 1892, p. 2; April 6, 1892, p. 5; January 29, 1893, p. 4; May 27, 1892, p. 8; June 1, 1892, p. 3; July 28, 1893, p. 4; August 16, 1893, p. 6; August 17, 1893, p. 2; October 25, 1893, p. 6; October 27, 1893, p. 8.

19. *Fort Worth Gazette*, January 6, 1890, p. 8; January 7, 1890, p. 8; March 24, 1890, p. 5; January 14, 1890, p. 8; January 21,1890, p. 4; January 28, 1890, p. 8; February 1, 1890, p. 8; *Fort Worth Weekly Gazette*, May 8, 1890, p. 8; *New York Times*, May 11, 1890, p. 8; Minutes of Meeting on Holding another Spring Palace, January 6, 1890, File 2F173, Letters 1900–1901, Buckley Burton Paddock Papers.

20. *Fort Worth Weekly Gazette*, May 8, 1890, p. 8; *Fort Worth Gazette*, May 6, 1890, p. 2; May 11, 1890, p. 7; May 15,1890, p. 2; *New York Times*, May 11, 1890, p. 8; May 22, 1890, p. 1; May 23, 1890, p. 5.

21. Knott, "Social Life in Texas in the 1890s," pp. 34–36; *New York Times*, May 31, 1890, p. 1; June 1, 1890, p. 8; *Fort Worth Weekly Gazette*, June 5, 1890, p. 3; *Fort Worth Gazette*, June 11, 1890, p. 2; July 30, 1891, p. 8; *Fort Worth Star Telegram*, September 19, 1934, p. 8.

22. *Fort Worth Weekly Gazette*, June 26, 1890, p. 4; *Fort Worth Gazette*, March 30, 1890, p. 16; March 27, 1892, p. 6.

23. *Fort Worth Gazette*, October 4, 1890, p. 2; October 14, 1890, p. 1; October 15, 1890, p. 6; November 8, 1890, p. 2; May 7, 1893, p. 10.

24. *Fort Worth Gazette*, September 21, 1891, p. 7; March 18, 1893, p. 15; July 27, 1891, p. 8; November 20, 1892, p. 4; March 17, 1892, p. 8; March 19, 1892, p. 8; April 20, 1892, p. 8; December 10, 1892, p. 2; December 14, 1892, p. 2; January 23, 1892, p. 5; February 3, 1891, p. 6; June 1, 1893, p. 4; April 19, 1891, p. 4; September 27, 1893, p. 4; *Fort Worth Daily Mail*, June 2, 1891, p. 1.

25. *Fort Worth Gazette*, May 30, 1894, p. 6; October 24, 1894, p. 4; November 2, 1894, p. 6; City Secretary's First Annual Report and the Mayor's Message, 1894, pp. 3–4, File 2F183, Fort Worth City Reports, Buckley Burton Paddock Papers.

26. *Fort Worth Gazette*, September 9, 1892, p. 8; September 19, 1892, p. 8; September 22, 1892, p. 4; April 19, 1893, p. 3; May 30, 1894, p. 6; June 13, 1894, p. 5; August 22, 1894, p. 6; October 24, 1894, p. 4; November 2, 1894, p. 6; April 10, 1895, p. 3; November 21, 1894, p. 8; Hundley, Jr., *Water and the West*, p. ix.

27. *Fort Worth Gazette*, August 31, 1891, p. 6; March 1, 1892, p. 2; April 28, 1892, p. 5; April 29, 1892, p. 5; May 29, 1892, p. 4; April 19, 1893, p. 3; *New York Times*, December 23, 1890, p. 4; December 25, 1890, p. 2; February 21, 1891, p. 1.

28. *Fort Worth Gazette*, March 7, 1892, p. 6; April 6, 1892, p. 8; June 8, 1892, p. 4; June 10, 1892, p. 8; October 18, 1893, p. 6; April 10, 1895, p. 3; October 30, 1895, p. 6.

29. *Fort Worth Gazette*, March 9, 1892, p. 6; March 22, 1892, p. 5; June 8, 1892, p. 4; June 9, 1892, p. 5; October 18, 1892, p. 6; October 19, 1892, p. 2; December 4, 1892, p. 2; January 4, 1893, p. 1; May 3, 1893, p. 4; June 21, 1893, p. 1; October 19, 1893, p. 6.

30. *Fort Worth Gazette*, January 9, 1894, p.1; January 17, 1894, p. 5; February 28, 1894, p. 2; April 10, 1895, p. 3; March 7, 1894, p. 8; April 1, 1894, p. 6; October 30, 1895, p. 6.

31. *New York Times*, July 11, 1893, p. 5; Jackson, *Crabgrass Frontier*, pp. 118–20.

32. *New York Times*, February 1, 1894, p. 6; February 2, 1894, p. 6; February 11, 1894, p. 6; November 12, 1894, p. 1; March 28, 1897, p. 24; *Fort Worth Gazette*, November 11, 1894, p. 6; November 12, 1894, p. 2.

33. *Fort Worth Gazette*, January 8, 1893, p. 2; July 15, 1892, p. 8; January 18, 1893, p. 2; January 23, 1893, p. 2; January 29, 1893, p. 4.

34. *New York Times*, January 12, 1893, p. 6; July 10, 1894, p. 2; February 14, 1895, p. 4; March 30, 1895, p. 4; May 11, 1895, p. 4; January 5, 1895, p. 9; October 17, 1895, p. 1; *Fort Worth Gazette*, July 2, 1891, p. 4; April 12, 1893, p. 6; April 14, 1893, section II, pp. 1–12; July 27, 1893, p. 1.

35. *Fort Worth Gazette*, March 4, 1893, p. 6, March 18, 1893, p. 10; June 5, 1895, p. 8; June 27, 1895, p. 4; August 4, 1895, p. 6; Gorman and Leclerc, "Past and Present," pp. 67–69; *Fort Worth Morning Register*, February 19, 1899, p. 5, December 23, 1898, pp. 10–11, Center for American History, The University of Texas at Austin.

36. *Fort Worth Gazette*, January 1, 1894, p. 1; November 14, 1893, p. 8; January 12, 1894, p. 8; April 11, 1894, p. 6; January 5, 1895, p. 1; *New York Times*, January 15, 1908, section AFR , p. 45.

37. *Dallas Times Herald*, July 8, 1896, p. 5; July 17, 1896, p. 5; *Fort Worth Register*, October 15, 1899, p. 8; Paddock and Montgomery, *Annual Report 1898*, p. 4.

38. *Graham (Texas) Leader*, February 12, 1898, p. 7; Paddock, *Central and Western Texas*, pp. 262–63, 267; *Fort Worth Register*, September 29, 1897, p. 8, October 29, 1897, p. 8; Gorman and Leclerc, "Past and Present," p. 67; Pate, *Livestock Legacy*, pp. 39–41; Hammond, *History of the Municipal Departments*, pp. 367–69; Paddock and Montgomery, *Annual Report 1898*, pp. 7–9.

39. Paddock to wife, September 19, 1895, Paddock Papers, Box GA 194, Folder 16; Paddock to wife, April 16, 1897, Paddock Papers, Box GA 194, Folder 17.

40. Gorman and Leclerc, "Past and Present," pp. 67–69; *Fort Worth Morning Register*, December 23, 1898, pp. 10–11, Center for American Studies The University of Texas Austin.

41. Paddock and Montgomery, *Annual Report 1898*, pp. 3–5.

42. Paddock and Montgomery, *Annual Report 1898*, pp. 3–5, 9–10.

43. Paddock and Montgomery, *Annual Report 1898*, pp. 5–7; *Fort Worth Register*, October 12, 1897, p. 1, October 13, 1897, p. 8, October 15, 1897, p. 8. The yellow fever scare began in New Orleans and spread to Houston and Galveston, which quarantined its residents after Texas State Health Officer Dr. R. M. Swearingen advised other Texas cities to refuse their refugees. Despite Paddock's denial of an official quarantine, there was a report of travelers from the south being turned away by some counties. A train from Houston received permission from all counties but Robertson County to go through at full speed; Robertson County forced the train to stop at Waxahachie. Upon the train's arrival in Fort Worth, five passengers were removed and placed on a southbound train because they could not convince questioners that they had gotten on at Waxahachie, and not Houston. After a few days the scare subsided, giving way to questions whether there had ever been an epidemic.

44. Paddock and Montgomery, *Annual Report 1898*, pp. 7–9.

45. Ibid.

46. Paddock to wife, undated. Paddock Papers, Box GA 194, Folder 17.

47. Paddock and Montgomery, *Annual Report 1898*, pp. 3–5, 9–10.

48. *Fort Worth Register*, January 26, 1897, p. 8.

49. *City Council Minutes*, Volume N, March 22, 1897, April 6, 1897, April 14, 1897, May 4, 1897; *Fort Worth Register*, January 26, 1897, p. 8, February 9, 1897, p. 8, February 13, 1897, p. 8, March 3, 1897, p. 4, March 6, 1897, p. 5; March 23, 1897, p. 5.

50. *Fort Worth Register*, October 2, 1897, p. 6, October 20, 1897, p. 5; *City Council Minutes*, vol. O, November 1, 1897; Gorman and Leclerc, "Past and Present," p. 68.

51. *City Council Minutes*, vol. O, September 7, November 1, 1897; *Fort Worth Morning Register*, March 3, 1899, p. 5; June 23, 1899, p. 2, Center for American History, The University of Texas at Austin; *Fort Worth Mail Telegram*, August 23, 1899, p. 8, Center for American History, The University of Texas at Austin.

52. *Fort Worth Register*, September 9, 1897, p. 8, September 12, 1897, p. 8, September 14, 1897, p. 8, October 5, 1897, p. 8, October 7, 1897, p. 8; Paddock and Montgomery, *Annual Report 1898*, p. 18; Knight, *Outpost on the Trinity*, p. 178.

53. Paddock to Dr. Captain, September 7, 1895, Paddock Papers, Box GA 195, Folder 11; Paddock to wife, September 21, 1895, Paddock Papers, Box GA 194, Folder 16; *City Council Minutes*, July 20, 1897, vol. N; *Dallas Morning News*, November 7, 1897, p. 3.

54. *Dallas Morning News*, November 7, 1897, p. 3, November 17, 1897, p. 3, December 17, 1899, p. 3; *City Council Minutes*, vol. O, September 21, 1897, November 16, 1897; *Fort Worth Register*, October 10, 1899, p. 8, October 21, 1899, p. 8, November 21, 1899, p. 8; December 17, 1899, p. 3; *Fort Worth Mail Telegram*, August 23, 1899, p. 8, Center for American History, The University of Texas at Austin; Blair

and Company to Paddock, August 23, 1899, File 2F172, Letters 1865–1899, Buckley Burton Paddock Papers; Robt. H. Weems of the Department of Finance of New York City to Paddock, January 23, 1900, File 2F173, Letters 1900–1901, Buckley Burton Paddock Papers.

55. Knott, "Social Life in Texas," p. 59.

56. *Fort Worth Gazette*, September 28, 1890, p. 6; September 24, 1890, p. 2; July 13, 1892, p. 4; Smith, *Things I Remember*, pp. 3–8, 23.

57. *Fort Worth Gazette*, June 10, 1893, p. 8; June 20, 1893, p. 8; September 6, 1893, p. 6; September 7, 1893, p. 6; June 2, 1897, p. 8.

58. *Fort Worth Gazette*, December 24, 1890, p. 6.

59. *Fort Worth Register*, March 3, 1897, p. 5.

60. *Fort Worth Register*, December 3, 1899, p. 8.

61. *Fort Worth Register*, July 13, 1897, p. 1, July 15, 1897, p. 8.

62. *Fort Worth Register*, July 14, 1897, p. 1.

63. *Fort Worth Gazette*, August 13, 1890, p. 2.

64. *Fort Worth Register*, July 3, 1897, p. 1, July 23, 1897, p. 8; Paddock and Montgomery, *Annual Report 1898*, pp. 21–22.

65. *Fort Worth Register*, July 24, 1897, p. 8, July 27, 1897, p. 8, August 3, 1897, p. 1, August 4, 1897, p. 1.

66. *City Council Minutes*, vol. O, March 3, 1899, March 17, 1899, April 21, 1899.

67. *City Council Minutes*, vol. O, May 5, 1899.

68. Ibid., vol. O, April 20, 1900; *Fort Worth Register*, August 27, 1899, p. 5.

69. *Fort Worth Register*, November 4, 1899, p. 8.

70. *Fort Worth Gazette*, July 3, 1892, p. 7.

71. *New York Times*, July 22, 1893, p. 3; September 7, 1892, p. 1; October 2, 1892, p. 11.

72. *Fort Worth Gazette*, August 29, 1895, p. 6; August 7, 1895, p. 6; September 5, 1895, p. 6; September 10, 1895, p. 6; Brogdon, "Political, Economic, and Social Aspects" p. 14; *General Directory of the City of Fort Worth, 1894–1895*, pp. 3–4, 375–76; *General Directory of the City of Fort Worth, 1896–1897*, pp. 1–2; *Fort Worth Register*, July 14, 1899, p. 2.

73. *New York Times*, December 24, 1897, p. 2; December 26, 1897, p. 1; Harkins, "History of Municipal Government," pp. 27–28; Brogdon, "Political, Economic, and Social Aspects," pp. 25–26; *Fort Worth Morning Register*, January 5, 1897, p. 8.

74. *Fort Worth Register*, September 12, 1897, p. 4, October 15, 1897, p. 8; *General City Directory 1896–1897*, pp. 18, 38, 50–52; *Graham (Texas) Leader*, May 21, 1896, p. 6; August 27, 1898, p. 6; Gorman and Leclerc, "Past and Present," p. 69; *Fort Worth Mail Telegram*, March 26, 1899, p. 15, Center for American History, The University of Texas at Austin; *Fort Worth Gazette*, May 18, 1893, p. 2.

75. *Fort Worth Register*, December 17, 1899, pp. 3,8; Gorman and Leclerc, "Past and Present," p. 67; *General Directory 1896–1897*, p. 40.

76. *Fort Worth Gazette*, January 1, 1894, p. 1; November 14, 1893, p. 8; January 12, 1894, p. 8; April 11, 1894, p. 6; January 5, 1895, p. 1; November 13, 1895, p. 6;

November 22, 1895, p. 6; February 14, 1896, p. 8; *New York Times*, January 15, 1908, section AFR, p. 45.

77. *Fort Worth Register*, March 16, 1897, p. 8, March 17, 1897, p. 8, March 23, 1897, p. 5, May 23, 1897, p. 1.

78. *Fort Worth Register*, August 12, 1897, p. 8.

79. *Fort Worth Register*, August 12, 1897, p. 8.

80. *Fort Worth Register*, August 19, 1897, p. 4, October 13, 1897, p. 8; Bateman, "Board of Trade," pp. 79–80.

81. *General City Directory 1896–1897*, p. 18.

82. Bateman, "Board of Trade," pp. 79–80; *Fort Worth Register*, October 14, 1899, p. 8, October 15, 1899, p. 4, October 24, 1899, p. 8, October 27, 1899, p. 8, November 18, 1899, p. 8, *Fort Worth Morning Register*, December 28, 1898, p. 8, Center for American History, The University of Texas at Austin.

83. *Fort Worth Register*, September 29, 1899, p. 8; September 30, 1899, p. 8; July 6, 1899, p. 8; July 7, 1899, p. 8.

84. *Fort Worth Register*, January 19, 1907, p. 8; January 26, 1897, p. 8; July 21, 1897, p. 1; November 17, 1899, p. 8; Arnold, "Study of the Social Life of a Texas City," p. 19.

85. Paddock, *Central and Western Texas*, pp. 262–63, 267. For a history of the arrival of the major packinghouses see Pate, *Livestock Legacy*; *Fort Worth Morning Register*, July 29, 1899, p. 5.

Chapter 4

1. Talbert, *Cowtown-Metropolis*, pp. 122–25; Schoen, "Immigrant to Capitalist," p. 29.

2. *Twelfth Census*, vol. 8, p. 994; Talbert, *Cowtown Metropolis*, p. 123.

3. *New York Times*, October 12, 1902, p. 33; *Twelfth Census*, pp. 868–69, 872–73.

4. *New York Times* September 26, 1900, p. 11; November 18, 1900, p. 17; *Twelfth Census*, vol. 1, pp. 41–42, 378, 388.

5. *Twelfth Census*, vol. 1, pp. 558–59, 562, 565; *Fort Worth Register*, July 28, 1901, p. 7; *Fort Worth Record*, July 14, 1901, pp. 7, 10; *New York Times*, October 12, 1902, p. 33; April 30, 1903, p. 3.

6. *Fort Worth Register*, February 10, 1901, p. 8; February 26, 1901, p. 8; April 9, 1901, p. 2; April 12, 1901, p. 1.

7. *Fort Worth Telegram*, April 7, 1903, p. 8; October 2, 1903, p. 1; October 4, 1903, p. 1. *Fort Worth Register*, April 1, 1902, p. 3; October 5, 1901, p. 4; Hammond, *History of the Municipal Departments*, pp. 367–69.

8. *Fort Worth Register*, May 16, 1901, p. 7; April 1, 1902, p. 3; October 16, 1901, p. 2; April 20, 1901, p. 3; *New York Times*, January 6, 1900, p. 2; October 12, 1901, p. 13; March 18, 1903, p. 3.

9. *Fort Worth Telegram*, April 7, 1903, p. 8; October 2, 1903, p. 1; October 4, 1903, p. 1; March 8, 1903, p. 16; March 15, 1903, p. 8.

10. *Fort Worth Register*, February 2, 1901, p. 5; July 7, 1900, p. 3; July 28, 1900,p. 5.

11. *Fort Worth Register*, February 2, 1901, p. 5; March 19, 1901, p. 8; April 9, 1901, p. 8; July 6, 1901, p. 5; August 17, 1901, p. 4; April 20, 1901, p. 4.

12. *Fort Worth Morning Telegram*, September 17, 1902, p. 5; September 25, 1902, p. 8; December 11, 1902, p. 6; *Fort Worth Telegram*, July 12, 1903, p. 1; July 15, 1903, p. 8; October 4, 1903, p. 1; September 22, 1903, p. 4; September 26, 1903, p. 1.

13. *Fort Worth Register*, January 1, 1901, p. 8, May 1, 1901, p. 6, November 11, 1900, p. 5; *City Council Minutes*, vol. P, October 19, 1900; November 9, 1900.

14. *New York Times*, August 31, 1900, p. 1; *Fort Worth Telegram*, February 22, 1903, p. 4; *Fort Worth Register*, June 19, 1902, p. 8; August 7, 1900, p. 8; May 24, 1901, p. 7; *City Council Minutes*, vol. P, February 1, 1901.

15. *Fort Worth Register*, November 16, 1901, p. 4; November 18, 1901, p. 8; November 22, 1901, p. 5; December 13, 1901, p. 4; January 18, 1902, p. 5; *City Council Minutes*, vol. Q, January 17, 1902.

16. *Fort Worth Register*, May 7, 1904, p. 5.

17. *Fort Worth Telegram*, April 14, 1903, p. 5; *Fort Worth Star Telegram*, December 19, 1915, p. 35.

18. Moore, "The Theater in Fort Worth," pp. 16–18, 42–44, 121–23.

19. *Fort Worth Register*, July 6, 1900, p. 3; July 7, 1900, p. 3; September 7, 1901, p. 5; September 9, 1901, p. 8; *Fort Worth Telegram*, March 30, 1903, p. 8; *New York Times*, November 15, 1901, p. 9; November 20, 1901, p. 6; November 21, 1901, p. 9; Moore, "The Theater in Fort Worth," pp. 8–9.

20. *New York Times*, June 18, 1900, p. 5; *Fort Worth Register*, August 29, 1899, p. 8.

21. *Fort Worth Register*, February 1, 1902, p. 4; April 5, 1902, p. 8; April 11, 1902, p. 5; May 13, 1902, p. 5; May 14, 1902, p. 8; June 3, 1902, p. 8; November 18, 1901, p. 5; January 17, 1902, p. 1; *Fort Worth Telegram*, February 11, 1903, p. 5; April 17, 1903, p. 2.

22. *Fort Worth Register*, May 13, 1902, p. 5; May 14, 1902, p. 8; June 3, 1902, p. 8; *Fort Worth Telegram*, September 7, 1902, p. 8; June 23, 1905, p. 3. Grimes wore badge 13, the same number worn by Lee Waller when he was killed in 1892 (see *Fort Worth Register*, May 28, 1902, pp. 4–5, and May 29, 1902, p. 8). The department dropped the number 13 in 1904 (see *Fort Worth Telegram*, May 29, 1904, p. 7).

23. *Fort Worth Telegram*, June 21, 1903, p. 14; *Dallas Times Herald*, January 4, 1903, p. 8; Cronon, *Nature's Metropolis*, p. 354; Link and McCormick, *Progressivism*, p. 87.

24. *Fort Worth Telegram*, April 24, 1903, p. 1; September 16, 1903, p. 8; September 17, 1903, p. 8; September 19, 1903, p. 1.

25. *Fort Worth Telegram*, September 4, 1903, p. 5.

26. *Fort Worth Register*, July 15, 1900, p. 3; August 12, 1900, p. 5; May 31, 1902, p. 8; *New York Times*, April 7, 1901, p. 17; April 21, 1901, p. 26.

27. *Fort Worth Telegram*, November 7, 1902, p. 5; November 26, 1902, p. 5.

28. *Fort Worth Register,* September 1, 1900, p. 8; September 2, 1900, p. 8; September 9, 1900, p. 8; September 20, 1900, p. 8; September 21, 1900, p. 8; October 17, 1900, p. 8; October 23, 1900, p. 2; November 2, 1900, p. 8; November 3, 1900, p. 8; November 4, 1900, p. 5; March 5, 1901, p. 8.

29. *Fort Worth Register,* November 3,1900, p. 8; November 4, 1900,p. 5; *From Frontier to Metropolis,* pp. 8–11; *New York Times,* October 12, 1902, p. 33.

30. *New York Times,* January 5, 1902, p. AFR 18, February 12, 1899, p. 2; Craig, *Fort Worth Stockyards,* p. 19; *Fort Worth Record,* July 8, 1906, p. 11.

31. *Twelfth Census,* vol. 9, pp. 399, 402, 403.

32. *Fort Worth Register,* October 14, 1900, p. 8; June 4, 1901, p. 8; July 21, 1901, p. 7, 10; August 1, 1901, p. 1; August 2, 1901, p. 8; January 7, 1902, p. 7; Cronon, *Nature's Metropolis,* p. 375; Bateman-Millican, *From Frontier to Metropolis,* pp. 8–11.

33. Ward, "Cowtown Success," p. 86; Craig, "Fort Worth Stockyards," p. 19; *Fort Worth Register,* October 13, 1900, p. 2; May 26, 1901, p. 3; May 30, 1901, p. 8; *Fort Worth Record,* September 29, 1916, p. 14.

34. *Fort Worth Register,* June 1, 1901, p. 8; June 4, 1901, p. 8; August 1, 1901, p. 1; August 2, 1901, p. 8; June 8, 1901, p. 8; August 18, 1901, p. 8; August 11, 1901, p. 3; Swift and Company to Paddock, October 1, 1902, File 2F174, Letters 1902, Buckley Burton Paddock Papers.

35. *Fort Worth Register,* May 26, 1901, p. 3; May 30, 1901, p. 8; August 21 1901, p. 8; September 25,1901, p. 8; April 2, 1901, p. 8; September 26, 1901, p. 8; October 8, 1901, p. 2; Thompson, "Factors Contributing to Growth," pp. 112–15.

36. *Fort Worth Register,* November 1, 1901, p. 8; January 10, 1902, p. 5; March 12, 1902, p. 3; March 13, 1902, p. 2; March 8, 1904, p. 2; *Fort Worth Telegram,* March 5, 1903, p. 1; March 6, 1903, p. 4; March 7, 1903, p. 1; August 2, 1902, p. 6; March 7, 1904, p. 1; March 8, 1904, p. 2; *Fort Worth Record,* March 6, 1904, p. 35.

37. *Fort Worth Telegram,* February 3, 1903, p. 2; February 13, 1903, p. 2.

38. *Fort Worth Record,* March 2, 1904, p. 10; March 8, 1904, p. 2.

39. *Fort Worth, 1903,* pp. 1–2. Local History Collection of the Fort Worth Public Library.

40. *Fort Worth Telegram,* May 17, 1903, section 4, p. 6.

41. *Fort Worth Telegram,* July 12, 1902, p. 8; *Fort Worth Register,* October 24, 1901, p. 5; October 26, 1901, p. 1; *General Directory of the City of Fort Worth, 1902–1903,* pp. 2–3.

42. *Fort Worth Telegram,* December 7, 1902, p. 8; November 16, 1902, p. 2; *Fort Worth Register,* August 11, 1901, p. 8; August 13, 1901, p. 8; August 21, 1901, p. 8; June 1, 1901, p. 8; April 22, 1902, p. 12; *Fort Worth Record,* January 25, 1906, p. 10; *General City Directory 1902–1903,* pp. 2–3.

43. *New York Times,* June 27, 1902, p. 12; July 3, 1902, p. 1; August 21, 1902, p. 14; January 4, 1903, p. AFR 4; Craig, *Fort Worth Stockyards,* p. 19; Cronon, *Nature's Metropolis,* pp. 244–47.

44. *Thirteenth Census,* vol. 3, pp. 781, 792.

Chapter 5

1. *Fort Worth Record*, April 9, 1905, pp. 1–2; January 11, 1906, p. 4; July 8, 1906, p. 11; May 3, 1908, p. 16; *New York Times*, April 9, 1905, p. 1.

2. Pate, *Livestock Legacy*, p. 295; *Fort Worth Record*, October 16, 1904, p. 15; July 8, 1906, p. 11; February 10, 1907, p. 3.

3. *Fort Worth Record*, July 8, 1906, p. 11; August 1, 1907, p. 4; May 2, 1908, p. 12; November 8, 1908, section 2, p. 6; November 10, 1908, p. 12; November 15, 1908, p. 16; December 10, 1908, p. 8; January 1, 1909, p. 1; December 2, 1908, p. 6; March 10, 1909, p. 1.

4. Steinberg, *Acts of God*, pp. xx, 70–71.

5. *Fort Worth Record*, May 24, 1908, p. 1; May 25, 1908, p. 1.

6. *Fort Worth Record*, January 8, 1908, p. 5; January 9, 1908, p. 3; January 27, 1909, p. 3; February 24, 1909, p. 12.

7. *New York Times*, April 4, 1909, p. 1; April 5, 1909, p. 9; *Fort Worth Record*, April 4, 1909, pp. 1,6, 10; April 5, 1909, p. 1; *Fort Worth Star Telegram*, April 3, 1909, p. 1; Bond, *History of Fort Worth, 1849–1928*, chapter 29.

8. *Fort Worth Morning Telegram*, July 9, 1902, p. 8; *Fort Worth Telegram*, June 30, 1906, p. 1; *Fort Worth Record*, February 14, 1904, p. 10; March 8, 1904, p. 2; May 22, 1904, section 1, p. 12; October 25, 1918, p. 10.

9. *New York Times*, July 12, 1904, p. 1; July 27, 1904, p. 1; September 7, 1904, p. 6; *Fort Worth Record*, July 13, 1904, p. 10; July 17, 1904, pp. 1, 20; July 23, 1904, p. 12; September 9, 1904, p. 6; September 10, 1904, p. 12.

10. *Fort Worth Record*, April 29, 1907, p. 10.

11. *Fort Worth Telegram*, February 18, 1903, p. 5; May 17, 1903, section 4, p. 1; Patricia Duncan, "Enterprise: B. B. Paddock and Fort Worth," p. 258; *Fort Worth Record*, May 27, 1904, p. 10; October 16, 1904, section 3, pp. 3, 16; October 3, 1905, p. 1; June 2, 1907, p. 1; June 23, 1907, pp. 9, 16; September 17, 1907, p. 1.

12. *Fort Worth Record*, October 16, 1904, section 3, pp. 1–3; October 3, 1905, p. 1; January 4, 1908, p. 1.

13. *Fort Worth Record*, August 1, 1907, p. 4; *Thirteenth Census*, vol. 9, pp. 1198–99.

14. *Fort Worth Record*, March 17, 1905, p. 12; October 16, 1904, section 3, p. 3; May 9, 1906, p. 12; May 13, 1907, p. 9; July 17, 1907, p. 14.

15. *Fort Worth Record*, May 29, 1909, p. 1; June 20, 1909, p. 19; *New York Times*, January 15, 1908, section AFR, p. 45.

16. *Fort Worth Telegram*, April 3, 1907, p. 4; May 5, 1907, p. 7; May 7, 1907, p. 1.

17. *Fort Worth Record*, January 23, 1905, p. 2; October 14, 1905, p. 12; January 19, 1908, p. 1; *Fort Worth City Directory, 1916*, p.48.

18. *Fort Worth Record*, October 16, 1904, section 3, pp. 1–3; May 19, 1907, p. 6; October 8, 1908, p. 7.

19. *Fort Worth Record*, October 14, 1906, pt. 5, p. 11.

20. Ibid.; *Fort Worth Record*, May 9, 1907, p. 7; May 13, 1907, p. 9; July 23, 1908, p. 12; July 2, 1907, p. 4; January 19, 1908, p. 1; December 17, 1916, p. 10; Cuellar,

"Stories from the Barrio," pp. 78–79, 134–39; McIlvain, "History of Hispanic Fort Worth," p. 16.

21. *Fort Worth Record*, June 21, 1908, p. 16; July 23, 1908, p. 12.

22. *Fort Worth Record*, July 10, 1904, p. 14; January 1, 1905, p. 4; *Fort Worth Telegram*, June 29, 1906, p. 5.

23. *Fort Worth Record*, December 28, 1906, p. 10; March 30, 1908, p. 8; October 11, 1909, p. 1; August 2, 1908, p. 9; August 9, 1908, p. 8; October 2, 1908, p. 3; *New York Times*, January 15, 1908, section AFR, p. 45.

24. *Fort Worth Record*, April 12, 1904, p. 12; June 26, 1909, p. 10; August 15, 1908; p. 4; August 16, 1908, p. 3; May 7, 1904, p. 6; May 6, 1905, p. 6; March 5, 1909, p. 8.

25. Jackson, *Crabgrass Frontier*, pp. 140, 144; *Fort Worth Record*, June 26, 1909, p. 2.

26. *Fort Worth Record*, May 9, 1907, p. 7; January 10, 1908, p. 10; February 10, 1909, p. 4; February 14, 1909, p. 8; February 16, 1909, p. 12; February 24, 1909, p. 7; March 2, 1909, p. 7; March 3, 1909, p. 4; March 4, 1909, p. 12; March 5, 1909, p. 8; March 12, 1907, p. 12; June 26, 1909, pp. 1, 2, 10; August 28, 1909, pp. 1, 4; *Fort Worth Star Telegram*, March 11, 1909, p. 1; June 29, 1909, p. 2.

27. *Fort Worth Record*, March 3, 1909, p. 4; March 4, 1909, p. 12; March 5, 1909, p. 8; March 12, 1907, p. 12; June 26, 1909, pp. 1, 10; *Fort Worth Star Telegram*, March 11, 1909, p. 1; June 29, 1909, p. 2.

28. *Fort Worth Record*, May 7, 1904, p. 6; May 6, 1905, p. 5; September 3, 1905, p. 7; August 12, 1906, p. 6; January 8, 1905, p. 6; January 21, 1905, p. 8; July 10, 1910, pt. 2, p. 5; September 2, 1910, p. 5; December 9, 1910, p. 10.

29. *Fort Worth Record*, October 2, 1906, p. 4; September 2, 1905, p. 4; November 18, 1906, p. 10; June 26, 1907, p. 14; June 27, 1907, p. 7; June 30, 1907, p. 3; July 7, 1907, section 3, p. 7; December 28, 1907, p. 10; March 1, 1908, p. 9; July 10, 1910, pt. 2, p. 5.

30. *Fort Worth Record*, September 12, 1908, p. 7; April 17, 1909, p. 5; April 21, 1909, p. 1; April 28, 1909, p. 5; September 26, 1909, p. 6; September 30, 1909, p. 12; July 10, 1910, pt. 2, p. 5.

31. *Fort Worth Telegram*, January 10, 1904, p. 1; *Fort Worth Record*, January 10, 1904, p. 16.

32. *Fort Worth Record*, November 28, 1904, p. 8; November 29, 1904, p. 5; *Fort Worth Telegram*, February 26, 1905, p. 1.

33. *Fort Worth Telegram*, December 16, 1904, p. 3; April 5, 1905, p. 3; *Fort Worth Record*, December 14, 1904, p. 3; October 14, 1905, p. 4; January 17, 1906, p. 8; Barth, *City People*, pp. 200–201.

34. *Fort Worth Telegram*, November 21, 1904, p. 8; December 30, 1904, p. 6; *Fort Worth Record*, January 12, 1905, pp. 8, 12; December 20, 1905, p. 12; December 21, 1905, p. 12.

35. *Fort Worth Telegram*, August 30, 1906, p. 10; August 31, 1906, p. 3; December 27, 1905, p. 5; *Fort Worth Record*, November 5, 1906, p. 3.

36. *Fort Worth Record*, December 23, 1906, p. 5; December 24, 1906, p. 4.

37. *Fort Worth Record*, December 30, 1906, pp. 1–2.

38. Ibid.

39. Ibid.

40. *Fort Worth Record*, January 9, 1908, p. 3.

41. *Fort Worth Record*, December 30, 1906, pp. 1–2.

42. *Fort Worth Record*, January 2, 1907, p. 8; January 3, 1907; January 5, 1907, p. 4; January 7, 1907, p. 8; January 10, 1907, p. 4; January 12, 1907, p. 6; January 14, 1907, p. 3; *Fort Worth Telegram*, January 5, 1907, p. 2.

43. *Fort Worth Record*, January 6, 1906, p. 3; July 25, 1906, p. 2; July 13, 1906, p. 3; December 4, 1906, p. 6; December 24, 1906, p. 4; January 1, 1907, p. 12; January 5, 1907, p. 4; *Fort Worth Telegram*, March 22, 1907, p. 2; March 23, 1907, pp. 1–2.

44. *New York Times*, March 29, 1907, p. 10; *Fort Worth Telegram*, March 22, 1907, p. 2; March 23, 1907, pp. 1–2; March 24, 1907, p. 7; March 29, 1907, p. 4; *Fort Worth Record*, April 2, 1907, p. 2; March 26, 1907, p. 5; May 4, 1907, p. 14; March 25, 1907, p. 4.

45. *Fort Worth Telegram*, June 27, 1907, p. 8; July 12, 1907, p. 1; August 14, 1907, p. 3; August 30, 1907, p. 1; *Fort Worth Record*, July 4, 1907, p. 12; July 17, 1907, p. 3; August 15, 1907, p. 7; September 3, 1907, p. 1; January 23, 1908, p. 12.

46. *Fort Worth Telegram*, June 27, 1907, p. 8; August 30, 1907, p. 1; *Fort Worth Record*, September 3, 1907, p. 1.

47. *Fort Worth Record*, September 8, 1907, pp. 1–2; *Fort Worth Telegram*, September 8, 1907, p. 1.

48. *Fort Worth Telegram*, September 10, 1907, p. 1; September 15, 1907, p. 7, September 17, 1907, p. 1; September 24, 1907, p. 1.

49. *Fort Worth Record*, November 1, 1908, p. 6; October 7, 1908, p. 8; *Fort Worth Telegram*, February 19, 1908, p. 5.

50. *Fort Worth Telegram*, September 15, 1907, p. 7; *Fort Worth Star Telegram*, June 7, 1909, p. 1.

51. *Fort Worth Star Telegram*, July 11, 1909, p. 11; August 13, 1909, p. 1, 9; August 14, 1909, p. 1.

52. *Fort Worth Record*, August 13, 1909, p. 1; *New York Times*, January 30, 1910, p. SM6.

53. *Fort Worth Star Telegram*, August 13, 1909, p. 1; August 14, 1909, p. 1; *Fort Worth Record*, August 14, 1909, p. 6; August 16, 1909, p. 3.

54. *Fort Worth Star Telegram*, August 23, 1909, p. 1; August 24, 1909, p. 1; August 23, 1909, p. 7.

55. *Fort Worth Telegram*, July 7, 1909, p. 1; September 5, 1909, p. 14; September 6, 1909, p. 2; September 8, 1909, p. 1; September 21, 1909, p. 1; September 11, 1909, p. 1; November 3, 1909, p. 1; July 15, 1910, p. 10.

56. *Twelfth Census*, vol. 1, pt. 1, p. 681; *Fort Worth Telegram*, March 16, 1904, p. 3; September 1, 1905, p. 2; September 16, 1905, p. 1; October 16, 1905, p. 1; October 21, 1905, p. 8; June 27, 1906, p. 1; December 30, 1908, p. 6; December 31, 1908, p. 2; January 1, 1909, p. 1; *New York Times*, March 16, 1904, p. 1; August 13, 1906, p. 5; *Fort Worth Record*, September 16, 1905, p. 12; October 3, 1905, p. 10;

November 16, 1906, p. 12; November 17, 1906, p. 7; Painter, *Standing at Armageddon*, pp. 219–20.

57. *Fort Worth Record*, July 19, 1907, p. 12; June 30, 1907, pt. 3, p. 5; August 11, 1907, p. 51 October 17, 1907, p. 12; November 10, 1909, p. 5; Knight, *Outpost on the Trinity*, pp. 135–36.

58. *Council Minutes*, vol. T, July 9, 1909.

59. *Fort Worth Record*, January 1, 1910, p. 4.

60. *Thirteenth Census*, vol. 9, pp. 1197–99; *Fort Worth Record*, July 10, 1910, pt. 2, p. 4.

61. *Thirteenth Census*, vol. 9, p. 1197; Paddock, *History of Texas*, p. 657; *Fort Worth Record*, April 2, 1912, p. 6.

62. *Fort Worth Register*, June 8, 1901, p. 4; June 28, 1901, p. 8; July 1, 1901, p. 5; July 2, 1901, p. 5; June 2, 1902, p. 5.

63. *Fort Worth Telegram*, February 18, 1903, p. 5; November 11, 1903, p. 6; *Fort Worth Record*, June 24, 1904, p. 3; June 25, 1904, p. 7; *New York Times*, May 20, 1907, p. 10.

64. *Fort Worth Record*, November 8, 1904, p. 10; August 6, 1905, p. 10; *Fort Worth Telegram*, February 18, 1903, p. 5.

65. *Fort Worth Record*, July 2, 1907, p. 4.

66. *Fort Worth Record*, July 14, 1907, p. 12.

67. *Fort Worth Record*, March 11, 1908, p. 1.

68. *Fort Worth Record*, April 4, 1905, p. 5; April 23, 1905, p. 20; May 23, 1905, p. 10; July 15, 1905, p. 5; October 17, 1909, p. 7.

Chapter 6

1. Bailey and Vick, eds., *The Fort Worth Story*, p. 55.

2. *Thirteenth Census*, vol. 3, pp. 781, 792, 795–96; *Twelfth Census*, vol. 3, pt. 1, pp. lxxix, 41–42, 378, 388; *Fort Worth Record*, September 24, 1910, p. 2; September 28, 1910, p. 1; December 12, 1910, p. 10.

3. *Fort Worth Star Telegram*, September 23, 1910, p. 1; October 30, 1949, merchandising section, p. 2; *Fort Worth Record*, September 28, 1910, p. 1.

4. *Fort Worth Star Telegram*, May 22, 1912, p. 14; *Fort Worth Record*, October 26, 1910, pp. 1, 9.

5. *Fort Worth Record*, May 13, 1913, p. 12.

6. These census figures clashed with a 1910 Texas State Labor Commission study showing Fort Worth with 42 factories, only six fewer than Dallas's 48, but crediting Fort Worth with greater total wages, $3,967,230 to $1,221,544, more than twice as many factory employees, 6,108 to 2,824, and a higher average annual wage, $650 to $433. The obvious contradictions between the 1910 census and the state report the same year suggest different bases of comparison. For example, in the 1910 census 6,621 wage earners worked in the city of Dallas, but the state study listed only 2,824 for all of Dallas County, which could only be

explained by faulty data or that the state considered wage earners separately from salaried personnel. The latter would not explain how the census found 147 manufacturers in just Fort Worth while the state reported only 42 in Tarrant County. The unexplainable inconsistency renders the state version unreliable.

7. *Fort Worth Record,* October 7, 1910, p. 13; October 8, 1910, p. 1; October 27, 1910, p. 1; December 15, 1912, pt. 5, p. 10; December 15, 1912, pt. 3, p. 3; *Fort Worth Star Telegram,* March 4, 1914, p. 1; *New York Times,* March 23, 1913, p. 1.

8. *Fort Worth Record,* September 24, 1910, p. 2; December 15, 1912, pt. 3, p. 3; February 22, 1911, p. 4; *Fort Worth Star Telegram,* June 23, 2004, p. 6B; May 22, 1912, p. 14; February 13, 1911, p. 1; *Fort Worth, Texas: The Gateway to the Great Southwest,* pp. 43–45; *Thirteenth Census,* vol. 9, pp. 1197–98.

9. *Fort Worth Record,* February 22, 1911, p. 4; *Fort Worth Star Telegram,* February 13, 1911, p. 1.

10. *Fort Worth Record,* March 15, 1911, pp. 1, 5; June 20, 1911, p. 1; December 31, 1911, p. 14; December 15, 1912, pt. 3, p. 3; Pate, *Livestock Legacy,* p. 295.

11. *Fort Worth Record,* February 11, 1910, p. 10; December 31, 1911, p. 14; January 2, 1913, pp. 14, 16; December 15, 1912, Pt. 3, p. 3; January 2, 1913, pp. 14,16; Pate, *Livestock Legacy,* p. 295.

12. *Fort Worth Record,* August 11, 1912, p. 16; *Fort Worth Star Telegram,* September 28, 1913, p. 20; *New York Times,* May 21, 1911, p. 12.

13. *Fort Worth Record,* December 15, 1918, pt. 4, p. 1; *Fort Worth Star Telegram,* June 14, 1914, pt. 4, p. 1; December 13, 1914, pt. 4, p. 7; Pate, *Livestock Legacy,* p. 295.

14. *Fort Worth Star Telegram,* December 13, 1914, pt. 4, p. 7; June 14, 1914, pt. 4, p. 1; *New York Times,* November 15, 1914, section XX, p. 6.

15. *Fort Worth Record,* March 29, 1910,p. 3; April 10, 1910, p. 11; May 4, 1910, p. 5; May 11, 1910, p. 1; June 11, 1910, p. 5; June 22, 1910, p. 4; June 23 , 1910, p. 9; July 1, 1910, p. 1; May 10, 1911, p. 5; December 16, 1910, p. 3; March 31, 1911, p. 5; May 22, 1912, p. 14; *City Council Minutes,* vol. V, August 9, 1911; August 19, 1911.

16. *Fort Worth Record,* December 16, 1910, p. 7; April 1, 1911, p. 3; August 20, 1911, pp. 3, 8; November 5, 1911, p. 1; July 28, 1912, p. 11; March 19, 1911, p. 12; December 17, 1911, p. 28.

17. *Council Minutes,* vol. U, April 11, 1911; *Fort Worth Record,* April 9, 1911, p. 13; August 8, 1911, p. 7; December 7, 1911, p. 7; Secretary Paul Palmer of the Board of Trade to Paddock, 1911, File 2F175, Letters 1911, Buckley Burton Paddock Papers. Note: When the board changed its name to the Chamber of Commerce it also named Paddock honorary president for life.

18. *Fort Worth Record,* October 2, 1910, p. 1; May 16, 1911, p. 3; September 1, 1912, pp. 7–8; October 13, 1912, p. 11; September 29, 1912, p. 9; October 26, 1912, p. 8.

19. Bralley, *Seventeenth Biennial Report,* p. 18.

20. *Fort Worth Record*, April 10, 1910, p. 10; September 2, 1910, p. 5; December 9, 1910, p. 10; December 11, 1910, p. 18; December 12, 1910, p. 7; June 18, 1911, p. 1; August 9, 1911, p. 9.

21. *Fort Worth Record*, December 30, 1910, p. 10; June 1, 1913, p. 12; Paddock to *Fort Worth Star Telegram*, circa 1914, File 2F177, Undated Letters, Buckley Burton Paddock Papers.

22. *Fort Worth Record*, June 20, 1911, p. 14; June 9, 1911, p. 4; July 9, 1913, p. 1; *Fort Worth Star Telegram*, September 18, 1913, p. 1.

23. *Fort Worth Record*, July 2, 1911, p. 12; September 8, 1911, p. 5; October 3, 1912, pp. 1, 5; November 2, 1912, p. 9; November 6, 1912, p. 1.

24. *Fort Worth Record*, November 2, 1912, p. 9; January 26, 1913, p. 18; May 2, 1913, p. 3; May 3, 1913, p. 16; May 11, 1913, p. 1; June 1, 1913, p. 2; *Fort Worth Star Telegram*, September 14, 1913, p. 1; October 16, 1913, p. 1; July 10, 1913, p. 1; December 5, 1913, p. 17; December 6, 1913, p. 17; August 13, 1914, p. 16.

25. *Fort Worth Record*, May 28, 1915, p. 6; July 20, 1915, p. 1; July 22, 1915, p. 1; July 23, 1915, p. 4; December 16, 1915, p. 14; January 7, 1916, p. 1; January 22, 1916, p. 1; April 16, 1916, p. 1; January 13, 1917, p. 8; February 11, 1917, p. 8; March 14, 1917, p. 16.

26. *Fort Worth Record*, March 16, 1912, p. 1; *New York Times*, January 13, 1912, p. 5; *Fort Worth Star Telegram*, April 7, 1914, p. 1; April 12, 1914, p. 8.

27. *Fort Worth Record*, February 16, 1913, p. 8; May 25, 1913, p. 10; *Fort Worth Star Telegram*, March 28, 1914, p. 1; March 31, 1914, p. 1; April 1, 1914, p. 10; September 16, 1914, p. 1; November 11, 1914, p. 9; September 1, 1916, p. 7.

28. *Fort Worth Record*, July 10, 1910, p. 9.

29. *Fort Worth Star Telegram*, August 19, 1911, p. 3; September 16, 1911, p. 1; October 28, 1911, p. 7; February 13, 1912, p. 10; September 19, 1913, p. 1; September 27, 1914, p. 14.

30. *Fort Worth Record*, January 9, 1910, p. 8; *Fort Worth Star Telegram*, February 28, 1911, p. 12; May 18, 1911, p. 1; November 21, 1911, p. 20.

31. *Fort Worth Record*, January 15, 1911, p. 8; May 5, 1913, p. 1; *Fort Worth Star Telegram*, October 2, 1910, p. 7; January 11, 1911, p. 2; October 14, 1913, p. 2; April 18, 1911, p. 1; *Council Minutes*, vol. U, April 18, 1911. The Dallas lawsuit had been brought by neighborhood residents who sued on the ground that the vice reservation devalued their property and sanctioned an activity prohibited under the Texas constitution (see *Fort Worth Record*, January 15, 1911).

32. *Fort Worth Star Telegram*, October 2, 1910, p. 7; January 11, 1911, p. 2; June 30, 1912, p. 8; October 14, 1913, p. 2; October 26, 1913, p. 20; *Fort Worth Record*, May 4, 1913, pp. 1, 3.

33. *Fort Worth Record*, January 14, 1912, p. 1; September 15, 1912, pp. 1–2; *New York Times*, November 15, 1911, p. 5; January 14, 1912; February 2, 1912, p. 13; September 15, 1912, p. 5; December 4, 1912, p. 2.

34. *Fort Worth Star Telegram*, April 24, 1911, p. 8; *Fort Worth Record*, April 21, 1913, p. 3; *New York Times*, May 13, 1912, p. 2.

35. *Fort Worth Record*, March 2, 1912, pp. 1, 3; March 3, 1912, pp. 1, 3; March 12, 1912, p. 3.

36. *Fort Worth Record*, March 3, 1912, p. 3; March 4, 1912, p. 1.

37. *Fort Worth Record*, March 28, 1912, p. 1; March 28, 1912, Extra Edition, p. 1; April 10, 1912, p. 1; April 25, 1912, p. 1; *Fort Worth Star Telegram*, December 9, 1913, p. 1; January 24, 1914, p. 1; September 9, 1916, p. 1. Norris remained controversial. In 1936, while serving as pastor of both Temple Baptist in Detroit and First Baptist in Fort Worth, he sued First Baptist for $85,200 and interest from a promissory note issued November 19, 1935 (see *Fort Worth Star Telegram*, July 17, 1936, p. 1).

38. *Fort Worth Record*, December 8, 1910, p. 11; December 9, 1910, p. 5; June 12, 1911, p. 2; June 6, 1911, p. 1; June 12, 1911, p. 2; July 24, 1911, pp. 1, 2; May 9, 1913, p. 5; May 6, 1912, p. 12; *Fort Worth Star Telegram*, July 2, 1915, p. 7; Wiebe, *The Search for Order*, pp. 56–57, 290–91.

39. *Fort Worth Record*, March 29, 1911, p. 6; April 6, 1911, p. 6.

40. *Fort Worth Record*, June 19, 1910, pt. 2, p. 6; May 31, 1911, p. 8; November 14, 1911, pp. 8–10; September 8, 1910, p. 8; March 12, 1911, p. 20; *Council Minutes*, vol. U, April 25, 1911; vol. V, August 12, 1911; *Fort Worth Star Telegram*, October 29, 1911, p. 4; November 14, 1911, pp. 10–12; November 15, 1911, p. 1; December 31, 1911, p. 10; January 28, 1912, p. 1; Painter, *Standing at Armageddon*, p. 385.

41. *Fort Worth Star Telegram*, January 22, 1910, p. 1; April 25, 1910, p. 14; April 27, 1910, p. 14; April 28, 1910, p. 7; *New York Times*, January 30, 1910, p. SM6.

42. *New York Times*, May 16, 1913, p. 6; *Fort Worth Star Telegram*, May 15, 1913, p. 1; May 16, 1913, pp. 1, 14; May 8, 1914, p. 5; March 9, 1914, p. 7; *Fort Worth Record*, May 16, 1913, p. 1.

43. *Fort Worth Star Telegram*, June 27, 1915, p. 1; October 14, 1915, p. 1; August 17, 1915, pp. 1, 15; August 22, 1915, p. 14; September 16, 1915, p. 7; April 15, 1916, p. 1; January 28, 1917, p. 1; June 17, 1918, p. 1; October 27, 1926, p. 1; *Fort Worth Record*, June 27, 1915, p. 1; August 17, 1915, September 6, 1915, pp. 1, 5.

44. *Fort Worth Star Telegram*, February 18, 1923, p. 14; June 21, 1935, p. 42.

45. *Fort Worth Star Telegram*, February 11, 1911, pp. 1, 7; February 28, 1911, pp. 1, 11; March 6, 1911, p. 1; *Fort Worth Record*, April 3, 1910, p. 11.

46. *Fort Worth Star Telegram*, January 2, 1916, p. 19; January 21, 1916, p. 1; January 1, 1917, p. 1.

47. *Fort Worth Star Telegram*, December 19, 1910, p. 9; July 5, 1910, p. 2; April 14, 1911, p. 11; October 6, 1911, p. 1; August 6, 1913, p. 2; *New York Times*, July 10, 1910, p. 3.

48. *Council Minutes*, vol. V, May 30, 1911; vol. X, May 12, 1914.

49. *Fort Worth Star Telegram*, November 12, 1911, p. 1; November 13, 1911, p. 10; November 24, 1911, p. 20; November 25, 1913, p. 11; *Fort Worth Record*, January 20, 1912, p. 12; July 10, 1910, p. 9.

50. *Fort Worth Record*, June 3, 1910, p. 3; *Fort Worth Star Telegram*, May 30, 1916, p. 1; July 3, 1916, p. 1; July 5, 1910, p. 2; *Council Minutes*, vol. Y, May 30, 1916, January 8, 1917, January 23, 1917.

51. *Fort Worth Record*, July 10, 1910, pt. 2, p. 1; October 7, 1910, p. 9.

52. *Fort Worth Record*, November 5, 1910, p. 4; February 8, 1911, p. 7; February 14, 1912, p. 1.

53. *Fort Worth Record*, March 7, 1912, p. 8; August 16, 1913, p. 1; *Fort Worth Star Telegram*, , September 9, 1913, p. 1; November 25, 1913, p. 1; January 29, 1914, p. 8; December 28, 1913, p. 3; January 24, 1914, p. 8; January 29, 1914, p. 14; February 1, 1914, p. 1. *New York Times*, September 6, 1913, p. 10.

54. *Fort Worth Record*, December 7, 1911, p. 7; *Fort Worth Star Telegram*, December 28, 1913, p. 3; November 20, 1913, p. 11; December 14, 1913, p. 11; February 25, 1913, p. 11.

55. *Fort Worth Record*, October 11, 1911, p. 10; July 10, 1912, p. 7, October 24, 1912, p. 3; October 29, 1912, p. 1.

56. *Fort Worth Star Telegram*, November 20, 1913, p. 11; *Fort Worth Record*, August 16, 1913, p. 1.

57. *New York Times*, November 6, 1914, p. 14; November 15, 1914, section XX, P. 6; January 31, 1915, section XX, p. 2; *Fort Worth Star Telegram*, December 13,1914, pt. 4, pp. 1–7; December 27, 1914, p. 25; December 12, 1914, p. 44; June 14, 1914, pt. 4, p. 1; February 25, 1915, p. 11.

58. *Fort Worth Record*, January 12, 1910, p. 7; *Fort Worth Star Telegram*, November 20, 1913, p. 11.

Chapter 7

1. *Fort Worth Star Telegram*, February 10, 2002, p. 25B; January 30, 2005, p. 9B; March 24, 1914, p. 3; *Fort Worth Record*, March 14, 1910, p. 1; March 24, 1914, p. 3; *Fort Worth Democrat*, April 20, 1882, p. 4; Knight, *Outpost on the Trinity*, pp. 135–36; Barr, *Black Texans*, p. 95; 1920 Report on Fort Worth School Enrollment and Expenses, September 25, 1920, File 2F177, Letters 1920–1921, Buckley Burton Paddock Papers. Parts of this chapter appeared in Rich, "A Distinctive Legacy," pp. 35–51.

2. Cortes, ed., *Mexican Experience in Texas*, appendix, p. 9; Rivas, "Study to Determine the Influence," p. 34; Miller, "Texas Mexican Baptist History," p. 4.

3. Jordan, "The 1887 Census," pp. 271–73. Hispanics declined from 6.5 percent of the Texas population in 1850 to 4.1 percent in 1887.

4. Cortes, ed., *Mexican Experience in Texas*, appendix, p. 16.

5. Jordan, "The 1887 Census," pp. 271–78.

6. Ibid.; *Graham (Texas) Leader*, October 21, 1898, p. 2.

7. McIlvain, "History of Hispanic Fort Worth," pp. vi and 2; Adams, *Texas Democrats; Texas State Gazetteer and Business Directory, 1914–1915; History of Texas Together with a Biographical History of Tarrant and Parker Counties*; McKinley, *The North Fort Worth Story*; Garrett, *Fort Worth*, p. 34.

8. Cuellar, "Stories from the Barrio," pp. 61–62; Cuellar, *Stories from the Barrio*, pp. 3–4.

9. Cuellar, "Stories from the Barrio," pp. 63–67; Cuellar, *Stories from the Barrio,* pp. 5–10.

10. Cuellar, "Stories from the Barrio," pp. 47, 69, 71–75; Cuellar, *Stories from the Barrio,* pp. 3–4; De León, *The Tejano Community,* pp. 88–91. In 1900 some 58.1 percent of Texas Hispanics worked at unskilled jobs, compared to 24.1 percent of Anglos.

11. Kibbe, *Latin Americans in Texas,* p. 124; McIlvain, "History of Hispanic Fort Worth," p. 7; Cuellar, "Stories from the Barrio," pp. 66–67; Paddock, *A History of Central and Western Texas,* pp. 266.

12. McIlvain, "History of Hispanic Fort Worth," p. 7; Cuellar, "Stories from the Barrio," pp. 66–67; for a history of the Acre see Selcer, *Hell's Half Acre.*

13. *Fort Worth Star Telegram,* February 18, 1923, p. 14.

14. Cuellar, "Stories from the Barrio," pp. 64–65.

15. Ibid., 46, 52–55; McIlvain, "History of Hispanic Fort Worth," p. 1–37; Pate, *North of the River,* pp. 137–38; Haynes and Wintz, *Major Problems in Texas History,* p. 371; Cortes, *Mexican Experience in Texas,* appendix, p. 16; Clinchy, *The Mexican American,* pp. 32–33.

16. Cuellar, "Stories from the Barrio," pp. 44–54, 399–400; *Fort Worth Record,* March 18, 1917.

17. Ibid.; *Fort Worth Star Telegram,* October 7, 1910, p. 9.

18. Cuellar, "Stories from the Barrio," pp. 79–82; *Fort Worth Star Telegram,* October 7, 1910, p. 9; Cuellar, *Stories from the Barrio,* pp. 14–15; *Fort Worth City Directory, 1918,* pp. 46–49; George W. Armstrong to Paddock, December 4, 1920, File 2F177, Letters 1920–1921, Buckley Burton Paddock Papers.

19. Cuellar, "Stories from the Barrio," pp. 44, 77–80; Cuellar, *Stories from the Barrio,* p. 11; Pate, *North of the River,* pp. 54, 137–38; McIlvain, "History of Hispanic Fort Worth," pp. 8–9; Arnold, "A Study of the Social Life of a Texas City," p. 32; Fort Worth Chamber of Commerce, *Industrial Fort Worth; Fort Worth Star Telegram,* October 7, 1910, p. 9; *Fort Worth Record,* March 18, 1917.

20. Cuellar, "Stories from the Barrio," pp. 79–80, 134–39; McIlvain, "History of Hispanic Fort Worth," p. 16.

21. *Fort Worth Star Telegram,* October 7, 1910, p. 9; *Thirteenth Census,* Abstracts and Supplement for Texas, p. 569.

22. McIlvain, "History of Hispanic Fort Worth," p. 8; *Fort Worth Telegram,* April 17, 1903, p. 2; *Fort Worth Star Telegram,* February 28, 1911, p. 12.

23. *Fort Worth Star Telegram,* October 7, 1910, p. 9.

24. Clinchy, *The Mexican-Americans,* pp. 32–35; Cuellar, "Stories from the Barrio," pp. 36, 43–45; Pate, *North of the River,* pp. 137–40; De León, "Mexicans and Mexican-Americans," pp. iii, 19, 25–27; McIlvain, "History of Hispanic Fort Worth," pp. 11–13; Cortes, *Mexican Experience in Texas,* appendix, pp. 10, 16; Rivas, "Study to Determine the Influence," p. 45; Cortes, *Mexican Experience in Texas,* appendix, p. 16.

25. McIlvain, "History of Hispanic Fort Worth," pp. 11–14; Cortes, *The Mexican Experience in Texas,* appendix, pp. 10, 16; Rivas, "Study to Determine the Influence,"

p. 45; De León, "Mexican and Mexican-Americans," pp. 18, 34; Clinchy, *The Mexican American*, pp. 33–35; Cuellar, "Stories from the Barrio," p. 48; Cortes, *Mexican Experience in Texas*, appendix, p. 16.

26. Cuellar, "Stories from the Barrio," pp. 91–92; *Fort Worth Press*, April 22, 1924; Zamora, *World of the Mexican Worker*, pp. 38–39; *Fort Worth Record*, March 8, 1917.

27. *Thirteenth Census*, Abstracts with Supplement for Texas, pp. 569, 642, 656; *Fourteenth Census*, vol. 2, pp. 47, 731; *Fifteenth Census*, vol. 3, pp. 68, 1016–17; Jordan, "The 1887 Census," p. 274.

28. Redistricting plan for Dallas City Council Districts, 2001 (www.dallascity hall.com/dallas/engpdf/Demographic.pdf); Redistricting Plan for Fort Worth City Council Districts, 2001 (www.fortworthgov.org/redistricting/plans).

29. Ibid.

Chapter 8

1. *Fort Worth Record*, January 11, 1916, p. 12; September 29, 1916, Booster Edition, p. 11; September 29, 1916, p. 3; January 1, 1916, p. 2; *Fort Worth Star Telegram*, February 25, 1915, p. 11.

2. *Fort Worth Record*, August 9, 1915, p. 1.

3. *Fort Worth Star Telegram*, February 25, 1915, p. 11; *Fort Worth Record*, October 31, 1915, pt. 3, p. 3; September 29, 1916, Booster Edition, pp. 9, 14.; Wiebe, *Search for Order*, pp. 266–67.

4. *Fort Worth Record*, September 29, 1916, Booster Edition, p. 14; September 3, 1915, p. 4.

5. *Fort Worth Record*, September 29, 1916, Booster Edition, pp. 11, 14; May 14, 1916, pp. 1, 10; December 30, 1916, p. 2; March 17, 1917, p. 1; September 3, 1915, p. 3; April 6, 1917, p. 5; Pate, *Livestock Legacy*, p. 295.

6. *Fort Worth Star Telegram*, February 25, 1915, p. 11; October 10, 1949, Automotive section, p. 11; *Fort Worth Record*, November 28, 1915, p. 11; December 29, 1915, pp. 1–2; July 2, 1916, p. 11; April 23, 1916, p. 11; April 15, 1917, p. 12; September 29, 1916, p. 3; April 11, 1916, p. 1; December 17, 1916, p. 10.

7. *Fort Worth Record*, July 8, 1917, pt. 2, p. 12; October 26, 1916, p. 1; April 1, 1917, pp. 1, 8; September 29, 1916, Booster Edition, pt. 2, p. 11; October 31, 1915, pt. 3, p. 3; Fitzgerald, *Texans and Their State*, pp. 12–13.

8. *Fort Worth Record*, September 29, 1916, Booster Edition, p. 11; Cashion, "What's the Matter with Texas, p. 9; *Fort Worth and the Billion Dollar Circle*.

9. *Fort Worth Record*, March 26, 1916, p. 3.

10. *Fort Worth Record*, May 11, 1916, p. 4.

11. *Fort Worth Record*, May 14, 1916, pp. 1, 10; June 2, 1916, pp. 1, 2; June 25, 1916, p. 7; June 28, 1916, p. 11; July 2, 1916, p. 11; July 4, 1916, p. 1; July 5, 1916, p. 1.

12. *Fort Worth Record*, April 1, 1917, p. 1; April 18, 1917, p. 1; April 16, 1917, p. 4; *Council Minutes*, vol. Z, May 22, 1917; April 16, 1917, April 23, 1917; *Fort Worth Star*

Telegram, April 29, 1918, p. 10; March 9, 1918, p. 1; October 13, 1918, p. 32; December 15, 1918, p. 6.

13. *Fort Worth Record ,* July 16, 1917, p. 1.

14. Maxfield and Jary, *Camp Bowie,* pp. 3–5, 7, 18, 26; *Fort Worth Record,* May 28, 1917, p. 8; June 12, 1917, pp. 1–2; July 16, 1917, p. 1; August 22, 1917, p. 1; September 4, 1917, p. 1; March 24, 1918, p. 8; April 12, 1918, p. 1.

15. *Fort Worth Star Telegram,* July 21, 2004, p. 7B; *Fort Worth Star Telegram,* October 13, 1918, p. 32.

16. *Fort Worth Record,* August 26, 1917, p. 16; August 24, 1917, p. 10; October 21, 1917, p. 15; Maxfield and Jary, *Camp Bowie,* pp. 3–5; *New York Times,* August 30, 1917, p. 8; February 24, 1918, p. 4; April 28, 1918, p. 82; *Fort Worth Star Telegram,* May 29, 2005, pp. 1, 8; Bond, *History of Fort Worth, 1849–1928.*

17. *New York Times,* July 28, 1918, p. 79; December 22, 1917, p. 3; December 25, 1917, p. 2; December 30, 1917, p. 4; February 14, 1918, p. 11; May 17, 1918, p. 3; February 16, 1918, p. 11; February 19, 1918, pp. 1, 24, 24; February 24, 1918, p. 4; April 28, 1918, p. 82; *Fort Worth Star Telegram,* May 29, 2005, pp. 1, 8; February 16, 1918, p. 8; *Fort Worth Record,* February 16, 1918, p. 1; February 25, 1918, p. 1. Twelve unfortunate pilots were buried in Greenwood Memorial Park.

18. *Fort Worth Star Telegram,* August 24, 1917, p. 1, 5; August 26, 1917, p. 5; December 11, 1917, p. 1; September 17, 1918, p. 4; February 2, 1918, p. 8; June 19, 1918; September 12, 1918, p. 2; September 13, 1918, p. 16.

19. *Fort Worth Star Telegram,* June 17, 1918, p. 1; October 7, 1919, p. 4.

20. *Fort Worth Star Telegram,* January 28, 1916, p. 2; March 31, 1916, p. 7; April 4, 1916, p. 1; September 14, 1916, p. 5; September 26, 1916, p. 1; *Fort Worth Record,* February 21, 1916, p. 4; March 5, 1916, p. 20; April 2, 1916, p. 1; September 16, 1916, p. 3; September 29, 1916, Booster Edition, p. 14.

21. *Fort Worth Star Telegram,* July 3, 1917, p. 1.

22. *Fort Worth Star Telegram,* March 4, 1917, p. 2; March 5, 1917, p. 1; March 16, 1917, p. 3.

23. *Fort Worth Star Telegram,* March 2, 1916, p. 11; March 3, 1917, p. 9; July 16, 1916, p. 4.

24. *Fort Worth Record,* March 21, 1917, pp. 1–2; March 25, 1917, pp. 1, 5; *Fort Worth Star Telegram,* March 20, 1917, p. 8.

25. *Fort Worth Star Telegram,* March 16, 1917, p. 3; March 5, 1917, p. 1; March 25, 1917, p. 9, 16, 18.

26. *Fort Worth Star Telegram,* March 16, 1917, p. 3; March 7, 1917, pp. 1, 3; March 6, 1917, p. 1; February 1, 1917, p. 2; *Fort Worth Record,* March 29, 1917, p. 5.

27. *Fort Worth Record,* March 17, 1917, p. 4; March 18, 1917, p. 7; March 21, 1917, pp. 1–2; March 25, 1917, p. 1, 5; November 21, 1917, p. 12; *Fort Worth Star Telegram,* March 25, 1917, p. 18; November 7, 1917, p. 5.

28. *Fort Worth Star Telegram,* March 22, 1917, p. 7; *Fort Worth Record,* March 22, 1917, p. 4; March 22, 1917, p. 4; March 23, 1917, p. 10; March 24, 1917, p. 17.

29. *Fort Worth Record,* November 21, 1917, p. 12.

30. *Fort Worth Record*, September 29, 1917, p. 3; *Fort Worth Star Telegram*, September 28, 1917, p.1; September 29, 1917, pp. 1–2.

31. Wiebe, *Search for Order*, pp. 287, 290–91, 295.

32. *Fort Worth Record*, July 8, 1917, p. 4; July 17, 1917, p. 1; July 12, 1917, p. 10; August 14, 1917, p. 1; September 14, 1917, p. 1; July 28, 1917, p. 5; September 28, 1917, p. 3; *Fort Worth Star Telegram*, August 26, 1917, p. 1; Painter, *Standing at Armageddon*, p. 333; Wiebe, *Search for Order*, pp. 287, 290–91.

33. *Fort Worth Record*, October 17, 1917, p. 9; September 17, 1917, pp. 1, 5; January 9, 1918, p. 12; March 10, 1918, p. 10.

34. *Fort Worth Star Telegram*, March 11, 1918, p. 4; March 28, 1918, p. 10; May 22, 1918, p. 1; June 25, 1918, p. 1; April 14, 1919, p. 16; July 20, 1918, p. 3; November 21, 1918, p. 7; January 16, 1919, p. 1; *Fort Worth Record*, March 2, 1918, p. 10; March 3, 1918, p. 1; March 10, 1918, p. 10; June 26, 1918, p. 1; March 22, 1918, p. 1; April 3, 1918, p. 12; April 5, 1918, p. 1; April 13, 1918, p. 6; April 15, 1918, p. 1; May 8, 1918, p. 10.

35. *New York Times*, January 27, 1918, p. 46; *Fort Worth Record*, October 10, 1917, p. 1.

36. *Fort Worth Record*, October 10, 1917, p. 1; October 11, 1917, p. 5; October 8, 1917, pp. 1, 2; October 19, 1917, p. 12; November 11, 1917, p. 1; December 21, 1917, p. 10; April 5, 1918, p. 1; *New York Times*, October 28, 1917, section SM, p. 6.

37. *Fort Worth Record*, March 18, 1918, pp. 1, 2; March 26, 1918, pp. 1, 3.

38. *Fort Worth Record*, April 6, 1918, p. 7; August 11, 1918, p. 3; October 10, 1917, p. 1; February 9, 1918, p. 1; *Fort Worth Star Telegram*, May 13, 1918, p. 5.

39. *Fort Worth Record*, January 14, 1916, p. 9; September 1, 1916, p. 7; January 1, 1918, p. 12; January 4, 1918, p. 4.

40. *Fort Worth Record*, October 3, 1918, p. 10; October 5, 1918, pp. 4, 10; October 10, 1918, p. 5; October 15, 1918, p. 10; October 16, 1918, p. 1; *Fort Worth Star Telegram*, October 23, 1918, p. 1; October 28, 1918, p. 3; May 4, 2009, pp. 1, 6; *Council Minutes*, vol. Z, October 21, 1918.

41. *Fort Worth Record*, November 1, 1918, p. 1; November 6, 1918, p. 12; November 14, 1918, p. 1; November 18, 1918, p. 6; *Fort Worth Star Telegram*, June 21, 1918, p. 13.

42. *Fort Worth Star Telegram*, March 9, 1918, p. 1; March 30, 1918, p. 11; *Fort Worth Record*, November 13, 1918, p. 8; December 11, 1918, p. 8; December 15, 1918, pt. 4, p. 1; January 1, 1920, Shriner's Edition, p. 10; Fitzgerald, *Texans and Their State*, pp. 12–13.

43. *Fort Worth Star Telegram*, February 25, 1915, p. 11; December 15, 1919, p. 1; *Fort Worth Record*, January 1, 1917, p. 6; February 21, 1918, p. 12; November 30, 1918, p. 10; December 13, 1918, p. 1; *New York Times*, August 25, 1918, p. 27; Buenger, *Path to a Modern South*, pp. 135–36; Schoen, "Immigrant to Capitalist," pp. 31–32. *Fourteenth Census*, vol. 8, p. 141; *Fort Worth and the Billion Dollar Circle*, pp. 5, 7, 26.

44. Buenger, *Path to a Modern South*, p. 135; *Fort Worth Star Telegram*, December 15, 1918, p. 1; *Fort Worth Record*, April 7, 1918, p. 10; December 8, 1918, p. 1;

December 10, 1918, p. 1; December 13, 1918, p. 1; December 14, 1918, p. 1; Bond, *History of Fort Worth*, Chapter 29; *New York Times*, February 1, 1920, p. 21; *Fort Worth and the Billion Dollar Circle*, p. 24, 26.

45. *Fort Worth Record*, December 8, 1918, p. 1; November 26, 1918, pp. 1, 5; November 3, 1918, p. 7; *Fort Worth Star Telegram*, December 21, 1918, section 3, p. 1; October 30, 1949, oil and gas section, p. 17.; *Fort Worth in Brief*.

46. *Fort Worth Star Telegram*, December 16, 1917, section 3, p. 2; February 25, 1919, p. 1; *Fort Worth Record*, November 2, 1918, p. 7; *New York Times*, April 14, 1919, p. 16; January 1, 1920, p. 20.

47. *Fort Worth Record*, January 13, 1918, p. 1; December 20, 1917, pp. 1, 4; March 4, 1918, p. 4; June 30, 1918, p. 7; March 10, 1918, p. 10; August 11, 1918, pt. 2, p. 8; April 14, 1918, p. 8.

48. *Fort Worth Record*, December 13, 1918, p. 12; November 22, 1918, p. 1; *New York Times*, September 12, 1919, p. 4; *Fort Worth Star Telegram*, January 1, 1919, p. 16; May 22, 1919, p. 11; May 16, 1919, p. 23. Nine army camps, including Camp Bowie, were auctioned on April 15, 1919, at Washington, D.C. See *New York Times*, March 28, 1919, p. 17.

49. *Fort Worth Star Telegram*, March 31, 1919, p. 1; August 17, 1919, p. 16; February 8, 1920, section 4, p. 1; February 10, 1920, p. 1; November 4, 1920, p. 5.

50. *Fort Worth Record*, February 13, 1918, p. 5; November 3, 1918, p. 5; June 16, 1918, pp. 1–2; September 1, 1918, p. 14; *Fort Worth Star Telegram*, August 21, 1919, p. 1. The Texas and Pacific Railroad was the city's largest taxpayer, paying in excess of $35,000 on a valuation of over $2 million.

51. *Fort Worth City Directory*, 1920, pp. 2–3; *Fort Worth in Brief*; *Fourteenth Census*, vol. 9, pp. 1451–52, 1449–50, 1460–61; Talbert, *Cowtown Metropolis*, p. 126; *Fort Worth and the Billion Dollar Circle*, p. 22.

52. *Fourteenth Census*, vol. 9, pp. 1449–50, 1460–63; Talbert, *Cowtown Metropolis*, p. 126

53. *Fourteenth Census*, vol. 9, pp. 1449–50, 1463; Talbert, *Cowtown Metropolis*, p. 126; *Fort Worth: The Story of Your City*, pp. 39–41.

54. *Fort Worth Star Telegram*, May 20, 1920, p. 2; June 13, 1920, p. 1; July 4, 1920, p. 6; August 27, 1920, p. 9; September 24, 1920, p.p. 1, 22; October 30, 1949, merchandising section, p. 2; *Thirteenth Census*, pp. 778, 781, 783, 784, 792; *Fourteenth Census*, vol. 3, pp. 105, 991, 995, 998, 1000, 1011, 1015; Paddock to *Fort Worth Record*, October 9, 1921, File 2F177, Letters 1920–1921, Buckley Burton Paddock Papers.

Conclusion

1. Painter, *Standing at Armageddon*, pp. 385–86.

2. *Fourteenth Census*, vol. 9, p. 1463.

3. *Fort Worth in Brief*; Schoen, "Immigrant to Capitalist," pp. 24, 30–31; Jackson. "Along Came a Spider," p. 23; Talbert, *Cowtown Metropolis*, pp. 126–27; Paddock, *History of Texas*, pp. 657–80.

4. Dykstra, *Cattle Towns*; Larsen, *The Urban West at the End of the Frontier*; Mahoney, *River Towns in the Great West*; Limerick, *Legacy of Conquest*.

5. *Fort Worth Star Telegram*, March 31, 1920, p. 1.

6. Paddock, *History of Texas*, pp. 657–80; *Fort Worth Record*, May 11, 1913, p. 8; Painter, *Standing at Armageddon*, pp. 385–86.

7. "Fort Worth Leads in War Production,," p. 11; *Fort Worth Star Telegram*, March 31, 2003, p. 1D; Schoen, "Immigrant to Capitalist," pp. 30–31.

Bibliography

Primary Sources

Newspapers

(Camp Bowie, Texas) Trench and Camp, 1917–1918
Daily Fort Worth Standard, 1876–1877
Dallas Morning News, 1897
Dallas Southern Mercury, 1891–1892
Dallas Times Herald, 1896
Fort Worth Daily Democrat and Advance, 1881–1882
Fort Worth Daily Mail, 1885–1891
Fort Worth Democrat (also as *Fort Worth Daily Democrat*), 1878–1881
Fort Worth Gazette (also as *Fort Worth Daily Gazette* and *Fort Worth Weekly Gazette*), 1883–1896
Fort Worth Mail-Telegram, 1899, 1902–1903
Fort Worth Record, 1904–1920
Fort Worth Register (also as *Fort Worth Morning Register*), 1896–1912
Fort Worth Standard, 1873–1875
Fort Worth Star Telegram, 1909–1923, 1933, 1936, 1945, 1949, 1962, 2003–2005
Fort Worth Telegram, 1902–1908
Graham (Texas) Leader, 1896, 1898
New York Times, 1880–1920

Collections

Buckley Burton Paddock Papers, 1865–1925. Dolph Briscoe Center for American History at the University of Texas at Austin.
Communities: Fort Worth History Papers. Tarrant County Archives. Fort Worth, Texas.
Julia Jenkins Garret Papers. Special Collections of the University of Texas at Arlington Library.

Myres, Sandra. Fort Worth 1870–1900, Notes and Documents 1968. Special Collections of the University of Texas at Arlington Library.
Paddock Papers. Special Collections of the University of Texas at Arlington Library.
Texas Writers' Project, 1941. Research Data: Fort Worth and Tarrant County, Texas. Fort Worth, Texas.

Remembrances/Autobiographies

Forney, John W. *What I Saw in Texas*. Philadelphia: Ringwalt & Brown, 1872.
Jones, John Oliver. *A Cowman's Memoirs*. Fort Worth: Texas Christian University Press, 1953.
Paddock, B. Buckley. *Early Days in Fort Worth, Much of Which I Saw and Part of Which I Was*. Fort Worth: n.d.
Terrell, J. C. *Remembrances of the Early Days of Fort Worth*. Fort Worth: Texas Christian University Press in cooperation with Texas Wesleyan University, 1999. (From the Texas Christian University Special Collections.)
Smith, Sam. *Things I Remember about Early Days in the History of Fort Worth*. n.p.: 1965.
Van Zandt, Khleber M. *Force Without Fanfare: The Autobiography of K. M. Van Zandt*. Edited by Sandra L. Myres. Fort Worth: Texas Christian University Press, 1968.

Directories/Chamber of Commerce Publications

Allen, E. D. *The Texas Spring Palace: A Complete and Categorical Description of This Marvelous Temple*. Fort Worth: Texas Printing and Lithographing Company, 1889.
Dexter, W. W. *Fort Worth Trade Review's Second Annual, Illustrated Edition*. Fort Worth: Fort Worth Chamber of Commerce, 1891.
———. *Fort Worth Trade Review's Second Annual, Subscription Edition*. Fort Worth: Fort Worth Chamber of Commerce, 1891.
Fort Worth, Texas: The Gateway to the Great Southwest. Fort Worth: The Fort Worth Chamber of Commerce, 1912.
Fort Worth: The Story of Your City. Fort Worth: Fort Worth Chamber of Commerce, 1925.
Fort Worth and the Billion Dollar Circle. Fort Worth: Fort Worth Chamber of Commerce, 1921.
Fort Worth City Directory, 1916. Dallas: R. L. Polk and Company, Compilers and Publishers, 1916.
Fort Worth City Directory, 1918. Dallas: R. L. Polk and Company, Compilers and Publishers, 1918.
Fort Worth City Directory, 1920. Dallas: R. L. Polk and Company, Compilers and Publishers, 1920.
Fort Worth in Brief. Fort Worth: Fort Worth Chamber of Commerce, 1922. (From the Amon Carter Museum of Western History, Fort Worth.)

From Frontier to Metropolis: Fort Worth Texas Diamond Jubilee. n.p.: Bateman-Millican Advertising Agency, 1923.

General Directory of the City of Fort Worth, 1882. Dallas: Gillespie, Work, and Walton, 1881.

General Directory of the City of Fort Worth, 1883–1884. Galveston: Morrison and Fourmy, 1884.

General Directory of the City of Fort Worth, 1885–1886. Galveston: Morrison and Fourmy, 1886.

General Directory of the City of Fort Worth, 1886–1887. Fort Worth: Morrison and Fourmy, 1887.

General Directory of the City of Fort Worth, 1888–1889. Fort Worth: Morrison and Fourmy, 1889.

General Directory of the City of Fort Worth Texas, 1898–1899. Fort Worth: Fort Worth Directory Association, 1898. (From the Special Collections of the University of Texas at Arlington Library, Arlington, Texas.)

General Directory of the City of Fort Worth, 1892–1893. Galveston: Morrison and Fourmy, 1891.

General Directory of the City of Fort Worth, 1894–1895. Galveston: Morrison and Fourmy, 1893.

General Directory of the City of Fort Worth, 1896–1897. Galveston: Morrison and Fourmy, 1896.

General Directory of the City of Fort Worth, 1899–1902. Galveston: Morrison and Fourmy, 1899.

General Directory of the City of Fort Worth, 1902–1903. Galveston: Morrison and Fourmy, 1902.

General Directory of the Inhabitants, Manufacturing Establishments, Institutions, Business Firms, etc., in the City of Fort Worth, 1890. Fort Worth: The Texas Printing and Lithographing Company, 1889.

Industrial Fort Worth. Fort Worth: Fort Worth Chamber of Commerce, 1930.

Industrial Fort Worth. Fort Worth: Fort Worth Chamber of Commerce, circa 1937.

Scoble, A. W., and H. L. Calhoun. *Annual Waterworks Report of A. W. Scoble, Superintendent, and H. L. Calhoun, Secretary, for Fiscal year Ending March 21, 1898.* Fort Worth: Texas Printing Company, 1898. (From the Amon Carter Museum of Western History, Fort Worth.)

Swasey, Charles J., and W. M. Nelson. *Directory of the City of Fort Worth.* Fort Worth: *Daily Democrat,* 1877.

Government Documents

Bralley, F. M. *Seventeenth Biennial Report of the State Department of Education for Years Ending August 31, 1909, and August 31, 1910.* Austin: Austin Printing Company, 1911.

Fort Worth City Council Minutes, 1880–1904.

Fourteenth Census of the United States. Washington, D.C.: Government Printing Office, 1922.

Mayfield, Allison. *Biannual Report of the Secretary of State of the State of Texas.* Austin: Ben C. Jones Company, 1897.

Ninth Census of the United States. Washington, D.C.: Government Printing Office, 1872.

Paddock, B. B., and John T. Montgomery. *Annual Report of the City of Fort Worth for Fiscal Year Ending March 21, 1898.* Fort Worth: Fort Worth Texas Printing Company, 1898. (From the Texanna Collection, Vance Memorial Library, Dallas Baptist University, Dallas, Texas.)

Tenth Census of the United States. Washington, D.C.: Government Printing Office, 1883.

Thirteenth Census of the United States. Washington, D.C.: Government Printing Office, 1913.

Twelfth Census of the United States. Washington, D.C.: Government Printing Office, 1901.

Smith, George W. *Biannual Report of the Secretary of State of the State of Texas.* Austin: Ben C. Jones Company, 1893.

Secondary Sources

Books and Articles

Adams, Frank Carter, ed. *Texas Democrats: A Centennial History of Politicians and Personalities of the Democratic Party, 1836–1936.* Austin: Democratic Historical Association, 1937.

All Roads Lead to Fort Worth. n.p.: circa 1907.

Arnold, Ann. *Camp Meeting to Cathedral: Fort Worth's Historic Congregations.* Arlington: Landa Press, 2004.

———. *History of the Fort Worth Legal Community.* Austin: Eakin Press, 2000.

———. *A History of the Fort Worth Medical Community.* Arlington: Landa Press, 2002.

Bailey, James M., and Nancy O. Vick. *The Fort Worth Story: Yesterday and Today.* Fort Worth: Fort Worth Schools, 1967.

Baker, James H., and Raymond E. Cage, II. *Indians in the History of Tarrant County, Texas.* Fort Worth: Tarrant County Archeological Society, 1962.

Barr, Alwyn. *Black Texans: A History of African Americans in Texas, 1528–1995.* Norman: University of Oklahoma Press, 1996.

Barth, Gunther. *City People: The Rise of Modern City Culture in Nineteenth-Century America.* New York: Oxford University Press, 1980.

Bateman, T. O. "The Fort Worth Board of Trade. *The Bohemian* 1, no.2 (1899): 79–80.

Bednarek, Janet R. Daly. *America's Airports: Airfield Development , 1918–1947.* College Station: Texas A&M University Press, 2001.

Blumberg, Louis, and Robert Gottlieb. *War on Waste: Can America Win Its Battle with Garbage?* Washington, D.C.: Island Press, 1989.

Bond, Tom Burke. *History of Fort Worth, 1849–1928.* n.p.: n.d.

The Book of Fort Worth. Fort Worth: Fort Worth Record, 1913.

Boorstin, Daniel J., *The Americans: The Democratic Experience.* New York: Random House, 1973.

Buenger, Walter L. *The Path to a Modern South: Northeast Texas Between Reconstruction and the Great Depression.* Austin: University of Texas Press, 2001.

Cashion, Ty. "What's the Matter with Texas?" *Montana, The Magazine of Western History* 55, no. 4 (Winter 2005): 2–15.

Calvert, Robert A., Greg Cantrell, and Arnoldo De León. *The History of Texas.* Arlington Heights, Illinois: Harlan Davidson, Inc., 1990.

Carter, James E. *Cowboys, Cowtown, and Crosses: A Centennial History of the Tarrant Baptist Association.* Fort Worth: Tarrant Baptist Association, 1986.

Clarke, F. M. "The New South. The City of Fort Worth." *New England Magazine* 2, no. 14 (December 1891): 538–47.

Clayton, Lawrence, and Joan Halford Farmer, eds. *Tracks Along the Clear Fork: Stories from Shackleford and Throckmorton Counties.* Abilene: McWhiney Press at McMurry University, 2000.

Clincy, Everett Ross. *The Mexican American: Equality of Opportunity for Latin-Americans in Texas.* New York: Arno Press, 1974.

Collins, Michael. *Those Daring Young Men: A History of the Automobile Pioneers in Fort Worth, 1902–1940.* Fort Worth: Frank D. Kent, produced by the *Fort Worth News Tribune,* 1985.

Cortes, Carlos, ed. *The Mexican Experience in Texas (The Chicano Heritage).* New York: Arno Press, 1976.

Craig, Horace. *Fort Worth Stockyards National Historic District: Longhorns, Cattle, Brands, Barbed Wire and a Tin Bucket, An Illustrated History and Guide.* Kearny, Nebraska: Morris Publishing, 1994.

Cronon, William. *Nature's Metropolis: Chicago and the Great West.* New York: W. W. Norton and Company, 1991.

Cuellar, Carlos E. *Stories from the Barrio: A History of Mexican Fort Worth.* Fort Worth: Texas Christian University Press, 2003.

David, Henry. *The History of the Haymarket Affair.* New York: Russell and Russell, 1936.

De León, Arnoldo. *The Tejano Community.* Albuquerque: University of New Mexico Press, 1982.

———. *They Called Them Greasers: Anglo Attitudes Toward Mexican-Americans in Texas, 1821–1910.* Austin: University of Texas Press, 1983.

Doyle, Don. *New Men, New Cities, New South.* The Fred W. Morrison Series in Southern Studies. Chapel Hill: University of North Carolina Press, 1990.

Duncan, Patricia L. "Buckley Paddock—Fort Worth's Biggest Booster, The Critical Years, 1873–1876." In *The E. C. Barksdale Student Lectures. 1976–1977,* 179–95. Austin: Published for the University of Texas at Arlington by the University of Texas Press, 1975.

Dykstra, Robert R. *The Cattle Towns.* Lincoln: University of Nebraska Press, 1968.

Elkins, Stanley, and Eric McKitrich. "A Meaning for Turner's Frontier." *Political Science Quarterly* 69 (1954): 321–53.

Elser, Max. *Fort Worth Almanac of 1883*. Fort Worth: Max Elser Printing, 1882.

Farman, Irvin. *The Fort Worth Club: A Centennial Story*. Fort Worth: The Club, 1985.

Fay, B. Winton. *Cowtown Keyboards: A Short History: From the First Piano in Fort Worth to Cliburn Competitions*. Fort Worth: Ink Blink Publishing, 2001.

Fitzgerald, Hugh Nugent. *Texans and Their State: A Newspaper Reference Work*. Fort Worth: The Texas Biographical Association, [1918].

Flores, Richard R. "The Corridor and the Emergence of Texas-Mexican Social Identity." *Journal of American Folklore* 105 (1992): 166–82.

"Fort Worth, Gateway to the Panhandle." *Frank Leslie's Illustrated Newspaper* (September 27, 1890): 7–13.

Fort Worth, 1903. n.p.: n.d. (From the Local History Collection of the Fort Worth Public Library.)

Fort Worth Business Directory. Fort Worth: Fort Worth Printing and Book Binding, 1884.

"Fort Worth Leads in War Production." *This Month in Fort Worth* 22, no. 3 (March, 1945): 11.

Fort Worth National Corporation/Annual Report, 1972; and Fort Worth National Bank/ Century One, 1873–1973. Fort Worth: The Bank, 1973.

The Fort Worth Press: We Believe in Fort Worth Book. Fort Worth: Monitor Publishing, 1926.

From Frontier to Metropolis: Fort Worth Texas Diamond Jubilee. n.p.: Bateman-Millican Advertising Agency, 1923.

Garrett, Julia Kathryn. *Fort Worth: A Frontier Triumph*. Fort Worth: Texas Christian University Press, 1972.

Garrett, Julia Kathryn, and Mary Daggett Luke, eds. *Down Historic Trails of Fort Worth and Tarrant County*. Fort Worth: Dudley Hogkins Company, 1949.

Gorman, Henrie, and Clara Leclerc. "Fort Worth: Past and Present." *The Bohemian* 1, no, 1 (Spring 1898): 67–69.

Graham, Richard. "The Investment Boom in British-Texan Cattle Companies 1880–1885." *Business History Review* 34, no. 4 (Winter 1960): 421–45.

Greenleaf, Sue. *About Fort Worth and Adjacent Country*. Fort Worth: C. M. Brown Publishing, n.d.

Hall, Flem. *Sports Champions of Fort Worth, Texas 1868–1968*. Fort Worth: John L. Lewis Publisher, 1968.

Hammond, W. J. *History of the Municipal Departments of the City of Fort Worth, Texas, 1873–1939*. n.p.: Federal Education Radio Project 705-3-9 sponsored by the United States Office of Education, Federal Security Agency, 1939.

Harrison, Margaret W. *The Story of Oakwood Cemetery*. Fort Worth: Oakwood Cemetery Association, 1970.

Haynes, Sam W., and Cary D. Wintz. "Major Problems in Texas History." In *Major Problems in American History*. Edited by Thomas G. Paterson. Boston: Houghton Mifflin Company, 2002.

History of Texas Together with a Biographical History of Tarrant and Parker Counties. Chicago: The Lewis Publishing Company, 1895.

Hoover, William R. *St. Patrick's: The First 100 Years.* Fort Worth: St. Patrick Cathedral, 1988.

Hundley, Norris, Jr. *Water and the West: The Colorado River Compact and the politics of Water in the American West.* Berkeley: University of California Press, 1975.

Jackson, Kenneth T. *Crabgrass Frontier: The Suburbanization of the United States.* New York: Oxford University Press, 1985.

Jennings, A. O. *Greater Fort Worth.* Fort Worth: A. O. Jennings, 1907.

Jordan, Terry G. "The 1887 Census of the Texas Hispanic Population." *Aztlan* 12 (Fall 1981): 271–78.

Kibbe, Pauline. *Latin Americans in Texas.* Albuquerque: University of New Mexico Press, 1946.

Knight, Oliver. *Fort Worth: Outpost on the Trinity.* Norman: University of Oklahoma Press, 1972.

Lane, Charles Fred. *Early Days in Fort Worth.* Fort Worth: Reimers-Taylor Publishing, n.d.

Larsen, Lawrence. *The Urban West at the End of the Frontier.* Lawrence: The Regents Press of Kansas / University Press of Kansas, 1978.

Licht, Walter. *Industrializing America: The Nineteenth Century.* The American Moment Series. Baltimore: The Johns Hopkins University Press, 1995.

Limerick, Patricia Nelson. *The Legacy of Conquest: The Unbroken Past of the American West.* New York: W. W. Norton and Company, 1987.

Link, Arthur S., and Richard L. McCormick. *Progressivism.* The American History Series, edited by John Hope Franklin and A. S. Eisenstadt. Wheeling, Illinois: Harlan Davidson, 1983.

Lynch, Vernon. "1879 in the *Echo:* A Year at Fort Griffin." *West Texas Historical Association Year Book* 41 (October, 1965): 51–79.

Mahoney, Timothy R. *River Towns in the Great West: The Structure of Provincial Urbanization in the American Midwest, 1820–1870.* Cambridge: Cambridge University Press, 1990.

———. *Provincial Lives: Middle-Class Experience in the Antebellum Middle West.* Cambridge: Cambridge University Press, 1999.

Makers of Fort Worth. Fort Worth: Fort Worth Newspaper Association, 1914.

Maxfield, Bernice Blanche Miller, and William E. Jary, Jr. *Camp Bowie, Fort Worth, 1917–1918: An Illustrated History of the 36th Division in the First World War.* Fort Worth: B. B. Maxfield Foundation, 1975.

McBeth, Leon. *Victory Through Prayer: A History of Rosen Heights Baptist Church 1906–1966.* Fort Worth: Rosen Heights Baptist Church, 1966.

McConnell, Joseph Carroll. *The West Texas Frontier: or A Descriptive History of Early Times in Western Texas, Containing an Accurate Account of Much Hitherto Unpublished History.* Jacksboro, Texas: Gazette Print, 1933–1939. (From the Texas Christian University Special Collections.)

McKinley, Dewitt. *The North Fort Worth Story.* Fort Worth: n.p., circa 1960.

Melosi, Martin V. *Garbage in the Cities: Refuse, Reform, and the Environment, 1880–
    1980.* College Station: Texas A&M University Press, 1981.

Merriner, James L. *Grafters and Goo Goos: Corruption and Reform in Chicago, 1833–
    2003.* Carbondale: Southern Illinois University Press, 2004.

Miller, Char, and Heywood T. Sanders, eds. *Urban Texas Politics and Development.*
    College Station: Texas A&M University Press, 1990.

Morrison, Andrew. *The City of Fort Worth and the State of Texas.* St. Louis and Fort
    Worth: George Engelhardt & Co., [1890].

Myers, Sandra. "Fort Worth 1870–1900." *Southwestern Historical Review* 72 (Octo-
    ber 1968): 200–22.

Our Celebration: All Saints Catholic Church Fort Worth, Texas. South Hackensack,
    New Jersey: Custombook Inc., 1977.

Overton, Richard Cleghorn. *Gulf to Rockies: The Heritage of the Fort Worth and
    Denver-Colorado and Southern Railways, 1861–1898.* Austin: University of Texas
    Press, 1953.

Paddock, B. B. "Fort Worth, Her Wonderful Progress." *The Bohemian* 5, no. 1
    (1907): 69–75.

———. *A History of Central and Western Texas.* Chicago: The Lewis Publishing
    Company, 1911.

———. *History of Texas: Fort Worth and the Texas Northwest Edition.* Chicago: Lewis
    Publishing Company, 1922.

———."Texas of Today." *The Bohemian.* Souvenir Edition (1904): 105–106.

———. *A Twentieth Century History and Biographical Record of North and West Texas.*
    Chicago: The Lewis Publishing Company, 1906.

Painter, Nell Irvin, *Standing at Armageddon: The United States, 1877–1919.* New
    York: W.W. Norton and Company, 1987.

Pate, J'Nell. *Livestock Legacy: The Fort Worth Stockyards, 1887–1987.* College Station:
    Texas A&M University Press, 1988.

———. *North of the River: A Brief History of North Fort Worth.* Chisholm Trail Series
    11. Fort Worth: Texas Christian University Press, 1994.

Pirtle, Caleb. *Fort Worth: The Civilized West.* Tulsa: Continental Heritage Press,
    1980.

Preuss, Gene B. "Differing Perceptions: Public School Teachers and Mexi-
    can Students in Texas, 1910–1930." *West Texas Historical Association* 72 (1996):
    119–29.

Putnam, Frank. "The Twin Cities of North Texas." *New England Magazine* 36 (1907):
    716–28.

Race, Lila Bunch. *Pioneer Fort Worth, Texas: The Life, Times and Families of South
    Tarrant County.* Dallas: Taylor Publishing Company, 1976.

Ratt, W. Dirk. *Revoltosos: Mexico's Rebels in the United States, 1903–1923.* College
    Station: Texas A&M University Press, 1981.

Reps, John W. *Cities of the American West: A History of Frontier Urban Planning.*
    Princeton: Princeton University Press, 1979.

———. *The Forgotten Frontier: Urban Planning in the American West Before 1890.*
    Columbia, Missouri: University of Missouri Press, 1981.

Rich, Harold. "A Distinctive Legacy: Settlement Patterns of Fort Worth's Hispanic Community." *West Texas Historical Journal* 82 (2006): 35–51.

———. "Strange Bedfellows: 'Longhair Jim' Courtright and Political Influence in
Fort Worth." *East Texas Historical Journal* 46, no. 1 (2008): 27–32.

Riney, James E., Maurice G. Fortin, Douglas M. Ferrier, et al. *Inventory of County
Records: Tarrant County Courthouse, Volume II.* The Texas County Record In-
ventory Project, North Texas State University Denton. Austin: Texas State
Library, 1977.

Roark, Carol E. *Fort Worth Then and Now.* Fort Worth: Texas Christian University
Press, 2001.

Sanders, Leonard. *How Fort Worth Became the Texasmost City.* Fort Worth: Amon
Carter Museum of Western Art, 1973.

Schmelzer, Janet. *Where the West Begins: Fort Worth and Tarrant County.* North-
ridge, California: Windsor Publishing, 1985.

Schmidt, Ruby, ed. *Fort Worth and Tarrant County: A Historical Guide.* Fort Worth:
Texas Christian University Press, 1984.

Selcer, Richard. *Fort Worth Characters.* Denton, Texas: University of North Texas
Press, 2009.

———. *Hell's Half Acre: The Life and Times of a Red Light District.* Chisholm Trail
Series 9. Fort Worth: Texas Christian University Press, 1991.

———. ed. *Legendary Watering Holes: The Saloons that Made Texas Famous.* College
Station: Texas A&M University Press, 2004.

Shirley, Glenn. *Heck Thomas Frontier Marshal: The Story of a Real Gunfighter.* Philadelphia: Chilton Books, 1962.

Skaggs, Jimmy M., "The Economic Impact of Trailing: One Aspect" *West Texas
Historical Association Year Book* 43 (October 1967): 18–30.

Smith, Edward J. *The Capitalist, or the City of Fort Worth (A Parody on the Mikado).* Fort
Worth: Smith, 1888. (From the Texas Christian University Special Collections.)

Speer, Bonnie. *Portrait of a Lawman: U.S. Deputy Marshal Heck Thomas.* Norman:
Reliance Press, 1996.

Spence, Vernon G. "Colonel Morgan Jones: Master Builder of Texas Railroads."
West Texas Historical Year Book 44 (October 1968): 15–25

Spring Palace, Fort Worth: A Parody on HMS Pinafore. Fort Worth: Texas Spring
Palace, 1889.

Stanley, Francis. *Longhair Jim Courtright: Two Gun Marshal of Fort Worth.* Denver:
World Press, 1957.

Steffen, Jerome O., ed. *The American West: New Perspectives, New Dimensions.* Norman: University of Oklahoma Press, 1979.

Steinberg, Ted. *Acts of God: The Unnatural History of Natural Disaster in America.*
New York: Oxford University Press, 2000.

The Story of Fort Worth from Outpost to Metropolis. Fort Worth: Fort Worth National Bank, n.d. [1960s].

Talbert, Robert Harris. *Cowtown Metropolis: Case Study of a City's Growth and
Structure.* Fort Worth: Leo Potishman Foundation, Texas Christian University,
1956. (From the Texas Christian University Special Collections.)

Taylor, Robert. *Fort Worth, 1800 to Now*. Fort Worth: *Fort Worth Star Telegram*, 1963.

Texas State Gazetteer and Business Directory, 1914–1915. Detroit: R. L. Polk and Company, 1914.

Uglow, Loyd M. *Standing in the Gap: Army Outposts, Picket Stations, and the Pacification of the Texas Frontier, 1866–1886*. Fort Worth: Texas Christian University Press, 2001.

Wade, Richard C. *The Urban Frontier: Pioneer Life in Early Pittsburgh, Cincinnati, Lexington, Louisville, and St. Louis*. Chicago: University of Chicago Press, 1959.

Ward, Celeste. "Fort Worth, A Cowtown Success: Its Stockyards and Packing Industries, 1870–1903." In *The E. C. Barksdale Student Lectures*, 84–95. Austin: Published for the University of Texas at Arlington by the University of Austin Press, 1978.

Webb, Walter Prescott. *The Great Plains*. Lincoln: University of Nebraska Press, 1981.

White, Richard. "Information, Markets, and Corruptions: Transcontinental Railroads in the Gilded Age." *The Journal of American History* 90, no. 1 (June 2003): 19–43.

White, Richard. *It's Your Misfortune and None of My Own: A New History of the American West*. Norman: University of Oklahoma Press, 1991.

Wiebe, Robert H. *The Search for Order, 1877–1920*. The Making of America, edited by David Donald. New York: Hill and Wang, 1967.

Wilson, Alexis. "Moments That Changed Our City: A History Lesson." *Fort Worth, Texas* 7, no. 12 (December 2004): 54–61.

———. "Moments That Changed Our City: A History Lesson." *Fort Worth, Texas* 8, no. 2 (February 2005): 36–41.

Williams, Mack, ed. *In Old Fort Worth: The Story of a City and its People as Published in the News Tribune in 1976 and 1977*. Fort Worth: Tribune Publishing Company, 1977.

Worster, Donald. *Under Western Skies: Nature and History in the American West*. New York: Oxford University Press, 1992.

Zamora, Emilio, Cynthia Orozco, and Rodolfo Rocha, eds. *Mexican-Americans in Texas History*. Austin: Texas State Historical Association, 2000.

Dissertations and Theses

Arnold, W. A. "A Study of the Social Life of a Texas City." Master of Arts thesis, Texas Christian University, 1919.

Ashburn, Karl Everett. "Fort Worth's Relation to the Texas Cotton Industry." Master of Arts thesis, Texas Christian University, 1928.

Ashburn, Katherine Travis. "History of Methodist Educational Work Among the Mexicans in Texas." Master of Arts thesis, Texas Christian University, 1934.

Bennett, Rossie Beth. "History of the Cattle Trade in Fort Worth, Texas." Master of Arts thesis, George Peabody College for Teachers, 1931.

Berrong, Verna Elizabeth. "History of Tarrant County from its Beginning until 1875." Master of Arts thesis, Texas Christian University, 1938.

Brogdon, Margaret Schell. "A View of the Political, Economic, and Social Aspects of Fort Worth from 1890 to 1900." Master of Arts thesis, Texas Christian University, 1967.

Copeland, David Ross. "Emerging Young Giant: Fort Worth 1877–1880." Master of Arts thesis, Texas Christian University, 1972.

Crisp, James Ernest. "Anglo-Texan Attitudes Toward the Mexican, 1821–1845." Ph.D. dissertation, Yale University, 1976.

Cuellar, Carlos Elisea. "Stories from the Barrio: A History of Mexican Fort Worth." Ph.D. dissertation, Texas Christian University, 1998.

De León, Arnoldo. "Mexicans and Mexican-Americans in Texas, 1910–1920." Masters of Arts thesis, Texas Christian University, 1971.

———. "White Racial Attitudes Toward Mexicanos in Texas, 1821–1900." Ph.D. dissertation, Texas Christian University, 1974.

Dickinson, James H. "The Supervision of Religious Education in Latin American Baptist Missions in Texas." Ph.D. dissertation, Southwestern Baptist Theological Seminary, 1951.

Duncan, Patricia Lenora. "Enterprise: B. B. Paddock and Fort Worth—A Case Study of Late Nineteenth-Century American Boosterism." Master of Arts thesis, University of Texas at Arlington, 1982.

Evans, Samuel Lee. "Texas Agriculture, 1880–1930." Ph.D. dissertation, University of Texas at Austin, 1960.

Goerte, Anne Lenore. "Some Phases of the Development of the Fort Worth School System, 1854–1930." Master of Arts thesis, University of Colorado, 1934.

Harkins, Thomas A. "A History of Municipal Government of Fort Worth." Master of Arts thesis, Texas Christian University, 1937.

Hendricks, Debra. "The History of Cattle and Oil in Tarrant County." Master of Arts thesis, Texas Christian University, 1969.

Hooks, Michael Q. "The Struggle for Dominance: Urban Rivalry in North Texas, 1870–1910." Ph.D. dissertation, Texas Technological University, 1979.

Jackson, Jill Carlson. "Along Came a Spider: Visions and Realities of Railroad Development in Fort Worth, Texas, 1873–1923, a Cartographic Approach." Master of Arts thesis, University of Texas at Arlington, 1996.

Knott, Gladys Louise. "Social Life in Texas in the 1890s." Master of Arts thesis, Texas Christian University, 1966.

Kurtzman, Ellen. "History of the Longhorn Council of the Boy Scouts of America." Master of Arts thesis, Texas Christian University, 1976.

Lane, Doris Ann. "A History of the Fort Worth Theater from 1880 to 1888." Master of Arts thesis, Texas Christian University, 1948.

McArthur, Daniel Evander. "The Cattle Industry of Texas, 1685–1918." Master of Arts thesis, University of Texas at Austin, 1918.

McGilvray, Byron Wendol. "A Brief History of the Development of Music in Fort Worth, Texas, 1849–1972." Master of Arts thesis, 1972.

Miles, James C. "Fort Worth and World War I." Master of Arts thesis, Southern Methodist University, 1946.

Miller, William Bricen. "Texas Mexican Baptist History or a History of Baptist Work Among Mexicans in Texas." Th.D. dissertation, Southwestern Baptist Theological Seminary, 1931.

Monroe, Orie Dexter. "Juvenile Delinquency and Juvenile Judicial Procedure in Fort Worth." Master of Arts thesis, Texas Christian University, 1929.

Montgomery, Mildred Gaskill. "Child-Placing Agencies in Fort Worth, Texas. Master of Arts thesis, Texas Christian University, 1927.

Moore, Harris Paxton. "The Theater in Fort Worth, 1902–1903." Master of Arts thesis, Texas Christian University, 1963.

Moore, Milton Harvery. "A School Building Program: Fort Worth, Texas." Master of Arts thesis, Texas Christian University, 1930.

Odom, Clayton Forman. "The Cats are King in Texas: A History of the Fort Worth Cats Baseball Club, 1888–1964." Master of Arts thesis, Texas Christian University, 1990.

Pearce, Paul. "The Fort Worth Zoological Park: A Sixty-Year History, 1909–1969." Master of Arts thesis, Texas Christian University, 1969.

Pointer, Bart Craig. "For the Public Good: Philanthropic Influence in Fort Worth, Texas." Ph.D. dissertation, Texas Christian University, 2000.

Plasters, Warren Howard. "A History of Amusements in Fort Worth from the Beginning to 1879." Master of Arts thesis, Texas Christian University, 1947.

Rich, Harold. "Twenty-Five Years of Struggle and Progress: The Fort Worth Police Department, 1873–1897. Master of Arts thesis, Texas Christian University, 1999.

———. "Beyond Outpost: Fort Worth, 1880–1918." Ph.D. dissertation, Texas Christian University, 2006.

Ritchie, Homer G. "The Life and Career of J. Frank Norris." Master of Arts thesis, Texas Christian University, 1967.

Rivas, Jose. "A Study to Determine the Influence of Ethnical and Social-Cultural Background upon the Religious Education of Baptist Students of Mexican Descent." Ph.D. dissertation, Southwestern Baptist Theological Seminary, 1966.

Rodriquez, Alicia Esther. "Urban Populism: Challenges to Democratic Party Control in Dallas, Texas: 1887–1900." Ph.D. dissertation. University of California, Santa Barbara, 1998.

Schoen, Leta S. "From Immigrant to Capitalist: The Evolution of O. B. Macaroni Company, 1899–1998." Master of Arts thesis, University of Texas at Arlington, 1998.

Shannon, Hallie D. "The Theater in Fort Worth from 1892 to 1896." Master of Arts thesis, Texas Christian University, 1950.

Summers, Nancy Katherine Yant. "Struggle for Existence: Fort Worth 1870–1876." Master of Arts thesis, Texas Christian University, 1968.

Thompson, Clarence Arnold. "Some Factors Contributing to the Growth of Fort Worth." Master of Arts thesis, Texas Christian University, 1933.

True, Clyde Allen. "Development of the Cattle Industry in the Southwest." Master of Arts thesis, Texas Christian University, 1928.

Wolz, Larry Robert. "A Survey of Concert Life in Texas During the Nineteenth Century." Master of Arts thesis, Texas Christian University, 1976.

Wright, Jhani Lou. "A Study of the Ranching Activities of the Snyder Brothers in Texas." Master of Science thesis, Texas Christian University, 1975.

Youngblood, A. C. "Family Housing Conditions in Substandard Areas of Fort Worth, Texas, in the Light of Biological Factors, Social Values, and the Functional Needs of Families." Master of Arts thesis, Texas Christian University, 1951.

Unpublished Papers

Copeland, David. "Hell's Half Acre: Fort Worth's First Amusement Center." Unpublished paper prepared for Dr. John A Carroll's History 8600.70 at Texas Christian University, 1969. In Texas Christian University Library open stacks.

King, Oliver and Carolyn Flatt. "Fort Worth and the Elections: 1888–1900." Unpublished research paper for Dr. John Kushma's History 5321 Class, June 25, 1981. In Local History Section of the Fort Worth Public Library.

Klein, Nathan. "Cowtown: A Fort Worth Birthright, A Brief History of the Fort Worth Stockyards." Honors paper at University of Texas at Arlington, 1998. In University of Texas at Arlington Library open stacks.

McIlvain, Jamie. "History of Hispanic Fort Worth." Honors paper in History at Texas Christian University, May 5, 1993. In Texas Christian University Library open stacks.

Miller, Richard. "City Building and Urban Growth: Fort Worth, 1870–1890." Typescript, University of Texas at Arlington. In University of Texas at Arlington Library open stacks.

Nichols, Liz. "Voices from the West: African-American Club Women and their Work in Fort Worth, Texas, 1896–1925." Unpublished research paper for Dr. Todd Kerstetter's American West Seminar at Texas Christian University, Spring, 2003. In possession of author.

Ohls, Gary. "German Heritage in Fort Worth, Texas." Unpublished research paper for Dr. Todd Kerstetter's American West Seminar at Texas Christian University, Spring, 2003. In possession of author.

Tucker, Jeff. "Frontier Firefighting: A Case Study of the Fort Worth Volunteer Fire Department, 1873–1893." Unpublished research paper for Dr. Todd Kerstetter's American West Seminar at Texas Christian University, Spring, 2003. In possession of author.

Web Sites

Patricia L. Duncan. "Paddock, Buckley Burton." *Handbook of Texas Online*, http://www.tshaonline.org/handbook/online/articles/fpa03), accessed March 6, 2013. Published by the Texas State Historical Association.

Redistricting Plan for Dallas City Council Districts, 2001. Available at http://www.dallascityhall.com/dallas/engpdf/Demographic.pdf

Redistricting Plan for Fort Worth City Council Districts, 2001. Available at http://www.fortworthgov.org/redistricting/plans

U.S. Census Bureau. University of Virginia Historical Census Data Web Site. Available at http://fisher.lib.virginia.edu/collections/stats/histcensus/

INDEX

Illustrations are indicated with italicized page numbers.

Canadian Royal Flying Corps, 186–87
Canapa, Manuel, 169
Cantey, Sam (congressman), 159
The Capitalist or the City of Fort Worth, 53
Capps, William, 74
Carruthers Field, 187
Case, A. B., 198
Casey, Martin, 65
Las Casitas Amarillas, 172
Cass Packing Company, 114
Castle, Vernon, 187
Cave (saloon), 129
Chamberlain, Humphrey B., 50, 74
Chamberlain Investments, 68, 74
Chamber of Commerce, 148, 162–65, 184–86, 199–200, 236n17
Chambers, A. J., 17, 18
Chevrolet, 182, 184, 203
Chicago, Ill., 6, 20, 39, 47, 49, 50, 53, 71, 75, 81, 87, 95, 97, 102–103, 105–107, 110, 112, 115, 143–45
Chicago and Fort Worth Packing Company, 77
Chicago and Rock Island Railway, 75, 77, 95, 147, 162, 172
Chicago Inter-Ocean, 54
Chicago Packing and Provision Company, 68, 110
Chinatown, 191
Chinese, 8, 14, 88
Chisholm Trail, 5
cholera, 72
Citizens Welfare League, 157
City Bakery, 33
City Council, 79, 85
city-county hospital, 153
City Market, 90
City Mills Company, 21, 22
City National Bank, 13, 27, 37, 74
Civil War, United States, 5, 166
The Clansman, 135
Clark, J. M., 75
Clark, M. C., 26
Cleburne, Tex., 16–18, 149

Cleburne Interurban (streetcar line), 149
Cleveland, Ohio, 98, 133, 149
Club Room (saloon), 33
coal, 20, 44, 56
cocaine, 99, 153
Coffenberry, J. B., 98
Coffey, Captain G. Frank, 158–59
Cold Springs, 222n47
College Heights, 135
College Hill, 13
Colorado, 122
Colorado City, Tex., 40
Comanche, Texas, 11, 18
Comanche National Bank, 43
commercial district, 13
commission (form of city) government, 119
Consolidated Vultee Aircraft Corporation, 7, 212
Continental Beef Company, 21
Cooke County, Tex., 82
Cooper, Ed, 159
Cooper, J. L., 90
Cooper, Tim, 159
Corn Palace (Denver, Colo.), 58
Corn Palace (Sioux City, Iowa), 57
La Corte, 170, 175
cotton, 3, 13, 20, 57, 73, 165
Cotton Belt Railroad (St. Louis Southwestern), 75, 172
Courtright, Timothy "Longhair Jim," 5, 30–37, 46, 219n4, 221n40
Crawford, David, 34
Cronon, William, 6
Crown (saloon), 100, 128–29
Cuban Revolution, 88
Cudahy Packing Company, 105, 181
Cuellar, Carlos, 169–70
Cullen, Addie, 64–65
Cummings, C. C., 25, 26
Cummings, Jorden Y., 130
Cummings, W. W., 80
Cunningham, W. B., 43
Curtiss JN-4, 187

Printed in the USA
CPSIA information can be obtained
at www.ICGtesting.com
LVHW051236191223
766490LV00029B/752/J

9 780806 144924